Virtue Jurisprudence

Also by Colin Farrelly

AN INTRODUCTION TO CONTEMPORARY POLITICAL THEORY

CONTEMPORARY POLITICAL THEORY: A Reader (*editor*)

JUSTICE, DEMOCRACY AND REASONABLE AGREEMENT

Also by Lawrence B. Solum

CIVIL PROCEDURE: PRINCIPLES AND THEORY

18 MOORE'S FEDERAL PRACTICE, 3rd edition (*with Susan Bandees*)

SEMIANNUAL RELEASES (*with Tom Rowe*)

DESTRUCTION OF EVIDENCE (*with Jamie Gorelick and Stephen Marzen*)

DESTRUCTION OF EVIDENCE: Supplement (*1989–2006 annual supplements*)

Virtue Jurisprudence

Edited by

Colin Farrelly

and

Lawrence B. Solum

palgrave
macmillan

First published 2008 by
PALGRAVE MACMILLAN
Houndmills, Basingstoke, Hampshire RG21 6XS and
175 Fifth Avenue, New York, N.Y. 10010
Companies and representatives throughout the world

PALGRAVE MACMILLAN is the global academic imprint of the Palgrave Macmillan division of St. Martin's Press, LLC and of Palgrave Macmillan Ltd. Macmillan® is a registered trademark in the United States, United Kingdom and other countries. Palgrave is a registered trademark in the European Union and other countries.

ISBN-13: 978–0–230–55289–0 hardback
ISBN-10: 0–230–55289–7 hardback

This book is printed on paper suitable for recycling and made from fully managed and sustained forest sources. Logging, pulping and manufacturing processes are expected to conform to the environmental regulations of the country of origin.

A catalogue record for this book is available from the British Library.

A catalog record for this book is available from the Library of Congress.

10 9 8 7 6 5 4 3 2 1
17 16 15 14 13 12 11 10 09 08

Printed and bound in Great Britain by
CPI Antony Rowe, Chippenham and Eastbourne

Contents

List of Contributors

Antony Duff, Professor of Philosophy, University of Stirling, Scotland.

Colin Farrelly, Associate Professor of Political Science, University of Waterloo, Canada.

Heidi Li Feldman, Professor of Law, Georgetown University Law Center, USA.

Robert P. George, McCormick Professor of Jurisprudence, University of Princeton, USA.

Kyron Huigens, Professor of Law, Cardozo School of Law, USA.

Rosalind Hursthouse, Professor of Philosophy, The University of Auckland, New Zealand.

Suzanna Sherry, Cal Turner Professor of Law and Leadership, Vanderbilt University Law School, USA.

Lawrence B. Solum, John E. Cribbet Professor of Law, University of Illinois, College of Law, USA.

Acknowledgments

The editors are grateful for permission to reprint the following material:

Robert P. George, *Making Men Moral* (Oxford: Clarendon Press, 1993), 19–47.

Heidi Li Feldman, "Prudence, Benevolence, and Negligence: Virtue Ethics and Tort Law", 74 *Chicago-Kent Law Review*, 1431 (2000).

Suzanna Sherry, "Judges of Character" 38 *Wake Forest Law Review*, 793 (2003).

Colin Farrelly, "Civic Liberalism and the 'Dialogical Model' of Judicial Review" 25 *Law and Philosophy*, 489 (2006).

Lawrence B. Solum, "Equity and the Rule of Law", *Nomos* XXXVI: The Rule of Law, 120 (1994).

Lawrence B. Solum, "Natural Justice", 51 *American Journal of Jurisprudence*, 65 (2006).

R. A. Duff, "Virtue, Vice, and Criminal Liability: Do We Want an Aristotelian Criminal Law?" 6 *Buffalo Criminal Law Review*, 147 (2003).

Kyron Huigens, "On Aristotelian Criminal Law: A Reply to Duff" 18 *Notre Dame Journal of Law, Ethics & Public Policy*, 465 (2004).

An Introduction to Aretaic Theories of Law*

Colin Farrelly and Lawrence B. Solum

1. Introduction

Contemporary legal theory has been dominated by the realist paradigm. The extreme version of realism is captured by the slogan of the critical legal studies movement: "Law is politics!" Other heirs to the realist tradition (including normative law and economics, the legal process school, legal pragmatism, and so forth) coalesce around what we might call *the instrumentalist thesis*—the point of legal institutions (especially courts) is to use the law as an *instrument* to achieve the goals of some normative theory (such as welfarism or deontology) or a political ideology (of the left, right, or center). There are, of course, opposing tendencies in contemporary legal theory. Some neoformalists emphasize the duty of adjudicators to follow the law and give the parties what they are due; in a rough and ready sort of way, these neoformalists adopt a deontological perspective on legal theory that competes with the consequentialism of contemporary neorealists.

In this introduction, we sketch an alternative direction for contemporary legal theory, an approach that we call "virtue jurisprudence." Our core idea is quite simple. In moral theory, virtue ethics offers a third way—an alternative to the deontological and consequentialist approaches that dominated modern moral philosophy until very recently. What would happen if we transplanted *virtue ethics* into normative legal theory? The essays in this anthology are part of a growing body of work that answers that question.

Before we go any further, we ought to say that the version of virtue jurisprudence offered in this brief introduction paper is hardly full blown. Rather, we will focus on one aspect of virtue jurisprudence—a virtue-centered theory of judging. That leaves a good deal of territory unmapped. In particular, we only skim the surface of the implications of virtue jurisprudence for the ends of law. An aretaic theory of legislation would naturally begin with the premise that the *telos* or proper end of law is the promotion of human flourishing. If the purpose of law is to enable humans to acquire, maintain, and exercise the human excellences or virtues, it seems likely that there will be important implications for familiar debates. Some argue that the central function of law is to prevent actions that harm offers or invade the moral rights of others. Virtue jurisprudence is naturally inclined to doubt this contention. Others argue that because the purpose of the law is the protection of property (understood in the wide sense that includes the person and liberty of individuals), it follows that it would be improper for law to aim at equality. Virtue jurisprudence is naturally inclined to the view that the law should enable and sustain the material and social conditions that would enable each and every individual to achieve the highest level of human functioning that is consistent with a similar level of functioning for all.

Instead of these topics, this introduction to the volume provides a brief intellectual history of the aretaic turn in legal theory, followed by a synopsis of the chapters in the volume.

2. The aretaic turn in legal theory

Contemporary legal theory endeavors to answer at least two big questions of practical jurisprudence[1]: First, *what is the aim of law?* Second, *how can legal institutions best do their job of resolving disputes?* Virtue jurisprudence offers distinctive answers to these questions.

For virtue jurisprudence, the final end of law is not to maximize preference satisfaction or to protect some set of rights and privileges: the final end of law is to promote human flourishing—to enable humans to lead excellent lives. Second, the best way to improve the ability of legal institutions to resolve disputes is not to populate the bench with economists or moral philosophers from either the left or the right; instead, achieving an excellent judiciary requires the selection of judges who possess the judicial virtues—civic courage, judicial temperament, judicial intelligence, wisdom, and, above all, justice. These answers to the big practical questions are unified by a central thesis: *the fundamental concepts of legal philosophy should <u>not</u> be welfare, efficiency, autonomy, or* *equality; the fundamental notions of legal theory should be virtue and excellence*. Thus, the contributors to this volume, while diverse and varied in the particulars of the topics and themes they address, share the unifying belief that jurisprudence should turn from an emphasis on ideology, rights, and utility to a focus on virtue.

What is the aretaic turn in legal theory? The word for virtue or excellence in classical Greek was *arête*, from which we derive the English word "aretaic," of, or pertaining to, excellence or virtue. Virtue jurisprudence is one way that legal theory can execute a move already made by moral philosophy and epistemology—*the aretaic turn*. On one hand, the aretaic turn represents a renewed concern with human excellence as a unifying normative and explanatory concept. On the other hand, the turn toward human excellence is a turn away from the reductive programs of both consequentialist and deontological legal theory. Virtue jurisprudence offers a rich and fruitful account of the nature, means, and ends of law that simultaneously dissolves old problems and poses a new set of challenges for legal theorists. The aretaic turn in legal theory moves away from degenerating research programs that disconnect the academy from the bench and bar and moves toward the reintegration of legal theory and practice.

3. Motivating the aretaic turn

Why virtue jurisprudence? What are the defects of the contemporary fusion of theory and practice? If all were well with modern jurisprudence, legal theorists would lack motivation to make the aretaic turn. But all is not well. Contemporary legal theory and practice are in serious trouble.

3.1 Modern moral philosophy and contemporary legal theory

There is a striking parallel between the state of contemporary legal theory after the turn of the millennium and the situation of modern moral philosophy in 1958, when Elizabeth Anscombe wrote her famous essay *Modern Moral Philosophy*.[2] Modern moral philosophy, Anscombe argued, has involved a competition between two great families of moral theories, consequentialism, and deontology. Both views face severe difficulties, and each provides a powerful critique of the other. Consequentialism has the advantage of providing a method that, in principle, is capable of resolving moral disputes but purchases its discriminatory power by leaving no room for inviolable human rights and independent consideration of fairness. Deontology has the disadvantage of an uncertain method and at least sometimes seems to exclude consideration of consequences that seem either relevant to or dispositive of the choice that must be made.

And what of the state of contemporary legal theory? Most readers will recognize the eerie parallels with Anscombe's sketch of the predicament of modern moral philosophy. Contemporary legal theory is characterized by two antinomies: *the antinomy of rights and consequences* and the *antinomy of realism and formalism*. Each antinomy captures a persistent controversy in contemporary legal theory that has proved resistant to resolution (or even clarification) through the practice of reasoned argument. In the less theoretical corners of the legal academy, many believe that legal scholars choose their position with respect to these antimonies on the basis of an *existential leap* as opposed to reasoned argument. In the pages of learned journals and in the introduction to learned monographs, readers may limn the contours of a struggle where rhetorical flourish and name calling take the place of careful scholarly analysis.

The antinomy of rights and consequences is the legal form of the modern philosophical debate between consequentialists and deontologists. In the legal academy, the flag of consequentialism is borne by the normative law and economics movement. An especially prominent and trenchant example is found in *Fairness versus Welfare*, a monumental law review article[3] and later book,[4] by Louis Kaplow and Steven Shavell of Harvard Law School, but normative law and economics has a long and distinguished pedigree.

If the flag of consequentialism is borne by normative law and economics, then surely the most prominent standard bearer for a rights-based approach to normative legal theory is Ronald Dworkin.[5] Dworkin's theory, law as integrity, emphasizes the idea that the parties have preexisting rights that oblige judges to decide cases on the basis of principle rather than policy. Of course, Dworkin is only one of many who carry the flag for deontology in the legal academy. When we describe the lay of the jurisprudential landscape as an antinomy of rights and consequences, we mean to make a bold assertion about the state of debate between the partisans of consequence and the advocates of rights. This debate does not seem to be progressing toward a conclusion; instead we seem to be in a state of perpetual conflict (at best) or mutual disengagement (at worst).

We should explain. On the one hand, there is considerable evidence for the proposition that normative legal theory is fragmenting. Normative law and economics has sufficient momentum so that it is institutionally feasible to proceed as if there were no deontological critique of the moral foundations of welfarism. Likewise, deontologists can debate among themselves, with egalitarians and libertarians arguing for their own preferred version of rights-based normative legal theory. Genuine dialog is rare. Genuine progress is even rarer. Kaplow and Shavell's *Fairness versus Welfare* certainly reignited the debate between the partisans of consequence and the advocates of rights, but we do not think it can fairly be said that much progress was made. Kaplow and Shavell's critics declared victory, but the normative law and economics movement proceeded as if nothing had happened.

If the *antinomy of rights and consequences* is characterized by perpetual warfare or mutual disengagement between two more or less equally matched forces, the *antinomy of realism and formalism* is reflected in a more fractured and less crystalline pattern of legal discourse. We can remind ourselves of the dialectic with a sweeping historical survey: the original legal realist movement of the 1920s and 1930s gave way to the law and process synthesis of the 1950s and 1960s, which in turn was challenged by the indeterminacy thesis advanced by the critical legal studies movement in the 1980s. Critical legal studies (CLS) gave way to a blistering critique of implausible claims about radical indeterminacy in the 1990s, only to see realist cynicism reach a new zenith in the wake of the United States Supreme Court's decision in *Bush v. Gore*.

Contemporary legal theory is of two minds about realism and formalism. The practitioners of legal theory have incorporated the standard realist moves into the conceptual toolbox. Who has not written an article or taught a class where one shows that a formal legal distinction masks decision making that is really driven by other considerations—politics, policy, economics, or something else? We are all realists. But legal formalism is surprisingly resilient to attempts to declare its demise. Once formalism is rescued from the realist caricature of a self-contained system of pure deduction, it is hard to deny that (1) there are easy cases and (2) while the law may underdetermine judicial decision making, it is rarely radically indeterminate. And neoformalism, in various forms, is on the rise. Originalism, textualism, and plain meaning—these are the watchwords of the neoformalists, a group which makes up in prominence and attention what it may lack in numerosity.

The point of adumbrating the two antimonies—rights and consequences, realism and formalism—is to convey the sense that contemporary normative legal theory, despite its vibrancy and sophistication, is stuck in certain recurring patterns of irresolvable argument. We hesitate to say that contemporary legal theory is a degenerating research program, but there is surely reason for dissatisfaction.

3.2 The argument from virtue ethics

If virtue ethics is the best available moral theory, then it seems quite likely that virtue jurisprudence must, in some sense, provide the best account of normative legal theory. Of course, stated at this level of generality and abstraction, the connection between virtue ethics and virtue jurisprudence certainly does not rise to the level of entailment. It might be the case that normative legal theory is independent of moral theory. The arguments for such independence might parallel those offered by John Rawls in his very famous essay, *The Independence of Moral Theory*, which claims that normative ethics does not shake out from metaethics.[6] Or it might be argued that virtue ethics (although true) is not appropriate as the basis for jurisprudence in a modern pluralist democracy. But given the claims made by virtue ethics, there are problems with any attempt to resist virtue jurisprudence that admits that the aretaic approach to ethics is the best one.

On this occasion, however, we shall not pursue the argument for virtue jurisprudence from virtue ethics—what might be called the *top-down strategy*. Pursuing that strategy would require that we make the case for virtue ethics and against deontology and consequentialism. That case might rely on arguments from both metaethics and normative ethics. The next step would be to move from virtue ethics to virtue politics, arguing that an aretaic approach to political philosophy is superior to its consequentialist and deontological rivals. Finally, one could try to show that acceptance of virtue ethics and virtue politics entails or supports acceptance of virtue jurisprudence.

Rather than pursue the top-down strategy, we shall begin with one of the core elements of virtue jurisprudence—an aretaic (or virtue-centered) theory of judging. And in the chapters that follow, which will we outline shortly, the connection between virtue and law is taken in different and interesting directions. Not only can the virtue ethics tradition help illuminate a theory of judging—one that goes beyond the minimal content outlined in this introduction—but it has also inspired new theories of criminal liability and negligence and offered new insights into the legitimacy of judicial review and the moral dilemmas lawyers often face. And so we think this volume offers philosophers, legal scholars, and political theorists a great deal. It highlights the important ways in which the virtue ethics tradition continues to be developed, refined, and applied.

4. A virtue-centered theory of judging

4.1 The uncontested judicial virtues

There is disagreement about the qualities that make for good judging. That disagreement is reflected in recent controversies about the selection of federal judges. Because judicial selection has largely been driven by the preference of political actors for certain outcomes on key issues (abortion, affirmative action, and so forth), political ideology has played a major role in the judicial selection process. This practical disagreement is reflected in legal theory as well. Legal scholars disagree on the criteria for a good legal decision, and hence they are likely to disagree about which judges are excellent as well. Nonetheless, it may be possible to identify a set of judicial excellences on which there is likely to be widespread agreement.

What is called for is a *theory* of the uncontested judicial virtues. "Uncontested" in this context reflects the notion that these virtues are based on uncontroversial assumptions about what counts as good judging and on widely accepted beliefs about human nature and social reality. By "virtue," we mean a dispositional quality of mind or will that is constitutive of human excellence, and the "judicial virtues" include both the human virtues that are relevant to judging and any particular virtues that are associated with the social role of judge.

4.1.1 Judicial incorruptibility and judicial sobriety

One judicial vice on which there is likely to be near universal agreement is "corruption." Judges who sell their votes undermine the substantive goals of the law because corrupt decisions are at least as likely to be wrong as they are to be substantively correct. Moreover, corrupt decisions undermine the rule of law values of productivity and uniformity of legal decisions and likewise undermine public respect for the law and public acceptance of the law as legitimate.

Even the most zealous advocate of ideological judicial selection is likely to accept the conclusion that judicial corruption is a vice. Of course, it is possible that some judges might accept bribes or political favors in a way that systematically favors a particular political ideology or that advances the interests of a particular political party. But the partisans of ideological judging would have good reason to think that even a corrupt judge who "votes the right way" is a bad judge. *Why?* Two reasons. First, corrupt judges are not reliable ideological allies—precisely because their decisions are for sale, they can be lured to the side of one's ideological opponents by a "better offer" or more attractive bribe. Second, there is always a risk that corruption will be exposed, and when exposed, a corrupt decision that favors one's cause may actually be counterproductive—delegitimating the ideology that it seemed to serve. Of course, these two prudential reasons are likely to be supplemented by the obvious reason of principle—corrupt decisions are morally wrong. We have no reason to believe that the partisans of ideological judging would not condemn corruption on moral grounds.

If we accept the conclusion that judicial corruption is a vice, then what is the corresponding virtue? This question could become complex—because there are a variety of character flaws that might lead to corruption. One such flaw is greed (or *pleonexia*), which may be an underlying cause of corruption because a desire for more than one's share (or entitlement) could lead a judge to accept bribes. All humans are at risk of mistaking wealth (which can only be a means) for a final end (something worth pursuing for its own sake). Some judges may resent the fact that they receive compensation that is sometimes only a fraction of that provided to their peers in private legal practice—some of whom may be less talented.

We do not need to identify all of the possible vices that could lead to corruption in order to see that *incorruptibility* is an uncontested judicial virtue. There is no real controversy over the proposition that judges should be disposed to resist the temptations that lead to corruption. We call this disposition the "judicial virtue of incorruptibility," even if it turns out that this virtue encompasses a variety of particular virtues, each of which corresponds to a particular human vice that could lead to corruption.

There is another vice that is closely related to corruption but is distinct from greed. Judges can become corrupted because their desires are not in order—because they crave pleasure or the status (and corresponding envy) conferred by the possession of fine things. Judges, like the rest of us, can be corrupted by a taste for designer shoes, fast cars, loose companions, or intoxicating substances. More subtly, a judge could be corrupted by a desire for the finer things of life, for example, a magnificent home, the ability to confer lavish gifts upon one's children, or the opportunity for luxurious travel.

Let us use some old-fashioned terminology and call the vice of disorderly desire "intemperance"—recognizing that modern ears may not be able to hear that word without summoning up an image of drunkenness caused by a craving for the pleasures of strong drink. Can a case be made that intemperance is not a judicial vice? One might argue that intemperance is a purely private vice—that a judge's preference for a third cosmopolitan, the latest from Jimmy Choo or Manolo Blahnik, or the company of good-looking youthful companions is his or her own business and hence irrelevant to the question whether she or he is an excellent judge. Of course, a proportionate and well-ordered desire for such things is simply not a vice—or at least not an *uncontested* vice. But a disposition to disproportionate desires for such pleasures can lead to more than corruption. Most obviously, a judge who is intoxicated (or high) on the bench is likely to be prone to error, for obvious reasons. The disordinate pursuit of less intoxicating pleasures can also impair judicial performance—by focusing a judge's attention and energy away from judicial tasks.

There is a counter argument. It is a common human experience to have a friend, colleague, or acquaintance who is intemperate, but nonetheless "gets the job done"—even performs brilliantly at times. Who has not encountered the lawyer who is a star by day, but a lush in the wee hours, or the friend whose life at work still holds together despite a drug problem. So, the argument goes, intemperance is not a *judicial vice*—at least not until it interferes with the performance of judicial duty. Even if the intemperate judicial candidate is a disaster at home, his or her intemperance should not disqualify him or her from judicial office if she or he performs at the office. This counter argument is ultimately unpersuasive. Of course, an intemperate judge can get lucky and "get away with it," either appearing to do well or even actually doing well despite disordered desires. But in such cases, "getting away with it" is a matter of luck; an intemperate judge is simply not reliable. A really damaging misstep is always just one cosmopolitan away.

The virtue that corresponds to the vice of intemperance could be called *temperance,* in the classical sense that encompasses the ordering of all the natural desires. But we propose that we use another term to refer to the judicial form of temperance. We have a saying that captures the intuitive sense that judges must have their desires in order: we say of a temperate human that she or he is "sober as a judge," and this suggests that we name this virtue "judicial sobriety."

4.1.2 Judicial courage

Fear is one of the most powerful and familiar of the emotions. For Aristotle, the virtue of courage relates to the morally neutral emotion of fear. Following the pattern of the moral virtues, courage represents a mean between a vice of excess—cowardice—and a vice of deficiency, which we might call "rashness" or "recklessness." We can agree that cowardice is a judicial vice, and judicial courage is a virtue.

We might usefully subdivide the virtue courage into two parts—which we shall call "physical courage" and "civic courage." That judges need physical courage in order to be excellent *as judges* is a lamentable fact in many societies. We have been reminded of this fact recently by the tragic experiences of federal district judge, Joan Lefkow, who was threatened by one defendant and whose husband and mother were murdered by a party to another case.[7] A judge who could be intimidated by threats of physical violence could not reliably do justice in our society—much less under conditions where violence (or threats of violence) was even more prevalent—as may be the case where narcoterrorism or violent ethnic conflict is pervasive.

Judicial courage has a second dimension. Judges, like most humans, care about their reputations and social standing. Like the rest of us, judges seek the approval and companionship of their fellows. So in addition to physical danger, judges may fear consequences of their actions that involve threats to status and social approval. This is because the law may require judges to make unpopular decisions. A judge who ordered school integration in the South might be shunned socially. In societies where the judicial branch wields significant power in cases involving hot-button issues (abortion, end-of-life disputes, and so forth), there will be occasions where doing what the law requires may be profoundly unpopular. For this reason, judges need the virtue of civic courage—the disposition to put the regard of one's fellows in proper place and to take it into account in the right way on the right occasions for the right reasons. A judge with this virtue will not be tempted to sacrifice justice on the altar of public opinion. A civically courageous judge understands that the good opinion of others is worth having if it flows from having done justice and that social approval for injustice is an impermissible motive for judicial action.

4.1.3 Judicial temperament and impartiality

Like fear, anger is an emotion both familiar and powerful.[8] Judges, like the rest of us, may be hot tempered or cool and collected. And like the rest of us, judges are likely to find themselves in situations where a hot temper could produce intemperate actions. This is especially true of trial judges, who are given the task of maintaining order in what may become emotionally charged circumstances. Litigants may ignore judicial authority or act with disrespect. Some lawyers may deliberately attempt to provoke the judge in order to elicit legal mistakes or "on the record" behavior that displays animus toward a party and serve as the basis for an appeal. In the face of such provocations, a judge with an "anger management problem" may "fly off the handle." Intemperate judicial behavior may lead the judge to misapply the law—misinterpreting the applicable legal standards in "the heat of anger." Moreover, a hot-headed judge may become partial—pulling against the party who is the object of anger and displaying favoritism to that party's opponent.

Aristotle identified *proates* or "good temper" as the corrective virtue for the vice of bad temper. In the judicial context, this virtue is so important that we have a phrase that expresses the virtue as a distinctively judicial form of excellence—"judicial temperament." This phrase reflects our sense that the virtue of "good temper" is essential for good judging.

Is judicial temperament also required for judges who do not supervise trials? Appellate judges work in a cooler environment—provocative behavior by appellate lawyers is rare although not unknown. The parties to an appellate proceeding frequently do not appear, and if they do, they sit in the audience without any formal participation in the appellate process itself. Some appellate courts proceed almost entirely on the basis of the briefs, dispensing with oral argument, and hence with the opportunity for "live and in person" provocations. Nonetheless, good temper is essential for excellence in appellate judging. Appellate judges hear cases in panels or en banc—creating opportunities for friction among the judges themselves. Hot tempers can destroy collegiality and with it the opportunity for compromise and mutual understanding. Moreover, even a brief can elicit anger, and if anger becomes rage, it can have a blinding effect, depriving the judge of the ability to recognize the merits of an argument or a weakness in the judge's own conception of the legal issues in a case.

If excessive anger is a vice, then what about its opposite? Is there a vice of deficiency with respect to anger? The Stoics are famous for answering this question in the negative: we might say that for the Stoics, the disposition to feel any anger in any circumstances is a vice.[9] The contrary view is that proportionate anger serves a valuable function—alerting us to wrongs and motivating us to respond to them. A simple way of framing the issue is to ask which character from the 1960s television series *Star Trek* would make the best judge—Captain Kirk, Dr. McCoy, or Mr. Spock. Mr. Spock resembles the Stoic sage—he feels no anger and acts only on the basis of logic; we imagine Judge Spock reacting with equanimity to even the most severe courtroom provocations. Dr. McCoy is hot tempered; we imagine him flying off the handle in response to outrageous behavior by the lawyer for a greedy corporation. Captain Kirk represents a mean between these two extremes; we imagine Judge Kirk as appropriately outraged by bad behavior and injustice but nonetheless remaining "in control," angered by the right things and responding in an appropriate manner. The virtue of judicial temperament consists in having appropriate anger—anger for the right reasons on the right occasions with a clear understanding of the consequences of its expression.

More concretely, when a party flouts the law or disrespects the participants in a legal proceeding, anger may be appropriate. Such appropriate anger alerts the judge to the existence of a "situation that must be dealt with." In some circumstances, the judge will properly display such anger, giving a lawyer, party, or witness "a stern warning." When a lawyer, party, or witness persists in bad conduct, sanctions may be warranted; in such cases, an appropriate sanction is the right way to act on the basis of appropriate anger. But judges with the virtue of a judicial temperament will not display their anger by ruling against an offending party on issues that are close or exercising discretion on incidental matters so as to disfavor the anger-provoking party.

One reason that anger is an especially dangerous vice for judges is that anger can produce bias. For this reason, the virtue of judicial temperament is closely related to another judicial virtue, "judicial impartiality." This virtue is a familiar feature of our conception of good judging. We want judges to be neutral arbitrators. A judge should be open to the law and evidence and not biased in favor of one side or another. Such impartiality should extend not just to the parties but should also encompass the causes, movements, special interests, and ideologies that may be associated with those parties. When a judge takes the bench or lifts his or her pen to write an opinion, she or he should put aside his or her allegiance to left or right, liberal or conservative, religiosity or secularism.

It is a mistake, however, to view impartiality as synonymous with disinterest. The virtue of impartiality is not cold-blooded. This is because the role of judge requires insight and understanding into the human condition. A good judge perceives the law and facts from a human perspective. Some facts are hot—charged with emotional salience. Some legal rules are righteous—engaging our sense of moral indignation when juxtaposed with violative behavior. So the impartial judge is not cold-blooded; she or he is not *indifferent* to the parties that come before him or her. Rather, the judge with the virtue of judicial impartiality has even-handed sympathy for all the parties to a dispute. When we say, "Impartiality is not indifference," we mean that the virtue of impartiality requires both sympathy and empathy without taking sides or favoring the legitimate interests of one side over those of the other.

4.1.4 Diligence and carefulness

Judging is hard work, involving its share of drudgery. Some trials are long and boring. Some opinions require long hours of research and even longer hours of careful drafting. The temptation to shirk this work is accentuated by the fact that judges are not (and should not be) closely supervised. And the lack of supervision is compounded in jurisdictions that grant judges life tenure or long terms in office. It is hard enough to remove a judge for outright corruption; one doubts that any American judge has been removed on the basis of sloth alone. But slothful or lazy judges can do real harm. They are tempted to delegate too much responsibility to judicial clerks, substituting the judgment of the clerk for the judge's own intellectual engagement with the case. Another temptation is to shape one's decision in order to minimize one's own workload. If granting the summary judgment motion takes a case off one's docket, the slothful judge might grant the motion for that reason alone, sacrificing justice on the altar of expediency.

What is the virtue that corresponds to the vice of sloth? We might call it diligence. The diligent judge has the right attitude toward judicial work, finding judicial tasks engaging and rewarding. But more than a good attitude is required. An excellent judge must have an appropriate "energy level"—a product of both physical and mental health. The combination of these traits should translate into a judge who is capable of hard work when hard work is required. Such a judge will put in the required hours and sweat out the difficult tasks. Such a judge will not hesitate to make the right decision, even if that makes more work for the judge. Nowadays, encouraging settlements may be an appropriate activity for judges, but a diligent judge will aim for just and efficient settlements and not for resolutions that serve the judge's own convenience.

Carefulness is closely related to diligence. No one can sensibly doubt that judicial carelessness is a vice. Careless decisions, careless drafting, careless research—any of these can lead to substantive injustice. Carefulness is especially important in the context of judging because excellent judging frequently requires meticulous attention to details. The lazy judge may shirk the unpleasant task of mastering the structure of a complex statute or avoid the painstaking task of making sense of the tangled body of precedent. Likewise, it requires diligence and care to draft an opinion in which each and every sentence is worded with careful appreciation of the importance of precision and accuracy. An excellent judge has an eye for detail and a devotion to precision.

4.1.5 Judicial intelligence and learnedness

Can anyone doubt that stupidity is a judicial vice? All humans need intelligence to function well, but some tasks require more intelligence on more occasions. Judging is the kind of task that sometimes requires extraordinary intelligence. Both law and facts can be complex. Only a judge with intelligence will be able to sort out the complexities of the rule against perpetuities or penetrate the mysteries of a complex statute. But more than intelligence is required. A truly excellent judge must also be learned in the law because one cannot start from scratch in each and every case and because there is at least some truth to the notion that the law is a seamless web. To put these same points the other way round: stupid and ignorant judges will be error prone, likely to misunderstand and misstate the law and unlikely to make findings of fact that are correct.

The need for judicial intelligence and learnedness is accentuated rather than diminished in an adversary system. It is true that good lawyering makes a judge's job easier; the lawyers can identify the relevant issues and call the judge's attention to the best arguments on each side of those issues that are in dispute. But in an adversary system, successful advocates will try to make "worse case appear the better," by deploying sophistry and rhetoric. Intelligent and learned judges can "see through" the obfuscation and look past the appeals to prejudice and preconception.

4.1.6 Craft and skill

So far, our investigation has focused on what Aristotle called the moral and intellectual virtues. These are dispositions of character and mind that make for human excellence. Good judging requires more than good character and intellectual ability. That is because judging includes elements of craft, and therefore, a good judge must possess a skill set—the particular learned abilities that are to good judging what good bowing technique is to archery or good draftsmanship is to architecture. A full account of judicial craft is far beyond the scope of this introduction, but one particular aspect of judicial craft and skill cries out for attention. Excellence in judging (especially good appellate judging) requires particular skill in the use of language. Good judges must be good communicators. This aspect of judicial skill includes at least two parts—oral and written. It is obvious that trial judges need good oral communication skills; they must deliver a variety of oral instructions to the various participants in both trial and pretrial proceedings. Among these, jury instructions are particularly important. Written communication skills are especially important for appellate judges in a common law system because of the doctrine of *stare decisis*. Because appellate opinions set precedent, a badly written opinion can misstate the law or state the law in a misleading way. A really well-drafted opinion, on the other hand, can clarify the obscure and illuminate the meaning of murky legal texts.

Good communication skills are also important to judges when they mediate between the parties to a dispute. A skilled judge can gain the trust and cooperation of the parties—resorting to the threat of sanctions only in those rare cases when force is truly necessary. In this way, good communication skills can increase the efficiency of judicial proceedings, allowing the judge to focus his or her attention on those issues and cases where settlement and cooperative processes are unavailing.

One advantage of a theory of judicial excellence is that it reveals a large zone of agreement. For all practical purposes, we can agree that judges should be incorruptible, courageous, good tempered, diligent, skilled, and smart. But these (mostly uncontested) virtues do not tell the whole story about judicial excellence. Even if we agree in our judgments about who the very worst judges are—the corrupt, ill-tempered, cowardly, lazy, incompetent, and stupid ones—there are strong and persistent disagreements about who the best judges are. The partisans of Lord Coke may deride the accomplishments of Lord Mansfield; the admirers of Justice Brennan may be among the critics of Justice Scalia.

Disagreements about judicial excellence are typically rooted in two disagreements about the nature of judicial virtue. The first disagreement is about the nature of the virtue of justice. The second disagreement concerns the role of equity and practical wisdom. On the one hand, some disagreements about judicial excellence turn out to be disagreements about and within conceptions of the virtue of justice—what some call "justice," others see as "unjust." On the other hand, other controversies hang on differences in the understanding of the role of practical wisdom in judging: some believe that wise judges will range far from the rules in the name of equity, while others believe that equity should be tightly constrained by the rule of law.

Two of the essays in this anthology are directed at these disagreements. "Natural Justice: An Aretaic Account of the Virtue of Lawfulness" addresses the disagreement about the nature of justice. In that essay, Lawrence Solum, one of the authors of this introduction and editors of this volume, argues that justice is best understood as lawfulness in a distinctive sense—a disposition constituted by internalization of the *nomoi*, the deeply held and widely shared social norms of a particular community. In "A Virtue-Centered Account of Equity and The Rule of Law," Solum argues that the virtue of practical wisdom or *phronesis* can reconcile the practice of equity (departure from the legal rules in response to particular fact situations) with the requirements of the rule of law. Together, the two essays suggest that practical wisdom and justice are the key judicial virtues and therefore that an excellent judge must be both *phronimos* and *nomimos*.

5. Overview of the chapters

Chapter 1 in this volume is an excerpt from Robert P. George's book *Making Men Moral*. In "The Central Tradition," George provides a useful introductory discussion of two of the main historical figures in the virtue ethics tradition—Aristotle and St. Thomas Aquinas. This perfectionist tradition is one that maintains that sound politics and good law are concerned with helping people to live moral lives. Indeed, George contends that a good political society may even justly utilize the coercive power of the state to help protect people from vice. But George is careful to distance the contemporary vision of perfectionist politics from the elitist and theological commitments of the historical figures of the central tradition. Contemporary proponents of virtue ethics give greater room to freedom and are more apprehensive about the use of law's coercive power than were Aristotle and Aquinas.

Moral goods are often goods that can only be realized via internal acts of will, not legal compulsion. And this provides government with a compelling reason not to try to eliminate every opportunity for immorality. A cavalier approach to diminishing vice could actually exacerbate a situation by creating morally worse evils (e.g. violating human rights) or impeding the realization of other important goods. Furthermore, a significant range of moral obligations are beyond the reach of law as a matter of principle. For example, if the government compelled citizens to express gratitude or the giving of gifts, this would alter the meaningfulness of such social practices. For these are practices that cannot be compelled. Gratitude and the giving of gifts require the parties involved to fulfill these obligations freely.

The fact that there are justice-based and prudential-based grounds for not repressing every vice does not, George argues, mean there are never valid reasons for prohibiting any vice on the grounds that it is immoral. While the law cannot directly make men moral—as it is not possible to compel people to realize moral goods—the state can nevertheless play a formative role in making men moral *indirectly*. So the law is a necessary, but by no means sufficient, means of establishing and maintaining what George calls a "healthy moral ecology." Moral laws help shape the framework of understandings and expectations that are necessary for any community.

George's contribution to this volume thus helps provide some necessary background and an introduction to the virtue ethics tradition and its concern for the relation between law and morality (e.g. virtue and vice). George's discussion of Aristotle, for example, should prove particularly helpful to those unfamiliar with the central tradition. Aristotle, one of the greatest philosophers of all time, believed that the central purpose of the *polis* (political community) is to make men moral. And George examines why Aristotle held this view and what its implications are for the role of law.

What constitutes a reasonable balance between safety and freedom? When is an individual or cooperation negligent and thus liable to compensate others for the harms they have caused? In "Prudence, Benevolence, and Negligence: Virtue Ethics and Tort Law," Heidi Li Feldman invokes the virtue ethics tradition to offer some valuable insights into the role of prudence and care in evaluating conduct. Tort law assesses negligence, and in order to determine what constitutes a reasonable negligence standard tort law assesses negligence according to the conduct of a reasonable person of ordinary prudence who acts with due care for the safety of others. Feldman argues that contemporary tort scholars only utilize a partial examination of this standard, one that focuses almost exclusively on the attribute of reasonableness. But this is problematic because it does not give due attention to the virtues of prudence and benevolence.

Feldman outlines the moral and economic traditions that have informed tort scholarship for the past half a century. Traditions such as Kantianism, utilitarianism, and social welfare economics place a premium on the concern for individual autonomy, maximizing pleasure and minimizing pain, and preference satisfaction. The virtue ethics tradition is a distinctive approach as it is interested in what lends worth to human lives, and thus it has an interest in the full range of human interests, needs, desires, aspirations, and activities.

A sovereign political system, argues Feldman, is one that permits the citizens to decide how carefully each must act to avoid personal injury to others. But it is simply not possible to hold a referendum each time somebody is going to act and might incidentally risk injuring others. What is needed, contends Feldman, is a way of expressing collective judgments about how carefully people should behave in particular circumstances. And civil negligence actions perform this function as juries apply a virtue-based standard of care. A virtue-based approach to negligence thus conceives of the negligence standard as a thought experiment that is best performed by lay people. And such an approach can inspire a radically democratic and populist tort theory.

In "Judges of Character," Suzanna Sherry attempts to transcend a long-standing debate in legal theory—the counter-majoritarian difficulty. The counter-majoritarian difficulty concerns the legitimacy of judicial review. The judges in the Supreme Court are not elected by the public and yet they have the power to invalidate laws passed by democratically elected officials. The antidemocratic nature of the institution of judicial review thus raises a problem for those who believe it does, and should, play an important and vital role in society. How does one justify the institution of judicial review? The answer, contends Sherry, lies with the idea of "judicial character."

To overcome the counter-majoritarian problem constitutional theorists must recognize that any constitutional theory must have nuances and exceptions and that it cannot satisfactorily account for every possible case. And in order to know when the theory applies, and when it does not, you need virtuous judges. Sherry addresses the judicial traits of humility and arrogance and courage and timidity. The value and limits of these different traits are illustrated through the consideration of different legal decisions, dealing with issues such as affirmative action and abortion. Rather than continuing the long-standing debate over the pros and cons of judicial review, Sherry suggests that it is more useful to invest our energies into the task of describing (and finding) individuals well suited to the task of judging.

The theme of judicial review is also the central concern in Colin Farrelly's chapter entitled "Civic Liberalism and the 'Dialogical Model' of Judicial Review." Farrelly attempts to revive the transformative potential of liberal democratic theory by endorsing a virtue-oriented conception of justice he calls *civic liberalism*. Unlike principle-oriented theories of distributive justice, which seek to protect the vulnerable in society by endorsing a version of either *judicial* or *legislative supremacy*, civic liberalism inspires a public philosophy that seeks to take seriously the moral and pragmatic demands of toleration, civility, and fairness. Such a public philosophy, Farrelly contends, ought to embrace a *dialogical model* of judicial review. Such a model currently informs Canadian Constitutional law, and Farrelly draws upon the Canadian experience in order to develop a virtue-oriented political theory that takes seriously what Robert Bork calls the "Madisonian dilemma."

Civic liberalism interprets the Madisonian dilemma as the dilemma between the moral demands of the virtues of toleration and civility. Respect for toleration leads us in the direction of limited government, government that does not unjustly interfere with individual liberty. This concern for individual rights provides the normative basis for constitutionalism. This can be contrasted with the moral demands of civility, demands that lead us to majority rule and the idea of self-government. If we take only the moral dimensions of these two virtues into account, it seems that we cannot resolve the Madisonian dilemma. For we have two contradictory prescriptions—limited government and self-government. But civic liberalism inspires a public philosophy that gives due attention to both the moral and *pragmatic* dimensions of these virtues. It does not seek to give an absolute priority to any of the moral demands of toleration or civility. Instead, it seeks to reconcile the diverse demands of toleration, civility, and fairness.

Civic liberalism does not see the Madisonian dilemma as paradoxical. Rather, this dilemma reinforces the need for a virtue-oriented approach rather than a principle-oriented approach to political theory. Civic liberalism defends a virtue-oriented conception of liberal democracy that takes both sides of the Madisonian dilemma seriously. A virtuous polity, argues Farrelly, is one that seeks a middle ground between judicial and legislative supremacy. Such a middle ground recognizes the importance, as well as the limitations, of different deliberative institutions (e.g. legislatures, courts).

In "A Virtue-Centered Account of Equity and the Rule of Law," the first of two chapters from Lawrence B. Solum, Solum examines the supposed tension between the ideals of the rule of law and equity. The rule of law has many different meanings, and one interpretation maintains that the rule of law requires a law of rules. This can be contrasted with the requirements of equity. A common understanding of equity is that legal decision makers sometimes ought to depart from the rules in order to do justice in particular cases. Thus, equity helps correct for the law's generality by filling gaps in the law. And so it appears that equity conflicts with the requirements of the rule of law.

Solum examines this alleged tension. He distinguishes between a number of different approaches to the conflict (e.g. characterizations of the conflict as a conceptual conflict, emphasizing the distinction between rules and discretion in adjudication) which help lay the foundation for his central argument—that a virtue-centered theory of judging grounds a reconciliation of equity with the rule of law. Solum's argument has important consequences for the attention we ought to give to the character of candidates for judicial office. Excellence in judging requires more than the avoidance of human vices, argues Solum. Excellent judges must possess many virtues (e.g. judicial intelligence, good temperament) and a moral vision and wisdom that can only be developed through experience.

In "Natural Justice: An Aretaic Account of the Virtue of Lawfulness," Solum argues that justice is a *natural virtue*. That is, justice is a natural characteristic of well-functioning humans and of well-functioning human societies. For Solum, natural justice is related to moral naturalism—the view that moral facts are natural facts (as opposed to being supernatural or transcendental). Solum's rich essay covers a diverse range of topics, from the fact-value distinction and the open-question argument to the fairness and lawfulness conceptions of justice. His investigation of natural justice is developed through three stages. From virtue ethics, he develops the idea of virtue jurisprudence. From natural goodness, he derives the notion of natural justice. And from natural justice, he comes to the theme of natural law.

A central tenant of the natural law tradition is the claim that "an unjust law is not true law." Solum modulates this slogan, via an appeal to virtue jurisprudence, into the slogan "defective norms are not true *nomoi*." An excellent judge is someone who grasps the importance of lawfulness and is disposed to act on the basis of the laws and norms of his or her community. A fully virtuous agent is not disposed to act in accord with social norms that undermine human flourishing or that lack legitimate authority. Solum believes that virtue jurisprudence provides the best contemporary expression of the natural law thesis that there is an essential connection between law and justice.

Chapters 7 and 8, by Antony Duff and Kyron Huigens respectfully, examine the merits and demerits of an Aristotelian account of criminal law. Duff, the critic, contends that while virtue and vice can play a useful role explaining some aspects of criminal liability, the grander ambitions of Aristotelian theorists are misguided. The criminal law should not take an interest in virtue or vice in the rich sense that in order to determine if someone is truly virtuous or vicious, we need to examine their emotional and appetitive dispositions, the patterns of feeling and desire which constitute their behavior.

When we try to determine whether a defendant's action was dishonest, argues Duff, we are not interested in whether another person's property appeared to him as a temptation he should resist, but gave in; or as something he assessed simply in terms of whether or not he could steal and get away without being detected. Nor are we concerned with the issue of whether or not he felt remorse after the crime. When it comes to criminal liability, our primary focus should not be on the character of an agent, but rather the character of their *action*. The focus on the latter is crucial if one wishes to set liberal limits on the extent to which the criminal law should be allowed to inquire or intrude into people's lives.

In "On Aristotelian Criminal Law: A Reply to Duff," Huigens responds to the criticisms made by Duff. Huigens begins by reviewing the shortcomings of the leading theories of punishment—utilitarian and retributive theories. The domination of consequentialist and deontological theories of punishment obscures the complexity and richness of the field of criminal law. Huigens argues that once due care is taken to distinguish between theory, end, and justification, the possibility of an aretaic theory of punishment becomes more obvious. Contra Duff, Huigens contends that the aretaic theory is compatible with the liberal tradition of limited government and that it supports the political ideal of deliberative normative community.

Huigens believes that Duff is correct when he claims that the place of vice in criminal law is, at best, a minor one. But Huigens claims that Duff is wrong in thinking that Aristotelian theories of punishment need to claim otherwise. The aretaic account of wrongdoing and fault is premised not on vice as a character trait but on a failure of practical reasoning. A free society is only sustainable when free individuals choose, in most situations, the right course of action. And thus Huigens does not see governance at the level of ends, desires, and motivations as jeopardizing liberal aspirations. Rather, such governance supports the liberal value of autonomy.

The last chapter in this volume is Rosalind Hursthouse's essay "Two Ways of Doing the Right Thing." Hursthouse's essay is a specially commissioned piece she wrote just for this volume. And we are very grateful that she kindly accepted our invitation to write an article on virtue and lawyers. This final chapter illustrates yet again the rich insights that the virtue ethics tradition can offer not only ethicists and legal scholars but also legal practitioners.

Lawyers' professional roles can often put a lawyer in difficult moral dilemmas. Dilemmas where their professional role requires them to do one thing—like maintain client confidentiality—and morality requires them to do the opposite. A famous example of such a dilemma is the Lake Pleasant Bodies Case, a case where the lawyers actually obtained information concerning the whereabouts of the bodies of the people their client had killed. If the lawyers made this information public, they could help minimize the harms imposed on the grieving families. But doing so would compromise the duty of confidentiality lawyers have to their clients. What are we to make of such dilemmas? Is it possible for someone to be a lawyer and be a virtuous person? Hursthouse argues that it is.

Hursthouse illuminates the insights of a virtue ethics analysis of such ethical dilemmas by drawing attention to the way virtuous agents react when they are placed in moral dilemmas. A virtuous lawyer must do a lot more than simply fulfill his or her role obligations. And they must do a lot more than *fulfil–them–with–an–appropriate–feeling of* regret. According to Hursthouse, virtuous lawyers must do the right thing in a virtuous way and, secondly, they must go the extra mile for justice. Doing this, she acknowledges, will not be easy. But no one ever said being virtuous would be easy.

Notes

1. We do not mean to imply that these two questions exhaust the tasks of contemporary legal theory. For example, a perennial question for legal theory concerns the nature of law—with natural law theory and legal positivism as the two leading contenders. Virtue jurisprudence can enter into that debate as well, although its contribution is outside the scope of this introduction.
2. Elizabeth Anscombe, *Modern Moral Philosophy* in Virtue Ethics: Oxford Readings in Philosophy, pp. 26–44 (originally 33 Philosophy (1958), reprinted in Religion, Ethics, and Politics, 3 The Collected Papers of G. E. M. Anscombe (1981) and in Ethics (Judith Thompson and Gerald Dworkin eds, 1968)).
3. Louis Kaplow and Steven Shavell, *Fairness versus Welfare*, 114 Harv. L. Rev. 961 (2001).
4. Louis Kaplow and Steven Shavell, Fairness versus Welfare (Cambridge, MA: Harvard University Press, 2002).
5. Ronald Dworkin, Law's Empire (1986); Ronald Dworkin, A Matter of Principle (1985); Ronald Dworkin, Taking Rights Seriously (1978).
6. *See* John Rawls, *The Independence of Moral Theory*, 48 Proceedings and Addresses of the American Philosophical Association 5–22 (1975).
7. Pam Hartman, How anger turns to 'social rage', Mobile Register, 2005, http://www.al.com/opinion/mobileregister/index.ssf?/base/opinion/1112545146171620.xml (visited June 12, 2007) (discussing murders caused by anger at judges); Susan Estrich, Now is a tough time to be a judge, The Sun News, March 25, 2005, http://www.myrtlebeachonline.com/mld/

sunnews/news/opinion/11226003.htm (stating "everyone was shaken up by what happened to the Lefkow family in Chicago, the cold-blooded murder of a judge's husband and aged mother").

8. Our view of the virtue of temperance has been improved by recent work by Nancy Sherman. See 2.2. Nancy Sherman, Aristotle, the Stoics, and Kant on Emotions, http://asweb.artsci.uc.edu/philosophy/news/colloqPresentations/Sherman.pdf (visited June 12, 2007).
9. *See* Plutarch, Moralia, On the Control of Anger; Seneca, On Anger.

1
The Central Tradition—Its Value and Limits

Robert P. George

1. The 'perfectionism' of the central tradition

Alasdair MacIntyre has defined a 'tradition' of thought and enquiry regarding justice and political morality as

> an argument extended through time in which certain fundamental agreements are defined and redefined in terms of two kinds of conflict: those with critics and enemies external to the tradition who reject all or at least key parts of those fundamental agreements, and those internal, interpretative debates through which the meaning and rationale of the fundamental agreements come to be expressed and by whose progress a tradition is constituted.[1]

This definition certainly makes sense of what Sir Isaiah Berlin refers to as 'the central tradition of western thought' about morality, politics, and law (and their interrelationships).[2] This tradition is indeed 'an argument extended through time' whose 'fundamental agreements' have been defined and redefined by internal debate as well as by disputation with external critics. Among these 'fundamental agreements' is the belief that sound politics and good law aspire not only to help make people safe, comfortable, and prosperous, but also to help make them virtuous. It is, above all, the belief that law and politics are rightly concerned with the moral well-being of members of political communities that distinguishes the central tradition from its principal rivals.

Mainstream contemporary liberalism (which, after the demise of Marxism, is surely *the* principal rival), challenges the 'perfectionism' of the central tradition as inconsistent with a due regard for human liberty. It rejects the central tradition's aspirations to help 'make men moral' on the ground that perfectionist laws and policies violate fundamental principles of justice and human rights. Orthodox liberals maintain that the moral perfection of human beings, while in itself desirable, is not a valid reason for *political* action. Hence, they advance 'anti-perfectionist' theories of justice and political morality that rule out 'morals laws' and other perfectionist policies as a matter of moral principle.

In *Making Men Moral* I defend the perfectionism of the central tradition. I shall argue that sound politics and good law *are* concerned with helping people to lead morally upright and valuable lives, and, indeed, that a good political society may justly bring to bear the coercive power of public authority to provide people with some protection from the corrupting influences of vice.[3] I am not prepared, however, to endorse everything that the principal architects of the central tradition have said regarding the legitimacy of political action undertaken for the sake of leading people to virtue. So in this chapter I shall lay out what I accept, and what I reject, and say why.

I shall focus on the perfectionism of Aristotle and Aquinas, the two thinkers who have most profoundly influenced the tradition. Although the tradition, as embodied in actual laws and policies as well as in the thinking of later philosophers, has not followed their teachings in every respect, it is imbued with their perfectionist understandings of justice and political morality. In rejecting perfectionism, orthodox liberals deny the validity of essential tenets of Aristotelian and Thomistic political theory. I concede that liberalism is rightly critical of important elements of the political teachings of Aristotle and Aquinas, but shall argue that, stripped of these mistaken ideas, their perfectionism is sound and defensible.

2. Aristotle on the role of the *polis* in making men moral

No one deserves more credit (or blame) than Aristotle for shaping the central tradition's ideas about justice and political morality. Centuries before the liberal assault on the tradition got into full swing, Aristotle himself anticipated, criticized, and firmly rejected what has become the defining doctrine of mainstream contemporary liberalism, namely, the belief that the law of a political community (*polis*) should be merely '(in the phrase of the Sophist Lycophron) "a guarantor of men's rights against one another"—instead of being as it should be, a rule of life such as will make the members of a polis good and just'.[4] Aristotle's argument in his *Politics* was that:

> any polis which is truly so called, and is not merely one in name, must devote itself to the end of encouraging goodness. Otherwise a political association sinks into a mere alliance, which only differs in space [i.e. in the contiguity of its members] from other forms of alliance where the members live at a distance from one another ... a polis is not an association for residence on a common site, or for the sake of preventing mutual injustice and easing exchange. There are indeed conditions which must be present before a polis can exist; but the presence of all these conditions is not enough, in itself, to constitute a polis. What constitutes a polis is an association of households and clans in a good life, for the sake of attaining a perfect and self-sufficing existence .... It is therefore for the sake of good actions, and not for the sake of social life, that political associations must be considered to exist.[5]

Making men moral, Aristotle supposed, is a—if not *the*—central purpose of any genuine political community. Why?

To answer this question, we must turn to Aristotle's writing on moral goodness and virtue. Near the end of the *Nicomachean Ethics*, he pointedly asks why sound moral arguments are not in and of themselves sufficient to lead men away from vice and toward virtue. Having provided, at least in outline, a philosophical account of 'the virtues, and also friendship and pleasure', Aristotle suggests the need for the project he undertakes in his *Politics*, observing that:

> while [moral arguments] seem to have power to encourage and stimulate the generous-minded among our youth, and to make a character which is gently born, and a true lover of what is noble, ready to be possessed by virtue, they are not able to encourage the *many* to nobility and goodness.[6]

Why not? Are 'the many' too stupid to understand moral arguments? People obviously differ in native intelligence; and it is plausible to think that only a minority of people have the intellectual capacity to follow the most subtle and complex philosophical arguments. Is it the case that, when it comes to the power of moral arguments to encourage and stimulate people to nobility and goodness, the difference between 'the many' for whom the arguments are insufficient, and the few for whom they are virtually all that is needed, is one of native intelligence?

No. While Aristotle suggests that 'the many' and 'the few' differ by nature, the relevant difference, as he sees it, is not, or at least not fundamentally, a difference in raw intellectual capacity to follow philosophical argumentation. Rather, it is from the start a difference in *character*. The problem with 'the many' is that:

> these do not by nature obey the sense of shame, but only fear, and do not abstain from bad acts because of their baseness but through fear of punishment; living by passion they pursue their own pleasures and the means to them, and avoid the opposite pains, and have not even a conception of what is noble and truly pleasant, since they have never tasted it.[7]

Is virtue, then, unattainable by 'the many'? Is the average person, 'living by passion', and lacking 'a character which is gently born, and a true lover of what is noble', simply incapable of living virtuously? Aristotle indeed concludes that moral argument is futile with such people. It is pointless to argue with them. Argument can merely inform people of the right thing to do; it cannot motivate them to do it. Thus argument is sufficient only for the already 'generous-minded' few who have been blessed by nature with a character 'ready to be possessed by virtue'. Nevertheless, Aristotle holds that other means may dispose those whose character is not 'gently born' to attain some measure of moral goodness:

> It is hard if not impossible, to remove by argument the traits that have long since been incorporated in the character; and perhaps we must be content if, when all the influences by which we are thought to become good are present, we get some tincture of virtue.[8]

What are these 'influences by which we are thought to become good'? How can 'the many' be brought under them? Plainly Aristotle supposes that character is, by and large, given by nature. Of nature's part in making men good, he says that it 'evidently does not depend on us, but as a result of some divine causes is present in those who are truly fortunate'. Nevertheless, he maintains that the character of the average person is not completely fixed by nature; it can be improved, if only slightly, by good influences. These influences can supply a bit (though apparently not much) of what nature has left out of the character of the average person, thus making it possible for him to 'get some tincture of virtue'.

Inasmuch, however, as the average person is moved by passion and not by reason, what is needed to prepare him for virtue is not argument, but coercion. 'In general', Aristotle says, 'passion seems to yield not to argument but to force.'[9] Therefore, if 'the many' are to have even the small measure of moral goodness of which they are capable, they must be forbidden from doing what is morally wrong and required to do what morality requires; and these commands must be backed by threats of punishment. If people have passionate motives (e.g. love of pleasure) for doing what is morally bad, they must be presented with more powerful countervailing passionate motives (e.g. fear of pain) not to do it. While people motivated by love of what is morally good can be expected to do the right thing *because* it is the right thing (once they understand it to be the right thing), people motivated by passion cannot be expected to do the right thing when they have a passionate motive not to do it and no more powerful countervailing passionate motive to do it. They can be expected to do what is right only when their passionate motives for doing so are more powerful than any competing passionate motives for not doing so. A lively fear of a sufficient punishment typically provides the countervailing motive needed to get the average person to do what is right and avoid doing what is wrong.

Building thus on an analysis of character and its formation, Aristotle develops his view of the role of law in providing the influences necessary to make men moral. Here again I shall let Aristotle speak for himself:

> But it is difficult to get from youth up a right training for virtue if one has not been brought up under right laws; for to live temperately and hardily is not pleasant to most people, especially when they are young. For this reason their nurture and occupations should be fixed by law; for they will not be painful when they have become customary. But it is surely not enough that when they are young they should get the right nurture and attention; since they must, even when they are grown up, practise and be habituated to them, we shall need laws for this as well, and generally speaking to cover the whole of life; for most people obey necessity rather than argument, and punishments rather than the sense of what is noble.[10]

Apparently referring to the teaching of Plato, he goes on to observe that:

> This is why some think that legislators ought to stimulate men to virtue and urge them forward by the motive of the noble, on

> the assumption that those who have been well advanced by the formation of habits will attend to such influences; and that punishments and penalties should be imposed on those who disobey and are of inferior nature, while the incurably bad should be completely banished. A good man ... will submit to argument, while a bad man, whose desire is for pleasure, is corrected by pain like a beast of burden. This is, too, why they say the pains inflicted should be those that are most opposed to the pleasures men love.[11]

It may seem from these passages that Aristotle has missed an elementary point about moral goodness, namely, that coercing people to do the right thing, even when it is successful, does not make them morally better; it does nothing more than produce external conformity to moral norms. Morality, however, is above all an internal matter, a matter of rectitude in choosing: one becomes morally good precisely, and only, by doing the right thing *for the right reason*. In other words, morality, unlike knowledge, or beauty, or even skillful performance, is a reflexive good, namely, a good that is (and can only be) realized in *choosing* uprightly, reasonably, well; a good into whose very definition *choice* enters.[12] A coerced choice, however, does not adopt the good and the reason which might have shaped the chosen option; instead one adopts that option for the sake of avoiding pain, harm, or loss to oneself. So, someone is not 'just and noble' for doing merely out of fear of punishment something that would truly be just and noble if done for the sake of what is good and right. If the legal enforcement of moral obligations does nothing more for the masses than present them with subrational motives for outward conformity with what morality requires, it does nothing toward making men moral.

Aristotle's point, however, is not that moral good is realized whenever the law produces in people outward behavior that conforms with what morality requires, even if that behavior is purely the product of fear of punishment. Rather, his point is that, given the natural tendency of the majority of people to act on passionate motives in preference to reason (i.e. love of the good), the law must first settle people down if it is to help them to gain some appreciation of the good, some grasp of the intrinsic value of morally upright choosing, some control by their reason of their passions. Mere arguments will not do the job, 'for he who lives as passion directs will not hear argument that dissuades him, nor understand it if he does'.[13] It is precisely inasmuch as the average man is given to passions that, 'like a beast of burden', he must be governed by fear of punishment. The law must combat his emotional motives for wrongdoing with countervailing emotional motives. Once the law is successful in calming his passions and habituating him to doing what is right and avoiding what is wrong, he—unlike a brute animal—may gain some intelligent, reasonable, and reflective control of his passion. Even the average person may then learn to appreciate the good a little, and, in choosing for the sake of the good, become morally better.[14]

Someone might object to Aristotle's claim that legal coercion can help put people into shape to appreciate the value of moral uprightness by settling them down and habituating them to virtue, on the ground that the more likely effect of such coercion is to instill resentment in people, and even incline them to rebellion. Here, too, Aristotle has an answer: 'While people hate *men* who oppose their impulses, even if they oppose them rightly, the law in its ordaining of what is good is not burdensome'.[15] What he appears to have in mind here is that, while resentment and rebellion can be expected where one person brings coercion to bear against another in an effort to prevent him from doing something morally wrong, people will accept coercion more readily when an immoral act is prohibited *generally*, that is, throughout a society, and by the *impersonal* force of the law.

Why, though, does Aristotle suppose that immoral acts must be prohibited by *public* authority as opposed to the authority of the head of the household or family? His argument is that:

> the paternal command ... has not the required force or compulsive power (nor in general has the command of one man, unless he be king or something similar), but the law has compulsive power, while it is at the same time a rule proceeding from a sort of practical wisdom and reason.[16]

It is, once again, the generality of legal prohibition that makes the difference. People, notably including children, are formed not only in households, but in neighborhoods, and wider communities. Parents can prohibit a certain act, but their likelihood of success in enforcing the prohibition, and transmitting to their children a genuine grasp of the wrongness of the prohibited act, will be lessened to the extent that others more or less freely perform the act.

For example, parents can forbid their teenage sons to look at pornographic magazines; if, however, other boys with whom they have contact are freely circulating such material, it will be difficult for the parents to enforce their prohibition. Moreover, the boys whose parents have forbidden them to have pornography are likely to experience that prohibition as more onerous to the extent of their knowledge that other boys are free to indulge their taste for pornography. They are more likely to feel resentment, and to rebel, when they are being deprived of a freedom that others enjoy. Whatever authority parents have over their own children, they lack the authority to deprive other people in the community, or other people's children, of the legal liberty to perform immoral acts; only public officials possess authority of that kind. If, however, public authorities fail to combat certain vices, the impact of widespread immorality on the community's moral environment is likely to make the task of parents who rightly forbid their own children from, say, indulging in pornography, extremely difficult.

Nevertheless, Aristotle argues that where the *polis* is failing to do its job, other institutions, including households, should do what they can to prevent immorality.

> Now it is best that there should be a public and proper care for such matters; but if they are neglected by the community it would seem right for each man to help his children and friends towards virtue, and that they should have the power, or at least the will, to do this.[17]

Indeed, he seems to recognize that the kind of moral formation that goes on in families, whatever its limitations, has certain advantages in the formation of moral character.

> For as in cities laws and prevailing types of character have force, so in households do the injunctions and habits of the father, and these have even more because of the tie of blood and the benefits he confers; for the children start with a natural affection and disposition to obey. Further, private education has an advantage over public; for while in general rest and abstinence from food are good for a man in a fever, for a particular man they may not be.... It would seem, then, that the detail is worked out with more precision if the control is private; for each person is more likely to get what suits his case.[18]

In short, families, unlike political authorities, can deal with individuals as individuals, taking into account their distinctive needs and circumstances. So, Aristotle finally implies, making men moral is not a task for the *polis* alone: political communities should do what they can to encourage virtue and prevent vice, while other institutions should do what they can to complement the work of the *polis*.[19]

3. Aquinas on the moral aims of law and government

More than fifteen hundred years after Aristotle's death, his greatest Christian disciple, St Thomas Aquinas, made his own enquiry into the point and purposes of human law in his *Summa Theologiae*, and reached similar conclusions about the need for law to concern itself with making men moral.[20] While Aquinas certainly seems more optimistic, as, perhaps, a Christian should be, about the universality of what he calls man's 'natural aptitude for virtue', he agrees with Aristotle that 'the perfection of virtue must be acquired by man by means of some kind of training'.[21] Moreover, he shares Aristotle's doubts that 'man could suffice for himself in the matter of this training, since the perfection of virtue consists chiefly in withdrawing man from undue pleasures, to which above all man is inclined, and especially the young who are more capable of being trained'.[22] With Aristotle, Aquinas acknowledges that there are some people 'who are inclined to acts of virtue by their good natural disposition, or by custom, or rather by the gift of God'; as for these, 'paternal training suffices, which is by admonitions'.[23] At the same time, however:

> since some are found to be dissolute and prone to vice, and not easily amenable to words, it was necessary for such to be restrained from evil by force and fear, in order that, at least, they might desist from evildoing, and leave others in peace, and that they themselves, by being habituated in this way, might be brought to do willingly what hitherto they did from fear, and thus become virtuous. Now this kind of training, which compels through fear of punishment, is the discipline of laws. Therefore, in order that man might have peace and virtue, it was necessary for laws to be framed.[24]

When Aquinas comments on the *Nicomachean Ethics*, he expounds what Aristotle says there without demurrer, suggesting that he is generally in agreement with it. In his advice to a Christian king, entitled *De Regno*, however, he gives a different (though not necessarily incompatible) rationale for the legal enforcement of morality, a peculiarly Christian rationale which, of course, never would have occurred to Aristotle.

Aquinas's basic premiss in *De Regno* is that what is good for everybody, in the end, is getting to heaven. The attainment of heavenly beatitude is the central common good of the people. The realization of this good (or goal) is not only what the Church is there for, it is the ultimate reason for the existence of public authority as well. The king serves the common good by getting the community into shape so that people are meeting their obligations to love their neighbors, thus fulfilling the second table of the Decalogue, and, through the redemption effected by Christ, getting themselves into heaven.

> Therefore since the beatitude of heaven is the end of that virtuous life which we live at present, it pertains to the king's office to promote the good life of the multitude in such a way as to make it suitable for the attainment of heavenly happiness, that is to say, he should command those things which lead to the happiness of Heaven and, as far as possible, forbid the contrary.[25]

How is the king to determine what leads to heavenly happiness? Aquinas says that 'What conduces to true beatitude and what hinders it are learned from the law of God, the teaching of which belongs to the office of the priest'.[26] Having been instructed by the priest as to the law of God, the king 'should have for his principal concern the means by which the multitude subject to him shall live well'.[27] The task of the king is to lead people to virtue by a gradual process: 'first of all, to establish a virtuous life in the multitude subject to him; second, to preserve it once established; and third, having preserved it, to promote its greater perfection'.[28]

Aquinas recognizes that a king who wishes to fulfill his duty to lead the people to virtue must establish and maintain the conditions for people to lead virtuous lives. These conditions are material as well as moral. First, he says, it is necessary for 'the multitude [to] be established in the unity of peace'. Second, the multitude, thus united, must be 'directed to acting well'. And third, 'it is necessary that there be at hand a sufficient supply of the things required for proper living, procured by the ruler's efforts'.[29] The material conditions, that is, 'a sufficiency of those bodily goods whose use is necessary for a virtuous life', while 'secondary and instrumental' to a man's living in a virtuous manner, must be secured if the ruler is to fulfill his duty.[30] Without the unity of peace, and other material goods, the political order will lack the stability it needs to function for the common good of its members. Indeed, security as well as stability, is needed; hence, the king must 'keep the multitude entrusted to him safe from the enemy, for it would be useless to prevent internal dangers if the multitude could not be defended from external dangers'.[31]

In *De Regno* Aquinas declares that the king should 'by his laws and orders, punishments and rewards... restrain the men subject to him from wickedness and induce them to virtuous deeds'.[32] Recognizing, however, that there are limits to what can be effectively and prudently commanded by public authority, he holds that evil-doing should be forbidden 'as far as possible'. In the *Summa Theologiae,* he explains these limits in reply to the famous question of 'whether it belongs to human law to repress all vices'.[33] His answer is that 'human law rightly allows some vices, by not repressing them'. His reasoning begins from the premiss that law should fit the condition of the people, many of whom will be quite imperfect in virtue and therefore incapable of living up to the highest standards of morality. 'Many things', he says, 'are permissible to men not perfect in virtue, which would be intolerable in a virtuous man'.

> Now human law is framed for the multitude of human beings, the majority of whom are not perfect in virtue. Therefore human laws do not forbid all vices, from which the virtuous abstain, but only the more grievous vices, from which it is possible for the majority to abstain; and chiefly those that are injurious to others, without the prohibition of which human society could not be maintained. Thus the law prohibits murder, theft and the like.

Aquinas is not here opposing in principle, as Joel Feinberg supposes he is,[34] the criminalization of victimless immoralities. Rather, he is acknowledging the need for any legislator to tailor the criminal law to fit the character and state of his particular society. Of course, Aquinas recognizes that some things must be forbidden in every society, for the simple reason that social life is impossible unless they are prohibited. Thus, no society can afford to leave its members generally free to kill or steal from each other. According to Aquinas, the law can and should go beyond the prohibition of these evils, however, to prohibit other serious wrongs that average people in the society can generally abstain from committing. Aquinas does not in the least deviate from Aristotle's view that the lawgiver should try to lead men to virtue. He merely notes the fact that the legal prohibition of their immoral acts cannot suddenly make men moral.

> The purpose of human law is to lead men to virtue, not suddenly, but gradually. Therefore it does not lay upon the multitude of imperfect men the burdens of those who are already virtuous, viz., that they should abstain from all evil. Otherwise these imperfect ones, being unable to bear such precepts, would break out into yet greater evils...

> the precepts are despised, and those men, from contempt, break out into evils worse still.[35]

The limits of legal prohibition of vice, for Aquinas, are not based on any supposed moral right of those whose actions might otherwise be prohibited. He does not suppose that people have a moral right to the legal liberty to perform immoral acts. He cites no principle of political morality which is transgressed by legislators who bring the coercive force of the law to bear against, say, putatively victimless immoralities. Rather, he judges it morally right to refrain from legally prohibiting vice where, given the condition of the people, the prohibition is likely to be futile or, worse yet, productive of more serious vices or wrongs. Citing Isidore, he holds that laws, if they are to serve the common good of leading the people to virtue, must be 'according to the customs of the country',[36] and 'adapted to place and time'.[37]

What Aquinas appears to have in mind is that laws which the multitude of a people generally find too difficult to comply with will produce a negative attitude toward the law in general, and lead to resentment and hardening of hearts, and possibly even rebellion. If, as Aristotle thought, the project of leading people to virtue requires that the law 'calm them down', and habituate them to doing the right thing, then the laws imposed on them toward these ends must be laws that they can bear. If a law provokes resentment and rebelliousness, then, far from calming passion-driven people so that they can become virtuous, the law will enflame their passions and make them less virtuous.[38] Hence, the prudent legislator will be careful to make the law fit the condition of the people, and not to make legal prohibitions too onerous.

Such reasoning might reasonably be described as prudential, and I will so describe it hereinafter. But its fundamentally moral character is made clear enough when later in the *Summa Theologiae* Aquinas discusses whether Christian rulers should tolerate the rites of Jews and infidels.[39] Such rites, he thinks, should be tolerated when not doing so will either lead to worse things or interfere with the achievement of better things. He cites an example from St Augustine's writings of the need sometimes to tolerate prostitution 'so that men do not break out in worse lusts'.[40]

On the precise question whether Christian political authorities ought to prohibit non-Christian worship, Aquinas holds that the rites of Jews should be legally tolerated, despite his belief that all Jews should now be Christians. He argues that there is still value in Jewish worship, which foreshadows and prefigures the full truth, despite its imperfection in failing to acknowledge Christ. To forbid such worship would be to lose that genuine, if incomplete, good.

He has no such irenical view toward the rites of infidels, however; he sees nothing of value in their worship. Nevertheless, he argues that they can rightly be tolerated, not to preserve any good, but to avoid greater evils. Which evils? Aquinas seems to be concerned first of all with the disruption and division that would be caused when infidels violate laws that suppress their rites. Moreover, he suggests, forbidding their rites would tend to harden them toward Christianity, thus closing their ears to the Gospel and making the task of evangelization more difficult. In other words, coercing them to avoid what is wrong might have the effect of impeding them from eventually doing what is right, that is, becoming Christians and accepting the divine offer of eternal life. This consequence is worse, he says, than tolerating their valueless worship.

When he turns to the crucial question of compelling *belief*, Aquinas holds that, since belief is by nature voluntary, it is useless to attempt to compel people who are not believers to believe or make the commitment of faith.[41] Nevertheless, he maintains that public authorities may rightly, and indeed should, compel Christians to hold to the religious commitments that they have made and to renounce heresy and apostasy.[42] Apparently he supposes that, while belief cannot be compelled, fidelity to a commitment based on belief can be. He argues that to hold the faith is a matter of moral obligation. His view of the matter is undoubtedly influenced by the norms according to which medieval society functioned: having made a commitment of fealty, one is bound by it; and people to whom one has made the commitment can hold one strictly to it.

Plainly, Aquinas is not thinking of religion as people do today (or as his own Church has come to understand it),[43] that is, as a matter of belief which, as such, must be and remain fully voluntary, and, therefore, uncoerced, if it is to be authentic and have any value. Rather, he is thinking of it as a commitment one has made to God, to which one is bound, and can be held bound by ecclesiastical and civil authority. Indeed, Aquinas goes so far as to defend the executing of heretics on the ground that tolerating heresy permits a cancer to spread in the body politic of political communities ordered and integrated around a religious faith;[44] inasmuch as what heretics do is more damaging to society (whose ultimate goal, after all, is to get people to heaven) than what counterfeiters do, he approves of the harsh way that medieval society dealt with them.

At the same time, he makes a justice-based (or as we would nowadays say, rights-based) argument as to why Christians, and the Christian state, should refrain from requiring baptism of non-Christian children. Recall that the whole point of political society is to help people to fulfill the moral law so that they can get to heaven. The saving of souls is the whole reason for the law. Now, Aquinas believed that, without baptism, people could not attain heavenly beatitude. Nevertheless, he held strictly to the principle that it is wrong to baptize Jewish children, for example, against their parents' wishes, even if doing so is indispensable to their salvation.

His objection to this practice, which many in his day apparently supported, is not merely that 'it would be detrimental to the [Christian] faith', because the forcibly baptized children, once they attain the age of reason, 'might easily be persuaded by their parents to renounce what they had unknowingly embraced'. More importantly, he maintains, the practice 'is against natural justice'. In *Summa Theologiae*, II-II, q. 10, a. 12, he sets out five arguments—more than the two or three he usually offers—for the proposition he means to reject. The number of these arguments, their seriousness, and the quality of the authorities he cites for them (including Augustine and Jerome) make it plain that he intends to take a strong stand on a live issue. His answer begins by putting forward the authority of the Church herself, whose traditions had rejected the idea of baptizing children against their parents' wishes, against her most esteemed theologians. He then argues that 'the parents' duty to look after the salvation of their children', who are, in a sense, 'a part of [them]' entails that 'it would be contrary to natural justice, if a child, before coming to the use of reason, were to be taken away from its parents' custody, or baptized against its parents' wishes'.

4. A Critique of Aristotle and Aquinas

While Aquinas does not say so explicitly, his view of the need for political authorities to uphold public morality by forbidding serious vice is undoubtedly reinforced by the Christian picture of pre-Christian Rome. The idea of what it was like, and what a horrible alternative it is, was spelled out vividly by Augustine:

> The worshippers ... of those gods, whom they delighted to imitate in their criminal wickedness, are unconcerned about the utter corruption of their country. 'So long as ... it enjoys material prosperity [they say], and the glory of victorious war, or, better, the security of

peace, why should we worry? What concerns us is that we should get richer all the time, to have enough for extravagant spending every day, enough to keep our inferiors in their place. It is all right if the poor serve the rich, so as to get enough to eat and to enjoy a lazy life under their patronage; while the rich make use of the poor to ensure a crowd of hangers-on to minister to their pride; if the people applaud those who supply them with pleasures rather than those who offer salutary advice; if no one imposes disagreeable duties, or forbids perverted delights; if kings are interested not in the morality but the docility of their subjects; if provinces are under rulers who are regarded not as directors of conduct but as controllers of material things and providers of material satisfactions, and are treated with servile fear instead of sincere respect. The laws should punish offences against another's property, not offences against a man's own personal character. No one should be brought to trial except for an offence, or threat of offence, against another's property, house, or person; but anyone should be free to do as he likes about his own, or with his own, or with others, if they consent. There should be a plentiful supply of public prostitutes, for the benefit of all those who prefer them, and especially for those who cannot keep private mistresses. It is a good thing to have imposing houses luxuriously furnished, where lavish banquets can be held, where people can, if they like, spend night and day in debauchery, and eat and drink till they are sick: to have the din of dancing everywhere, and theatres full of fevered shouts of degenerate pleasure and of every kind of cruel and degraded indulgence. Anyone who disapproves of this kind of happiness should rank as a public enemy: anyone who attempts to change it or get rid of it should be hustled out of hearing by the freedom-loving majority.'[45]

In these passages, Augustine depicts the kind of public life that can be expected when the law prescinds from questions of 'private' virtue and seeks only to protect one man from another as each struggles to achieve his own satisfactions. His view is that the law cannot be morally neutral in the way that orthodox contemporary liberalism supposes: either it will promote virtue, or it will facilitate vice.

Perhaps every generation must learn for itself that 'private' immoralities have public consequences. In our own time, we have ample reason to doubt that orthodox liberalism's distinction between private and public immorality can be maintained, at least with respect to the types of immoral acts that the central tradition has proposed to forbid or restrict by law. It is plain that moral decay has profoundly damaged the morally valuable institutions of marriage and the family,[46] and has, indeed, largely undercut the understandings of the human person, marriage, and the family that are presupposed by the very idea of sexual immorality and by the ideals of chastity and fidelity which give family life its full sense and viability. It is one thing for radicals or relativists who believe that traditional marriage and family life are oppressive, or merely 'one option among equally valid alternatives', to condemn laws premised on the idea of sexual vice; it is quite another thing, though, for liberals to maintain that even adherents of traditional moral views should accept their critique of morals laws on the ground that the legal prohibition of 'private' immorality serves no public good.[47]

The idea that public morality *is* a public good, and that immoral acts—even between consenting adults—can therefore do public harm, has not been refuted by liberal critics of the central tradition. On the contrary, the idea is vindicated by the experiences of modern cultures which have premissed their law on its denial. The institutions of marriage and the family have plainly been weakened in cultures in which large numbers of people have come to understand themselves as 'satisfaction seekers' who, if they happen to desire it, may resort more or less freely to promiscuity, pornographic fantasies, prostitution, and drugs. Of course, recognition of the public consequences of putatively private vice does not mean that liberalism is wrong to be critical of morals legislation. For, as we shall see in later chapters, contemporary liberals make a variety of moral arguments against such legislation that do not depend on the propositions that public morality is not a public good or that private immorality cannot do public harm. It does mean, however, that a crucial premiss of the tradition's case against moral *laissez-faire* remains unshaken: societies have reason to care about what might be called their 'moral ecology'.

The tradition, as embodied in the sorts of laws and public policies to which orthodox liberalism objects, has not followed Aristotle and Aquinas in every detail. It has come to give greater room to freedom, and to be more circumspect in the use of the law's coercive power, than Aristotle and Aquinas would have thought necessary or appropriate. I shall argue that, where the tradition has developed in these ways, it has been right to do so. Although Aristotle and Aquinas were correct in supposing that the law may justly and appropriately seek to combat vice and encourage virtue, and while the whole tradition, including Aristotle and Aquinas, is superior to liberalism in allowing, in principle at least, for the quasi-paternalistic (and, in some cases, even the paternalistic) and educative use of the law to forbid certain immoralities, their analyses of these questions were flawed in various ways. And, indeed, there are certain respects, especially those touching upon religious liberty, in which the influence of liberalism on the tradition has been salutary.

While ancient and medieval life was not without diversity, Isaiah Berlin is probably correct to criticize the tradition for failing to understand the diversity of basic forms of good and the range of valid pluralism.[48] Aristotle, for example, plainly failed to allow room in his ethical and political theory for the diversity of irreducible human goods which, considered as providing basic reasons for action and options for choice, are the bases for a vast range of valuable, but mutually incompatible, choices, commitments, and plans and ways of life. And he lacked anything like a good argument for his view that there must be a single superior way of life, or a uniquely highest life for those capable of it; nor did he provide anything approaching a plausible theory of where those not capable of what he believed to be the highest life fit into a society that treats that way of life as the best.

Without adopting the relativistic view which sees the good as so radically diverse that whatever people happen to want is good, we can and should recognize a multiplicity of basic human goods and a multiplicity of ways that different people (and communities) can pursue and organize instantiations of those goods in living valuable and morally upright lives. Our recognition of (non-relativistic) value pluralism opens up something that Aristotle never clearly saw: people are not simply disposed by nature (and/or culture) well or badly; they dispose themselves, and can dispose themselves, well or badly, in a vast variety of ways. Human beings put their lives together in different ways by making different choices and commitments based on different values that provide different reasons for choice and action. There is no single pattern anyone can identify as the proper model of a human life, not because there is no such thing as good and bad, but because there are many goods. Moreover, people are fulfilled in part by deliberating and choosing for themselves a pattern of their own. Practical reasoning is not merely a human capacity; it is itself a fundamental aspect of human well-being and fulfillment: a basic dimension of the human good consists precisely in bringing reason to bear in deliberating and choosing among competing valuable possibilities, commitments, and ways of life.[49]

Lacking an appreciation of the diversity of basic human goods, and thus the diversity of valuable ways of life ordinarily available to people, Aristotle wrongly supposed that people have preordained stations in life, and that the wise legislator who is concerned to promote virtue will therefore have the job of slotting people into their proper stations and seeing to it that each person fulfills the duties of his particular station. Working from an implausibly limited and hierarchical view of human good, Aristotle failed to perceive that persons, as loci of human goods and of rational capacity for self-determination by free choices, are *equal in dignity*, however unequal they are in ability, intelligence, and other gifts: hence his élitism, not to mention his notorious doctrine of 'natural slaves'.[50]

Aristotelian élitism is a fundamental and gross error, which is itself rooted in a failure to appreciate the diversity of basic human goods that fulfill the persons in and by whom they are instantiated and realized. It is this diversity that confounds every attempt to identify a 'highest' or 'best' life to which those who are by nature suited to that life (and are thus the 'highest' or 'best' examples of human beings) should aspire. In any event, whatever may have been the case in Aristotle's Athens, legislators in modern representative democracies are unlikely to be morally superior to the people who elect them. One might even argue that, given what it takes to achieve public office, the average legislator today is likely to be generally less strict in the observance of certain moral norms than the average voter.

At the same time, there is in normal circumstances no reason to suppose, as Aristotle did, that the great mass of people are incapable of being reasonable and need to be governed by fear. Nor is there any reason to believe in the existence of a moral élite whose members need only understand moral truth in order to live up to its demands. The fact is that all rational human beings are capable of understanding moral reasons; yet all require guidance, support, and assistance from others. All are susceptible to moral failure, even serious moral failure; and all are capable of benefiting from a milieu which is more or less free from powerful inducements to vice. All require freedom if they are to flourish; but unlimited freedom is the enemy, not the friend, of everyone's well-being.

Once we have brought into focus the diversity of human goods, it becomes clear that legislators concerned to uphold morality cannot prohibit all that much. At most, they can legitimately proscribe only the fairly small number of acts and practices that are incompatible with any morally good life. Paternalism is strictly limited by the diversity of goods whose recognition makes nonsense of the idea of assigning people to 'natural' or 'appropriate' stations in life. Of course, there are morally valuable institutions, such as marriage, which, while not morally obligatory for everyone, are nevertheless worthy of protection. To defend such institutions from forces and developments in a society that may threaten them, legislators will need to understand their nature, value, and vulnerability. It will be complicated, then, for legislators to design laws that protect institutions such as marriage. To ban an act such as adultery on the ground of its intrinsic immorality is fairly straightforward (if difficult to enforce); to design just and good laws pertaining to marital break-up, divorce, and the care of children, however, is not so simple.

Of course, even where intrinsic immorality is not a question, political authorities can rightly regulate the pursuit of certain plans of life, and even forbid them to certain persons because of their lack of ability or appropriate training, in order to protect the public from, say, incompetent physicians, lawyers, accountants, or teachers. In any event, the recognition of a variegated human good, and the consequence of a multiplicity of possible good plans of life, will both limit the scope of the legislation validly aimed at encouraging virtue and discouraging vice, and render the job of legislators concerned to uphold public morality a task more complicated than Aristotle imagined.

Turning to Aquinas, the fundamental and (to the modern reader) obvious problem with his view is that it assumes the propriety of legislating not only morals, but also faith, and indeed of legislating morals precisely in so far as they are accepted on religious authority and are the means to an end (i.e. heavenly beatitude) that religious faith puts forward but reason by itself cannot identify. Aquinas makes the first principle of politics a matter of religious belief, thus proposing a radical establishment of religion that is utterly inconsistent with a due regard for religious liberty. I shall later argue that religion, considered as a basic human good within the grasp of practical reason, can indeed provide a reason for political action. It cannot, however, provide a reason for compelling or forbidding religious belief or practice. Aquinas's approach, in so far as it imperils religious freedom, jeopardizes the value of religion itself.

Aquinas himself, as we saw, perceives that justice, as well as prudence, requires respect for some measure of religious freedom: hence his willingness to tolerate the rites of non-Christians and his principled opposition to requiring the baptism of children against their parents' wishes. He fails, however, to see that the reasons for civil authorities to respect religious liberty extend to everybody, including heretics and apostates. Recognition of the moral grounds of the right to freedom of religion renders unacceptable Aquinas's semi-theocratic (or sacral/consecrational) view of political community and authority.

As we have seen, Aquinas does recognize important prudential limits to the political pursuit of beatitude. He astutely suggests that prudent legislators will tailor the criminal law to the character of the people and the moral state of their society in order to avoid the likely bad consequences of imposing on people burdens that they cannot bear. This point remains valid even when we consider laws to uphold public morality for the sake of virtue as such, rather than as means to getting people to heaven. Taking a cue from Aquinas, we can identify other prudential (and, as such, morally significant) considerations which might militate in favor of a policy of tolerating certain moral evils: for example, (1) the need to avoid placing dangerous powers in the hands of governments that are likely to abuse them; (2) the danger that criminalization of certain vices may have the effect of placing monopolies in the hands of organized criminals who will market and spread the vices more efficiently; (3) the risk of producing secondary crimes against innocent parties; (4) the risk of diverting police and judicial resources away from the prevention and prosecution of more serious crimes; (5) the concern that the power to enforce moral obligations will be exploited by puritanical, prudish, or disciplinarian elements in society to repress morally legitimate activities and ways of life whose genuine value these elements fail to appreciate; (6) the danger of establishing too much authority and creating a situation in which people relate primarily to a central authority whom they must constantly work to avoid offending, thus discouraging them from building genuine relationships with each other to the point of true friendships and valuable communities.

5. The value and limits of perfectionist law and policy

Aquinas is right to say that immorality must sometimes be tolerated in order to avoid morally worse evils, or because, in certain circumstances, the failure to tolerate a certain vice will impede the realization of important goods. These considerations have more extensive implications, however, than Aquinas works out or that people who agree with him in principle commonly suppose. Virtue is instantiated, and virtuous characters are established, by (and only by) choosing right against choosing wrong. Thus any tightly disciplinary regime of law, even if it succeeds in producing outward conformity to moral rules, will tend, as a result of overly aggressive efforts to combat some vices, to create a milieu in which other vices flourish. Wise legislators whose goal is to encourage true moral goodness, and not merely the outward behavior that mimics true virtue, will therefore seek to secure and maintain a moral ecology that is inhospitable not only to such vices as pornography, prostitution, and drug abuse, but also to the vices of moral infantilism, conformism, servility, mindless obedience to authority, and hypocrisy.

Commenting on the situation in Catholic colleges and universities in the United States in the late 1950s, Germain Grisez has remarked on the dangers posed to the moral and spiritual life by approaches to personal formation that fail to take full cognizance of the difference between mere outward conformity to moral rules and genuine moral action.

> This formation involved outward conformity to a detailed set of rules and practices, but it did not guarantee any inward acceptance or conversion. The freedom of the student was not elicited to make a commitment to values which might have grounded the practices he was expected to enact.[51]

Any legislator who understands the human good well enough to be trusted to legislate for any community—political, religious, or even familial—will recognize that there are many important goods that people ought to realize in their lives whose realization is possible only if people freely choose to do 'the right thing'—more exactly, to adopt a morally upright option in situations where at least one option that they are rejecting would be to do the morally wrong thing. Moral goods are 'reflexive' in that they are reasons to choose which include choice in their very meaning; one *cannot* participate in these goods otherwise than by acts of choice, that is, internal acts of will, and the internal disposition established by such choices. As internal acts, they are beyond legal compulsion. Such goods get instantiated precisely in people's choices to do things that they should do when they could willfully fail to do them, or to refrain from doing things that they should not do when they could choose to do them. In light of the reflexivity of moral goods, there would be a compelling reason not to even try to eliminate every opportunity for immorality. Even if, *per impossibile*, a government could do so without damaging people's participation in important non-moral human goods, such an attempt necessarily involves an effort to eliminate choice and directly impede people's participation in the reflexive good. It would therefore be unjust or, as we now say, a violation of a human right.[52]

Moreover, governments have conclusive reasons not to attempt to enforce certain obligations which are essential to valuable social practices whose meaningfulness depends on the parties fulfilling their obligations freely. For example, compelling the expressing of gratitude, or the giving of gifts, or the acknowledging of achievements, where people ought to express gratitude, give gifts, or acknowledge achievements, would have the effect of robbing these important practices of their meaning and value in social life. The reasons for not bringing coercion to bear with respect to such practices do not depend on the circumstances; they are not merely prudential. And they place significant ranges of morality beyond the reach of legislation as a matter of principle.

Nevertheless, the existence of justice- or rights-based grounds, as well as prudential reasons, for 'not repressing every vice', does not entail that there are never valid reasons to legally prohibit *any* vice on the ground of its immorality. The legal prohibition of a vice may be warranted precisely to protect people from the *moral* harm it does to them and their communities. I have already observed that people do not become morally good by merely conforming their outward behavior to moral rules. Someone who refrains from a vice merely to avoid being caught and punished under a law prohibiting the vice realizes no moral good (though he may avoid further moral harm). Laws can compel outward behavior, not internal acts of the will; therefore, they cannot compel people to realize moral goods. They cannot, in any direct sense, 'make men moral'. Their contribution to making men moral must be indirect.

People become morally bad by yielding to vice; and they can be protected from the corrupting influence of powerfully seductive vices by laws that prohibit them (in so far as they are manifest in outward behavior) and prevent them from flourishing in the community. By suppressing industries and institutions that cater to moral weakness, and whose presence in the moral environment makes it difficult for people to choose uprightly, such laws can protect people from strong temptations and inducements to vice. To the extent that morals laws help to preserve the quality of the moral environment, they protect people from moral harm.

Any social environment will be constituted, in part, by a framework of understandings and expectations which will tend, sometimes profoundly, to influence the choices people actually make. People's choices, in turn, shape that framework. The significance of common understandings and expectations with respect to sex, marriage, and family life is obvious. The point extends well beyond these matters, however: the moral environment as constituted, in part, by the framework of understandings and expectations which exists in a particular society will affect everything from people's tendency to abuse drugs, to their driving habits on the highways, to their honesty or dishonesty in filling out their tax returns. If people's moral understandings are more or less sound, and if these understandings inform their expectations of one another, the moral environment thus constituted will be conducive to virtue. In contrast, if human relations are constituted according to morally defective understandings and expectations, the moral environment will seduce people into vice. In neither case will the moral environment eliminate the possibility of moral goodness and badness, for people can be good in bad moral environments and bad in good moral environments. The point remains, however, that a good moral ecology benefits people by encouraging and supporting their efforts to be good; a bad moral ecology harms people by offering them opportunities and inducements to do things that are wicked.

A physical environment marred by pollution jeopardizes people's physical health; a social environment abounding in vice threatens their moral well-being and integrity. A social environment in which vice abounds (and vice might, of course, abound in subtle ways) tends to damage people's moral understandings and weaken their characters as it bombards them with temptations to immorality. People who sincerely desire to avoid acts and dispositions which they know to be wrong may nevertheless find themselves giving in to prevalent vices and more or less gradually being corrupted by them. Even people who themselves stand fast in the face of powerful temptations may find their best efforts to instill in their children a sense of decency and moral integrity thwarted by a moral environment filled with activities and images or representations which, in the unfashionable but accurate phrase of the common law, 'tend to corrupt and deprave'.

Moreover, even people who wish to perform immoral acts but fear doing so lest they be caught and punished, or who would wish to perform them if their opportunities to do so had not been eliminated by the effective enforcement of a morals law, can be protected by effective laws from the (further) moral harm that they would do to themselves. A morals law may prevent moral harm, thus benefiting a potential wrongdoer, simply by protecting him from the (further) corrupting impact of acting out the vice. It is not that the person deterred solely by the law from wrongdoing realizes a moral good by not engaging in the vice. Moral goods cannot be realized by direct paternalism. Rather, it is that he avoids, albeit unwillingly, the bad impact of (further) involvement in the vice on his character.

Of course, it is a mistake to suppose that laws by themselves are sufficient to establish and maintain a healthy moral ecology. It is equally a mistake to suppose, however, that laws have nothing to contribute to that goal. Even apart from their more direct effects in discouraging particular vices or eliminating occasions for people to commit them, morals laws can help to shape the framework of understandings and expectations that helps to constitute the moral environment of any community. As Aristotle and Augustine rightly held, a community's laws will inevitably play an important educative role in the life of the community. They can powerfully reinforce, or fail to reinforce, the teachings of parents and families, teachers and schools, religious leaders and communities, and other persons and institutions who have the leading roles in the moral formation of each new generation.

Although Aristotle was correct in observing that parents sometimes require the assistance of the general and impersonal force of the law to provide their children with a sound moral upbringing, he was wrong to ascribe to the law the role of primary moral educator. As he himself seemed to perceive, sound moral education requires close attention to the moral development of persons who, as individual moral agents, instantiate moral goodness and badness in their choices and actions. Parents, teachers, and pastors can attend to, understand, and work with individual persons in ways that the law simply cannot. Law, as a more or less impersonal guide, must aspire to nothing more than a supporting or secondary role.

At the same time, inasmuch as vice itself often damages and weakens families, schools, and religious institutions, the contribution of law to upholding public morality may be crucial to enabling these institutions to flourish and fulfill their roles as primary moral educators. As modern exponents of the central tradition have carefully explained, however, law goes wrong—it weakens these valuable 'subsidiary'[53] institutions and damages people's moral well-being—when it usurps their role and sets itself up as the primary moral teacher.

Critics of morals legislation often point out that law is a 'blunt instrument'. There is truth in this claim: law really is poorly suited to dealing with the complexities and details of individual's moral lives. Laws can forbid the grosser forms of vice, but certainly cannot prescribe the finer points of virtue. Nevertheless, laws that effectively uphold public morality may contribute significantly to the common good of any community by helping to preserve the moral ecology which will help to shape, for better or worse, the morally self-constituting choices by which people form their character, and in turn affect the milieu in which they *and others* will in future have to make such choices.

Notes

1. *Whose Justice? Which Rationality?* (Notre Dame, Ind.: University of Notre Dame Press, 1988), 12.
2. Isaiah Berlin, *The Crooked Timber of Humanity: Chapters in the History of Ideas* (New York: Alfred A. Knopf, 1991). Writing from the perspective of a forceful

critic of this tradition, it is plain that Berlin does not mean to confer some mark of moral approval upon it by describing it as 'central'. And, while I am considerably more sympathetic to this tradition, I do not make the claim—which would, in any event, be merely tendentious—that this tradition is today more 'central' to Western legal and political institutions than is the tradition of liberalism; hence, I referred to in the Introduction to *Making Men Moral* as the central *pre-liberal* tradition in the West. Nevertheless, liberalism has not simply displaced this tradition. The situation is too complicated to be summed up so neatly. Our institutions are, I think, informed by elements of both traditions, coexisting sometimes in harmony and other times in varying degrees of tension.

3. Certain influential contemporary thinkers have mounted a challenge from within the tradition of liberalism to the mainstream or orthodox view that excludes perfectionism from political theory. Joseph Raz, for example, has severely criticized anti-perfectionist liberalism, and proposed, as an alternative, a perfectionist theory of political morality, according to which 'it is the goal of all political action to enable individuals to pursue valid conceptions of the good and to discourage evil or empty ones' (*The Morality of Freedom* (Oxford: Clarendon Press, 1986), 133). Raz stands with contemporary liberalism, and against the central tradition, however, in his view that 'victimless immoralities' may not legitimately be forbidden by law. I consider Raz's perfectionist liberalism in Ch. 6 of *Making Men Moral*.
4. *Pol*, iii. 5. 1280^{b}; quotations are from the translation by Ernest Barker, in *The Politics of Aristotle* (Oxford: Clarendon Press, 1946). Barker's use of the term 'rights' here is somewhat anachronistic; the modern use of the term is foreign to Greek and Roman thought, and Aristotle's quotation from Lycophron would be more exactly rendered 'guarantor of reciprocal justice'.
5. Ibid.
6. *Nic. Eth.* x. 9. 1179^{b}; quotations are from the translation by W. D. Ross in *The Basic Works of Aristotle* (New York: Random House, 1941).
7. Ibid.
8. Ibid.
9. Ibid.
10. Ibid. x. 9. 1179^{b}–1180^{a}.
11. Ibid. x. 9. 1180^{a}. Cf. Plato's analyses in *Laws*, 722 D ff., and *Protagoras*, 325 A.
12. By such a choice, one *adopts* the good inherent in the right reasons that shaped the option one thus chooses. One determines and integrates one's character, to a greater or lesser degree, around that good and that reason for acting.
13. *Nic. Eth.* x. 9. 1179^{b}.
14. Much later in the tradition, Aristotle's view is echoed by Kant: 'Man must be trained, so as to become domesticated and virtuous later on. The coercion of government and education make him supple, flexible and obedient to the laws; then reason will rule' *Gesammelte Schriften*, xv. 522–3 (Prussian Academy edn., 1923); quoted from the translation by G. Kelly, in *Idealism, Politics and History* (London: Cambridge University Press, 1969).
15. *Nic. Eth.* x. 9. 1180^{a}.
16. Ibid.
17. Ibid.

18. *Nic. Eth.* x. 9. 1180^b.
19. Aristotle's view of the matter appears to be unstable, however, for in *Pol.* i. 1. 1252^b 13–30 he assumes that the household or family is merely an association for the sake of life, while the *polis* is an association for the sake of the good life; and, in *Pol.* viii. 1. 1337^a 23–32, he concludes that education is the responsibility of the *polis* and not (or at least not primarily) the responsibility of parents.
20. *'Summa Theologiae*, I-II, q. 95, a. 1; quotations are from the translation by the Fathers of the English Dominican Province, in *The 'Summa Theologica' of St. Thomas Aquinas* (London: Burns, Oates & Washburn, 1915).
21. Ibid.
22. Ibid.
23. Ibid.
24. Ibid.
25. *De Regno*, iv (i. 15) [115]; quotations are from the translation by Gerald B. Phelan, in *St. Thomas Aquinas On Kingship* (Toronto: The Pontifical Institute of Mediaeval Studies, 1949).
26. Ibid., iv (i. 15) [116].
27. Ibid.
28. Ibid. [117].
29. Ibid. [118].
30. Ibid.
31. Ibid. [120].
32. Ibid.
33. I-II, q. 96, a. 2.
34. See Joel Feinberg, *Harmless Wrongdoing* (New York: Oxford University Press, 1988), 341–2. For a critique of Feinberg's reading of Aquinas on this point, see Robert P. George, 'Moralistic Liberalism and Legal Moralism' *Michigan Law Review*, 88 (1990), 1415–29, at 1421–2.
35. *Summa Theologiae*, I-II, q. 95, a. 1.
36. Ibid. q. 96, a. 2.
37. Ibid. q. 95, a. 3.
38. Here Aquinas, as a Christian thinker, had the advantage of St. Paul's reflections in Ch. 7 of the *Letter to the Romans* on the tendency of the law to make people rebellious.
39. II-II, q. 10, a. 11.
40. Citing Augustine, *De Ordine*, ii. 4. Whatever Augustine's view of the matter, one should not conclude that Aquinas is here endorsing the legalization of prostitution. Whether prostitution ought to be legally prohibited or tolerated is not the issue. He is simply exemplifying the prudential consideration that he has just laid down, and citing Augustine as an authority for it.
41. *Summa Theologiae*, II-II, q. 10, a. 8.
42. Ibid. q. 11, a. 3.
43. See the Declaration on Religious Liberty of the Second Vatican Council, *Dignitatis Humanae*.
44. On the 'sacral' or 'consecrational' nature of medieval political communities, see Jacques Maritain, *True Humanism* (London: Geoffrey Bles, 1941), 135–51.
45. *De Civitate Dei*, ii. 20; quoted from the translation by Henry Bettenson, in *The City of God* (Harmondsworth: Penguin Books, 1972), 71.

46. See William A. Galston, *Liberal Purposes* (Cambridge: Cambridge University Press, 1991), 283–7.
47. In light of the data he considers regarding family break-up, out-of-wedlock births, and the tragic consequences of these phenomena for family life in contemporary America, Galston urges his fellow liberals to reject both 'the proposition that different family structures represent nothing more than "alternative lifestyles"', and 'the thesis that questions of family structure are purely private matters not appropriate for public discussion and response' (ibid. 285).
48. This theme runs through Berlin's essays in *The Crooked Timber of Humanity*.
49. See John Finnis, *Natural Law and Natural Rights* (Oxford: Clarendon Press, 1980), 88–9.
50. For a proper understanding of this doctrine, see W. W. Fortenbaugh, 'Aristotle on Slaves and Women', in J. Barnes, M. Schofield, and R. Sorabji (eds.), *Articles on Aristotle*, ii (London: Duckworth, 1975). Also see Daniel N. Robinson's exceptionally valuable analysis in *Aristotle's Psychology* (New York: Columbia University Press, 1989). It is worth noting here that Professor Robinson, whose penetrating and meticulous scholarship I greatly admire, has proposed an interpretation of Aristotle's eudaimonism that goes far toward the sort of *pluralistic* perfectionism that I myself defend. Interpreted in this way, I find Aristotle's practical philosophy considerably less objectionable. As Professor Robinson points out, however, there are certain 'unavoidable differences in the interpretation of Aristotle's subtle and sometimes inconsistent treatises' (ibid., p. xi).
51. 'American Catholic Higher Education: The Experience Evaluated', in *George A. Kelly (ed.), Why Should the Catholic University Survive?* (New York: St John's University Press, 1973), 44.
52. Mark Twain's *The Man That Corrupted Hadleyburg* calls attention to the dangers *to the moral life* inherent in the effort to ensure that people never make immoral choices.
53. 'Subsidiary' here again means not merely secondary, but assistance-giving: *subsidium* translates into English as 'helpful'.

2

Prudence, Benevolence, and Negligence: Virtue Ethics and Tort Law

*Heidi Li Feldman**

1. Introduction

Tort law assesses negligence according to the conduct of a reasonable person of ordinary prudence who acts with due care for the safety of others.[1] This standard assigns three traits to the person whose conduct sets the bar for measuring negligence: reasonableness, ordinary prudence, and due care for the safety of others. Yet contemporary tort scholars have almost exclusively examined only one of these attributes, reasonableness, and have wholly neglected to carefully examine the other elements key to the negligence standard: prudence and due care for the safety of others. It is mistaken to reduce negligence to reasonableness or to try to understand the sense of reasonableness contemplated by the negligence standard without reference to the virtues of prudence and benevolence. Taken together and analyzed in relation to one another, these three traits define a distinct evaluative perspective, according to which some actions expose oneself and others to inappropriate risk of physical harm, and others do not. In this chapter, I only partially articulate this evaluative perspective, focusing on its dimensions defined by prudence and care and leaving to one side the dimension defined by reasonableness. I have restricted the exposition partly because of limits, of the article format,[2] and partly to counterbalance

*Professor of Law, Georgetown University, affiliated Associate Professor of Philosophy, Georgetown University Law Center, Ph.D., Philosophy University of Michigan, 1993; J. D. University of Michigan, 1990; A. B. Brown University, 1986.
The author thanks Jeffrey Bub, David Luban, Naomi Mezey, and Robin West for comments on drafts of this chapter and thanks Matt Warren for dedicated research assistance in preparing the manuscript for publication.

the overattention to reasonableness that has characterized tort scholarship of the last fifty years.

The dominant tort theories of the previous half century have attempted to explain and shape the normative bite of the negligence standard by incorporating into it intensely moralized conceptions of reasonableness, usually borrowed from Kantianism or utilitarianism and its public policy counterpart, neoclassical welfare economics.[3] Certainly, a comprehensive interpretation of the reasonable person standard needs a satisfactory account of the reasonableness element of that standard.[4] But by itself no account of reasonableness can capture completely negligence law's approach to appraising conduct. The full negligence standard—set by the conduct of a person who is not only reasonable but also duly prudent and careful—advances a more fulsome conception of moral personhood, one that sets as the legal standard a figure who is not only reasonable but also prudential and careful.

This chapter diagnoses contemporary tort scholars' inattention to the full figure that animates negligence law. I explore the moral and economic traditions—Kantianism, utilitarianism, and social welfare economics—that have informed tort scholarship of the past fifty years. These philosophical and economic traditions themselves neglect virtues such as prudence and care, and legal scholarship rooted in them not surprisingly ends up also ignoring these virtues and their centrality to the negligence standard. I introduce an alternative philosophical tradition, virtue ethics, to gain purchase on the role of prudence and care in evaluating conduct. One novel feature of the virtue ethics approach is that, while it relies on character traits as a way of appraising conduct, it does not appraise actions according to the actual subjective motives or character traits of the actor. In other words, virtue ethics does not think that acts inherit their moral worth from the motive of the actor. Instead, virtue ethics identifies particular traits as more or less worthy, asks what sort of acts these traits dispose a person to perform, and then rates acts according to whether or not they are of the kind a person possessed of worthy character traits would perform. This approach to moral epistemology—to the identification of virtuous acts—parallels the inquiry tort law asks juries to make when evaluating whether a defendant's actions were or were not negligent. As I argue below, a standard of conduct based on virtues achieves prescriptivity—the capacity to license or condemn particular acts—via the performance of thought experiments, in which the experimenter "predicts" the behavior of the idealized virtuous person and then sees whether the conduct under judgment coincides or differs from the act forecasted by the thought experiment. In a civil tort action, the fact finder—usually a jury—performs this sort of thought experiment to ascertain how a person possessed of two specific virtues, prudence and due carefulness, would behave in a specific situation. Through this experiment, the jury discovers whether negligence law permits or proscribes the conduct of the alleged tortfeasor.

Viewing the reasonable person standard as a thought-experiment apparatus, which people can use to arrive at conclusions about which acts are inspired or rejected by the virtues of reasonableness, prudence, and due care together, will disquiet those who seek a more reductionist definition of negligence. In general, virtue ethics opposes reductionist interpretations of moral and ethical concepts, denying that we can decide upon good or worthy conduct by applying formulas or algorithms. Much recent tort scholarship has attempted to reduce the meaning of negligence to economic inefficiency or utility-minimization. While this may make calculating negligence easier for those entities supposedly set up to achieve economic efficiency or utility-maximization—that is, the modern corporation—it displaces the sort of context-sensitive, deliberative evaluation of actions traditionally invited by the reasonable person standard. Contrary to the plain language of jury instructions and case law, economic accounts of the reasonable person standard remake the person who animates American negligence law in the image of homo economicus, perhaps to make it easier for corporate persons to align themselves with the image of personhood put forth by tort law.

Aside from the hermeneutic problems with this makeover—the fact that it simply ignores the language of the negligence standard—it raises other, perhaps deeper, concerns. Using the jury to calibrate the meaning of negligence through context-sensitive, case-specific thought experiments allows the citizenry to continuously revisit a fundamental political question: the proper balance between safety and freedom. In a community whose members want to pursue their life plans, each member needs to be safe from risk of personal injury and have the scope to take action. The results of the thought experiments juries perform in civil negligence actions are guideposts to the balance the citizenry endorses. In a political system that assigns sovereignty to the citizenry, it is the citizens who should decide how carefully each must act in an effort to avoid personal injury to others. We cannot hold a referendum each time somebody is about to act and incidentally risk injuring others. We need, therefore, another way of forming and expressing collective judgments about how carefully people should proceed in particular circumstances. Civil negligence actions, in which juries apply a virtue-based standard of care, perform this function.

Viewing negligence through the lens of virtue ethics brings the elements of ordinary prudence and due care into the foreground of our understanding of the negligence standard of care. This in itself sets the virtue-based interpretation apart from tort theory of the past fifty years. But the implications of the virtue-based interpretation extend beyond assigning significance to the elements of ordinary prudence and due care. Because a virtue-based approach conceives of the application of the negligence standard as a thought experiment best performed by lay people, the virtue-based approach is radically democratic and populist, in contrast to most major tort theories advanced from the 1960s through the 1990s.

These theories generally treat the tort system as a vehicle for social engineering. Different theories assign different outputs as the objective, ranging from economically efficient conduct to the realization or protection of Rawlsian equality or Kantian equality, or the implementation of the formal requirements of corrective justice. If these outputs were in fact the dominant point of the tort system, lay jurors and even civil tort actions would be largely superfluous. Lay jurors possess no particular expertise in economic analysis, liberal political and moral philosophy, or the structure of corrective justice. Civil negligence actions do not ask jurors to apply a standard of care that even refers to these matters. To construe the common law of negligence developed via judicial doctrine and jury verdicts as a mechanism of social engineering geared toward any of the goals I listed above is tantamount to rating the common law of negligence a failure. Neither the negligence standard nor the process for developing and applying that standard would be sensible components of an engine meant to churn out economic efficiency, Rawlsian equality, or Kantian autonomy.

One somewhat plausible response to this observation would be to scrap the negligence standard or the common law approach to accidental injury, or both, in favor of a legal or political institution designed specifically to achieve one's preferred output. Even if such measures could be instituted—a doubtful prospect—they are not a good idea. Eliminating the negligence standard and the jury's role in applying it would sacrifice something of political and social importance: the opportunity for popular, collective judgments about how each citizen should conduct herself or himself when the pursuit of her or his own objectives creates the risk of injuring somebody else. Jury verdicts in negligence actions give social content to the virtues of prudence and due care, repeatedly providing concrete conclusions about the sort of conduct that is consistent or inconsistent with these dispositions. In this chapter, I argue that ordinary people are cognitively well-equipped to reach these conclusions through collaboratively comparing a specific defendant's conduct to that of a fictional person endowed with the virtues of prudence and due care who is faced with the circumstances confronted by the actual tort defendant. Jury verdicts reached by such a process preserve popular sovereignty over the appropriate balance between safety and freedom, a fundamental and persistent political question in a society in which people's liberty to act consistently exposes themselves and others to risk of physical injury.

2. Virtue ethics in the landscape of moral theory

For most of the twentieth century—the century of modern tort theory—the majority of moral and political philosophers have been either Kantians or utilitarians. Kantian moral theory focuses primarily on questions of individual autonomy and equality; Kantian political theory focuses on distributive justice, working from the premise that the allocation of resources fundamentally influences autonomy and equality. Utilitarianism focuses on maximizing pleasure and minimizing pain. Utilitarian moral and political philosophy begot microeconomic social welfare theory, the dominant theoretical approach to political economy in the United States for at least the second half of the twentieth century. In the realm of public policy, neoclassical economists have defined the central issue as efficiently maximizing overall social welfare, a project cast in terms of satisfying as many preferences as possible rather than as a problem of increasing pleasure or decreasing pain.[5]

In contrast to these moral and economic traditions, virtue ethics does not concern itself with individual autonomy, social equality, or the monolithic centrality of pleasure or desires in human life. Nor does it fundamentally address distributive justice or the objective of satisfying as many people's preferences as possible (the maximization of social welfare). What unites philosophers in the virtue ethics tradition—a tradition that ranges from ancient Greece to contemporary western societies[6]—is their concern with the quality of human life and an effort to identify both what counts as a life of high quality or worth and the character traits it takes to achieve one.[7]

The virtue ethics enterprise differs in kind from Kantianism, utilitarianism, and welfare economics. Kantianism asks, Which acts accord with moral law, a law that preserves the autonomy of the agents who answer to it? Autonomy and freedom are of central moral importance, and other human concerns fall outside the domain of ethics. Utilitarianism asks, Which acts promote pleasure and diminish pain? These experiential states are all that are relevant to moral life. Welfare economists ask, Which measures maximize the satisfaction of preferences? Subjective desires are the only variable relevant to deciding social policy. Virtue ethics has a more expansive conception of morality and public welfare than any of these other, later traditions. Virtue ethics expands morality to cover many kinds of value that figure in human life, treating as relevant to both individual and social decision making whatever enhances or diminishes the overall quality of human lives. This leads virtue ethicists to an interest in what lends worth to human lives and, therefore, to an interest in the full range of human interests, needs, desires, aspirations, and activities.[8]

This naturalistic humanism separates virtue ethics from Kantianism. According to Kant, if a person acts from desire, need, or want, that person acts heteronomously or instrumentally, in accord with a merely hypothetical imperative; and such action does not qualify as moral.[9] In less technical terms, Kant's point was that human needs, wants, and desires vary from person to person and even from time to time for a single person. Thus, acts motivated by need, desire, or want are contingent upon the existence and content of the need, desire, or want. Kant argued that this sort of contingency has no place in morality.[10] According to him, moral law obtains universally and categorically.[11] It extends to all rational agents, regardless of their needs, wants, and desires; and it cannot be identified by consulting these natural human characteristics. Therefore, according to Kant, action directed toward satisfying human needs, wants, and desires is not moral action.[12] Indeed for Kant morality sits in opposition to what is most natural about humans. Since the satisfaction of human needs, wants, and desires plays an important role in human flourishing, the ideal central to virtue ethics, Kant's moral theory simply does not speak to what matters most from the virtue ethics perspective.

Classical utilitarianism differs from Kantianism in that it makes certain sensations experienced by human beings central to the project of morality. This means that utilitarianism is naturalistic. But in its singular focus on pleasure and pain, utilitarianism is not really humanistic: it does not take seriously the idea of each individual's potential to achieve a rich, full life, the sort of multifaceted flourishing important in virtue ethics. In classical utilitarianism, pleasure is the single good, and morality requires us to act so as to increase pleasure and decrease pain.

Human needs, wants, and desires matter to utilitarians because their satisfaction or disappointment influences the total amount of pleasure or pain in the world. But by focusing morality solely on the production of pleasure and the diminishment of pain, utilitarianism shifts our attention to the overall state of the world at any given moment—to how much pleasure or pain it contains at time T1, T2, T3.... For the utilitarian, morality does not require attention to discrete individuals and the total quality of their lives. Our lives are simply vehicles for experiencing pleasure and pain and our individual actions morally significant only as triggers of pleasure and pain.

Virtue ethics, in contrast to both Kantianism and utilitarianism, regards the entirety of each individual's life as the locus of value. Ethical value does not reside in specific acts that conform to a nonnaturalistic moral law, nor does it reside exclusively in the production or diminishment of pleasure and pain. The good life encompasses many things, including projects, skills, talents, activities, relationships, and sensations. Virtue ethicists approach the question of what makes for a good life by identifying examples of good lives, and then examining the character traits of the individuals who have had them.

Character traits are psychological features of people that dispose them to regularly act in certain ways. They do this by guiding both our perception of and our response to the world around us. Depending upon the character traits a person has, different features of the world stand out to him or her; and, therefore, the world calls for certain responses from him or her.[13] In other words, a person's character traits define his or her evaluative perspective on the world, making some things matter more than others and inducing him or her to perform certain actions rather than others. For example, a funny person appreciates or sees the humor in a situation, and this moves him or her to crack a clever joke about it. To take another trait, a gentle person who sees or appreciates another person's need to be treated tenderly and quietly offers a soothing comment or a reassuring touch.

Just as funny or gentle people do, prudent or duly careful people see situations in a particular light and find certain actions natural or called for in those situations. A prudent person sees opportunities for betterment or gain and ways to realize those opportunities. A duly careful person notices his own and others' vulnerability to injury that he might inadvertently cause, and takes steps to reduce that vulnerability. A person who is both prudent and duly careful is simultaneously sensitive to opportunities for gain and to reducing the risk of injury to others and himself.

3. Prudence, carefulness, and negligence

The qualities of prudence and care, both singled out in the negligence standard, have received attention from virtue ethicists. Both of these qualities go directly to the central concern of virtue ethics: the characteristics that make people's lives better or worse. Acting prudently involves making good judgments about what ends one should have and the most appropriate and effective ways to achieve those ends; acting carefully involves reflecting upon how one's conduct may imperil other people's safety, a prerequisite to their well-being. While virtue ethicists have specifically cited the quality of prudence as a virtue, they have generally referred to benevolence rather than care as the virtue that disposes us to care about other people's flourishing. In this instance, I think the law outruns virtue-ethical theory by taxonomizing concern for others in a more fine-grained way. Due care or consideration for other people's safety is a species of benevolence, part of caring about other people generally. Other legal spheres pertain to other species of benevolence. Family law, for example, takes the best interests of the child as the basic test for settling custody disputes. This test calls for concern for the well-being of children rather than interested adults, and, like due regard for the safety of others, this is a species of a more general concern for others, benevolence. The law of fiduciary duties regulates the conduct of those who handle other people's money (or other financial assets), and this topic focuses on yet another species of benevolence, the concern a trusted or powerful agent must show for others' financial well-being. Precisely because the law governs a variety of particular relationships between individuals across a range of settings, it has developed nuanced species of benevolence, the more general virtue historically discussed in virtue ethics.

3.1 Prudence: in virtue ethics and in the law of negligence

From early in the tradition, virtue ethicists have singled out as a virtue a trait that involves good judgment in the choice and pursuit of one's ends. Aristotle discusses phronesis, sometimes translated as practical wisdom[14] and sometimes as intelligence.[15] Aristotle explains,

> Now it is thought to be the mark of a man of practical wisdom to be able to deliberate well about what is good and expedient for himself, not in some particular respect, e.g., about what sorts of thing conduce to health or to strength, but about what sorts of thing conduce to the good life in general.[16]

Practical wisdom "is a true and reasoned state or capacity to act with regard to the things that are good or bad for man."[17] Later virtue ethicists refer explicitly to prudence. In the medieval period, Thomas Aquinas discussed prudentia, which he describes as the "right reason of things to be done."[18] Adam Smith, a virtue ethicist of the Enlightenment period, regarded prudence as the foundational virtue for achieving one's own well-being.[19] Smith wrote, "The care of the health, of the fortune, or the rank and reputation of the individual, the objects upon which his comfort and happiness in this life are supposed principally to depend, is considered as the proper business of that virtue which is commonly called Prudence."[20] Philippa Foot, a contemporary virtue ethicist, calls Aristotelian phronesis "wisdom" and writes: "Wisdom, as I see it, has two parts. In the first place the wise man knows the means to certain good ends; and secondly he knows how much particular ends are worth."[21]

While philosophical discussion of good ends and practical wisdom or prudence and right reason might sound lofty and high-blown relative to the stuff of tort law—everyday activity that can lead to injury—virtue ethicists themselves have regarded practical wisdom or prudence as a trait called for in everyday life. Aristotle considers such worldly objects as prosperity, friendship, and political power important to flourishing.[22] Since prudence enables us to deliberate about the nature of and means to flourishing,[23] it follows that the Aristotelian conception of prudence includes deliberation about things like prosperity and how to achieve it. Aquinas specifically argues that the body is necessary to achieve human happiness.[24] He goes on to argue that the body requires external goods such as food, drink, and wealth, which serve "as instruments to happiness."[25] Remarks such as these demonstrate that virtue ethicists associate practical wisdom or prudence with the identification and efficacious pursuit of ordinary goals such as wealth or prosperity, convenience, and saving time—the sort of goals that animate our everyday acts, acts which can create more or less risk of injury to other people depending upon how carefully we pursue these goals.

Tort scholars of the early twentieth century undertook the task of giving the doctrinal use of negligence an intellectually coherent interpretation, and their work emphasized the role identifying and pursuing worthwhile ends play in the concept.[26] In 1915, Professor Henry T. Terry published a list of factors relevant to deciding whether conduct constitutes negligence.

> (1) The magnitude of the risk. A risk is more likely to be unreasonable the greater it is.
> (2) The value or importance of that which is exposed to the risk, which is the object that the law desires to protect, and may be called the principal object. The reasonableness of a risk means its reasonableness with respect to the principal object.
> (3) A person who takes a risk of injuring the principal object usually does so because he has some reason of his own for such conduct—is pursuing some object of his own. This may be called the collateral object. In some cases, at least, the value or importance of the collateral object is properly to be considered in deciding upon the reasonableness of the risk.
> (4) The probability that the collateral object will be attained by the conduct which involves risk to the principal; the utility of the risk.
> (5) The probability that the collateral object would not have been attained without taking the risk; the necessity of the risk.[27]

While tort scholars have construed Terry's mention of utility and probabilities as indications that he was groping toward a cost-benefit model of negligence,[28] the text as a whole does not support this interpretation. By citing the importance of the "collateral object"—the actor's own chosen end—and the need to take a risk to achieve that, Terry is describing factors relevant to a person of prudence, somebody who is spotting opportunities and figuring out which conduct would realize them effectively. Terry's list suggests that acting nonnegligently involves noticing which ends are worthwhile from a social perspective and which from a personal one, balancing the importance of each, and taking effective means to achieve this balance. This process differs from economic cost-benefit analysis in a number of ways. It does not characterize the worth of ends in terms of preference satisfaction; it does not suggest that maximal preference satisfaction is always the appropriate balance; and it does not mandate that the balance always be achieved in the most economically efficient fashion.

Another famous tort scholar of the first half of the twentieth century, Professor Warren A. Seavey, claimed that tort law imposes upon people "a duty not to permit [their] activities . . . to create an undue risk of harm to any protected interest of another." Seavey explained that tort law seeks to reconcile "competing interests" when assessing whether risk is undue:

> Persons who act necessarily create risks to others, and unless activity is to be entirely at the risk of the actor it is only where the risk becomes

> excessive that liability is imposed. Since the public is interested in having activities conducted, the law recognizes a privilege for a person who acts in the advancement of his own interests, the interests of a third person, or those of the public, to create risks of harm to third persons which are not disproportionate to the interests sought to be advanced or protected.[29]

Like Terry's, Seavey's understanding of undue risk contemplates a balancing of ends, including the ends of advancing one's own and others' interests in being free from physical harm as well as a variety of other interests, some more personal than others. He does not suggest that this balancing is identical to welfare or utility maximization nor that cost-benefit analysis is the way to judge the appropriate balance. Rather, he writes that the standard qualities relevant to judging this balance are "such knowledge, intelligence, and consideration for the interests of others as is possessed by the normal person in the community."[30] Seavey's emphasis on knowledge and intelligence intimates that the virtue Aristotle called phronesis, Aquinas called prudentia, Smith called prudence, and Foot calls practical wisdom—the virtue of deliberating wisely about what ends contribute to human flourishing and how to achieve them—is a trait valorized in American negligence law.

3.2 Benevolence and care: in virtue ethics and in tort law

Both Terry and Seavey discuss a general regard for others' interests as well as one's own when they interpret the meaning of negligence. In contrast, early virtue ethicists did not delineate a virtue of caring generally about others' welfare, although Aquinas did introduce to Aristotelian ethics the virtue of beneficence, a disposition to give to others, particularly those connected to oneself.[31] The idea of a more general disposition to care about others' well-being, even if not to always actively promote it, enters virtue ethics through the British moral tradition, especially in the work of David Hume and Adam Smith. These philosophers also expressly understood one's character traits to shape one's particular evaluative perspective on the world, both framing how one views any given situation and how one responds to it, especially on an emotional level.

Hume attributed to people sympathy, a psychological tendency to share, literally, other people's feelings.[32] In a Humean moral psychology, sympathy functions as the engine of benevolence. If we literally feel other people's feelings, we will be disposed to care about how they feel because our own feelings vary accordingly. Thus, we will be disposed to act to promote good feelings in others so that we may, through the mechanism of sympathy, enjoy good feelings ourselves. As in Hume's theory, sympathy is foundational to Adam Smith's account of the moral. Smith begins his treatise *The Theory of Moral Sentiments* by noting our tendencies toward sympathy and benevolence: "How selfish soever man may be supposed, there are evidently some principles in his nature, which interest him in the fortune of others, and render their happiness necessary to him, though he derives nothing from it except the pleasure of seeing it."[33]

Unlike Hume, though, Smith does not think that we care about the happiness of others because we actually share directly their feelings. "As we have no immediate experience of what other men feel, we can form no idea of the manner in which they are affected, but by conceiving what we ourselves should feel in the like situation."[34]

Smithean sympathy operates because we can conceive of ourselves in the situation of another and then appreciate how he would feel. "Sympathy, therefore, does not arise so much from the view of the passion, as from that of the situation which excites it."[35] Sympathy leads us to put our own interests and feelings into a broader social perspective.

> [A]s nature teaches the spectators to assume the circumstances of the person principally concerned, so she teaches this last in some measure to assume those of the spectators. As they are continually placing themselves in his situation, and thence conceiving emotions similar to what he feels; so he is constantly placing himself in theirs, and thence conceiving some degree of that coolness about his own fortune, with which he is sensible that they will view it. As they are constantly considering what they themselves would feel, if they actually were the sufferers, so he is as constantly led to imagine in what manner he would be affected if he was only one of the spectators of his own situation. As their sympathy makes them look at it, in some measure, with his eyes, so his sympathy makes him look at it, in some measure, with theirs, especially when in their presence and acting under their observation: and as the reflected passion, which he thus conceives, is much weaker than the original one, it necessarily abates the violence of what he felt before he came into their presence, before he began to recollect in what manner they would be affected by it, and to view his situation in this candid and impartial light.[36]

Sympathy sets the stage for benevolence by inspiring people to conceive of other people's feelings and to efface their conceptions of their own feelings. Benevolence tempers the prudential disposition to promote our own flourishing exclusively rather than aid the flourishing of others.

While Smith, like Hume, thinks that sympathy operates most powerfully with regard to those whom we directly and regularly encounter, he does not preclude its extension to strangers. Not only does Smith think we sympathize with fellow members of our society whom we do not personally know, but he also believes "our good-will is circumscribed by no boundary, but may embrace the immensity of the universe."[37] He claims that, via our imagination, our benevolence extends potentially universally. "We cannot form the idea of any innocent and sensible being, whose happiness we should not desire, or to whose misery, when distinctly brought home to the imagination, we should not have some degree of aversion."[38] This desire for others' happiness and aversion to their misery disposes us to act benevolently toward strangers, to those whose emotions we do not directly observe—so long as we "form an idea" of them.

4. Judgments of negligence: thought experiments in prudence and due care

Virtue ethicists recognize that we do not always act in accord with the virtues available to us. But according to virtue ethics, we naturally have the capacity to see what these traits ask of us. We can take up the perspective of a virtuous person to see how she or he would conduct herself or himself in a particular situation. The more naturally certain virtues come to us, the more easily we can inhabit the perspective they define. In the previous section, I discussed two traits that virtue ethicists have thought particularly amenable to human beings: prudence and benevolence. I noted that expositors of the civil negligence standard seem to presuppose that actions arising from or in accord with these traits are not negligent. In this section, I discuss how jurors can take up the evaluative perspective defined by prudence and benevolence to ascertain the particular actions to be expected from a person of these virtues.

In a civil negligence trial, the judge instructs the jury on the nature of negligence, using definitions such as the following. Note especially that these instructions make no mention of cost-benefit or risk-utility analysis[39] nor any sort of Kantian measure according to which nonnegligent action would be action whose underlying maxim could be universalized to all rational beings.

> Negligence is lack of ordinary care. It is a failure to use that degree of care that a reasonably prudent person would have used under the same circumstances. Negligence may arise from doing an act that a reasonably prudent person would not have done under the same circumstances, or, on the other hand, from failing to do an act that a reasonably prudent person would have done under the same circumstances.[40]

> Negligence is the doing of something which a reasonably prudent person would not do, or the failure to do something which a reasonably prudent person would do, under circumstances similar to those shown by the evidence. It is the failure to use ordinary or reasonable care. Ordinary or reasonable care is that care which persons of ordinary prudence would use in order to avoid injury to themselves or others under circumstances similar to those shown by the evidence.[41]

> Negligence is the doing of some act which a reasonably prudent person would not do, or the failure to do something which a reasonably prudent person would do, when prompted by considerations which ordinarily regulate the conduct of human affairs. It is, in other words, the failure to use ordinary care under the circumstances in the management of one's person or property, or of agencies under one's control.[42]

These instructions typify those given throughout American jurisdictions.[43] According to such instructions, to decide whether a defendant acted negligently, jurors must compare his or her conduct to the exemplar formulated in tort doctrine. Jurors must engage in a thought experiment of a kind: they must ascertain the conduct of a fictional person possessed of particular ethical traits in circumstances like those the actual defendant faced when he or she[44] acted in a way that ultimately caused injury to another person. This thought experiment produces something akin to a prediction of an actual person's behavior in situations where his or her conduct has the potential to injure other people. The completion of the thought experiment yields, I argue below, a politically legitimate, normative expectation that proscribes or permits that particular conduct in similar situations.

Philosophers of mind have advanced two theories about how people might conduct the sort of thought experiment called for by the jury instructions given in negligence actions—that is, how people might cognize in order to predict other people's actions. The older theory, folk psychology, claims that people assume that other people have contentful attitudes that cause them to act in specific ways.[45] That is, when we anticipate another person's actions, we attribute to them certain beliefs, desires, and other attitudes that then move them to act one way or another. When we interpret an action somebody has already taken, we do so by assuming that particular beliefs, desires, and attitudes moved them to act in that particular way. Either way, we view the other person more or less independently of our own beliefs, desires, and attitudes, arriving at predictions and interpretations by making definite hypotheses about the content of their beliefs, desires, and attitudes and postulating a causal role for them.

An alternative theory, simulation theory,[46] accords more closely with Smith and Hume's understanding of how people relate to one another, and, therefore, may accord more readily with a virtue ethics approach to predicting and understanding how a virtuous person acts. Simulation theorists claim that people interpret and predict another person's actions by imaginatively projecting themselves into the other person's position, imaginatively assuming his traits and feelings. Rather than going through a process of hypothesizing that person's beliefs, desires, and attitudes, we assume his evaluative, emotional outlook and then see how we would act.[47] We imaginatively run our own cognitive capacities from the perspective inhabited by the person we aim to interpret or predict, and thereby reach a conclusion about his or her likely conduct.

Empirically, people may combine the two methods.[48] It might be that, in order to assign beliefs, desires, and attitudes to somebody else in a way that enables successful prediction of his or her actions, we might first have to imaginatively simulate facing his or her situation with his or her traits and feelings. Likewise, it might not be possible to perform this imaginative feat without attributing at least some beliefs, desires, and attitudes to the person one is attempting to simulate. Grant that people folk-psychologize, simulate, or combine the two methods in order to interpret and predict one another's actions. These theories from philosophy of mind suggest how jurors might handle the cognitive demand placed on them by instructions that ask them to meaningfully ascertain the actions of a fictional exemplar of reasonableness, prudence, and due care for the safety of others. The instructions themselves inform the jurors of the relevant characteristics of the person they must imagine. A trial gives jurors information about the specific circumstances they should assume the exemplar faces as well as information about the beliefs, desires, and goals the defendant had when she or he was in those circumstances. Then, via folk psychology, simulation, or both, jurors arrive at conclusions about how a reasonably prudent, duly careful person would have acted in those circumstances.

A jury verdict in a negligence action constitutes a communal normative expectation based on the counterfactual prediction the jury made in applying the negligence standard. Whenever we predict one another's behavior, we develop expectations based on those predictions, expectations that may be met or disappointed. This gives expectations normative force, the capacity to guide others to act in accordance with them. The expectation of conduct embodied in a judgment of negligence or nonnegligence clearly has legally normative force: it informs members of the society of what sorts of conduct will generate a legally enforceable requirement that an injurer compensate a victim. What gives ethical normative force to the expectation implied by a jury's judgment of negligence is that this expectation arises from a counterfactual prediction of the conduct of how a person with specifically ethical traits—ordinary prudence and due carefulness—would behave.

Viewing the jury as performing a particular epistemic and political function when it conducts a thought experiment about how a person possessed of particular virtues would act in certain circumstances also bolsters virtue ethics as a moral theory. Within moral philosophy, virtue ethics has been vulnerable to the complaint that it lacks definitive prescriptivity because virtue ethics requires an interpreter—generally the virtuous person—to translate virtuous dispositions into specific actions. This has led some philosophers to argue that virtue ethics cannot supply a complete moral theory since a moral theory must not only tell us what character traits to have but also what actions to take. The law's treatment of the virtue-based negligence standard, however, provides virtue ethicists with a response to this criticism. Virtue ethics can arrive at prescriptivity when it is operationalized. Even if there is no formulaic way to deduce appropriate actions from definitions of the virtues, tort law's thought-experiment procedure for inferring specific prescriptions based on the possession of particular virtues in particular situations shows that virtue-based evaluative inquiry can yield specific prescriptions for or against particular acts.

5. Accounting for the absence of virtue ethics in contemporary tort theory

Perhaps tort theory of the past fifty years has overlooked virtue theory because many tort theorists appear to think of negligence law as fundamentally concerned with either furthering justice or efficiency.

Actually, that statement oversimplifies the current landscape of American tort law scholarship. Some tort scholars have not attempted such univocal interpretations.[49] Others accept that tort law serves a variety of purposes, but highlight one particularly.[50] Still others claim that although it may seem that tort law concerns itself with multiple objectives—for example, justice and efficiency—these apparently different goals actually collapse into one.[51] Nevertheless, the basic claim stands: issues of justice and efficiency dominated tort theory of the late twentieth century, with the result that tort theorists have not attended to the virtues of prudence and due care for other people's safety, the virtues specified in the tort law's actual negligence standard.[52]

Tort theorists of the 1960s and 1970s picked up on then-current developments in political philosophy and economics. To appreciate this era of tort law scholarship, it helps to examine more closely the state of political philosophy and economics in the late 1960s and early 1970s. The centerpiece of this study is John Rawls' landmark book, *A Theory of Justice*, published in 1971.[53] In this work, Rawls compiled ideas he had been exploring in publications that appeared throughout the 1950s and 1960s. Finally, in *A Theory of Justice*, Rawls presented both a decision procedure for selecting principles of distributive justice for the basic structure of society and two substantive principles, which he argued would emerge from applying this procedure.[54] Rawls explicitly fashioned the proposed decision procedure to vindicate and guarantee commitments to a Kantian conception of personhood, with its emphasis on autonomy and rational agency. The principles Rawls claims would be chosen by his Kantian decision procedure place principles of liberty and equality above considerations of efficient utility or welfare maximization. Rawls' theory of justice, therefore, rivals both utilitarian and economic approaches to social policy.

Both in *A Theory of Justice* and in his subsequent writings, Rawls has insisted that neither the Kantian decision procedure nor the two principles of justice apply beyond the basic structure of society. Whether common law doctrines fall within the basic structure is a difficult question, one Rawls himself does not address.[55] In any event, in 1972, torts scholar George Fletcher published *Fairness and Utility in Tort Theory*,[56] a piece with a decidedly Rawlsian flavor. Fletcher introduces "the paradigm of reciprocity,"[57] which he summarizes as a "principle of fairness": "all individuals in society have the right to roughly the same degree of security from risk."[58] Fletcher then overtly places this principle in relation to Rawls:

> By analogy to John Rawls' first principle of justice, the principle might read: we all have the right to the maximum amount of security compatible with a like security for everyone else. This means that we are subject to harm, without compensation, from background risks, but that no one may suffer harm from additional risks without recourse for damages against the risk-creator. Compensation is a surrogate for the individual's right to the same security as enjoyed by others. But the violation of the right to equal security does not mean that one should be able to enjoin the risk-creating activity or impose criminal penalties against the risk-creator. The interests of society may often require a disproportionate distribution of risk. Yet, according to the paradigm of reciprocity, the interests of the individual require us to grant compensation whenever this disproportionate distribution of risk injures someone subject to more than his fair share of risk.[59]

Fletcher's label—the paradigm of reciprocity—can be a bit confusing because Rawls himself considers his first principle of justice a principle of reasonableness. Nonetheless, Fletcher, like Rawls, means to contrast a principle of fairness with principles of utility or welfare maximization. Fletcher's paradigm of reciprocity opposes the paradigm of reasonableness, which he regards as a fundamentally utilitarian framework.

According to Fletcher, the paradigm of reasonableness in tort law emerged in the nineteenth century.

> The new paradigm challenged the assumption that the issue of liability could be decided on grounds of fairness to both victim and defendant without considering the impact of the decisions on the society at large. It further challenged the assumption that victim's right to recovery was distinguishable from the defendant's duty to pay.... The core of this revolutionary change was a shift in the meaning of the word "fault."...Recasting fault...into an inquiry about the reasonableness of risk-taking laid the foundation for the new paradigm of liability. It provided the medium for tying the determination of liability to maximization of social utility, and it led to the conceptual connection between the issue of fault and the victim's right to recover.[60]

Fletcher concludes that the reasonable person standard is a vehicle for utilitarian social policy.

> The reasonable man became a central, almost indispensable figure in the paradigm of reasonableness. By asking what a reasonable man would do under the circumstances, judges could assay the issues both of justifying and excusing risks. Reasonable men, presumably, seek to maximize utility; therefore, to ask what a reasonable man would do is to inquire into the justifiability of the risk.[61]

I reject Fletcher's conclusory connection between the reasonable person standard and utilitarianism. Grant that the reasonable person of ordinary prudence who acts with due care for the safety of others emerged as the negligence regime's central standard during the nineteenth century. As I noted at the outset of this chapter, the full language of the standard does not invoke utilitarianism, and we need not automatically substitute the neoclassical economically rational actor for the reasonable person represented in tort law. Nothing compels tort theory to include neoclassical economics' controversial conception of rationality, according to which acting rationally just amounts to efficiently maximizing preference satisfaction.[62] In a sense, Fletcher realizes this, attempting to advance a nonutilitarian theory of negligence law. But his effort seems blindered. *Fairness and Utility in Tort Theory* reads as if a Rawlsian interpretation of negligence law was the only conceivable alternative to a utilitarian approach. Had Fletcher paid attention to the full doctrinal representation of the reasonable person, which depicts her as not only reasonable but also prudential and concerned for the safety of others, Fletcher might have noticed that negligence law invites attention to certain virtues and hence to virtue ethics.

Fletcher was not alone in his neglect of the full doctrinal representation, however. He was presenting his theory to rival the burgeoning law and economics movement in tort theory, a movement whose central and primary expositor, Richard Posner, did cast the reasonable person standard in neoclassical economic terms, and hence in the utilitarian tradition. In 1972, Posner published *A Theory of Negligence*,[63] another landmark in tort theory. A progenitor of the law and economics interpretation of American tort law, Posner argued that the "dominant function of the fault system is to generate rules of liability that if followed will bring about, at least approximately, the efficient—the cost-justified—level of accidents and safety."[64] He summarized his theory as follows:

> Under this view, damages are assessed against the defendant as a way of measuring the costs of accidents, and the damages so assessed are paid over to the plaintiff (to be divided with his lawyer) as the price of

> enlisting their participation in the operation of the system. Because we do not like to see resources squandered, a judgment of negligence has inescapable overtones of moral disapproval, for it implies that there was a cheaper alternative to the accident. Conversely, there is no moral indignation in the case where in which the cost of prevention would have exceeded the cost of the accident. Where the measures necessary to avert the accident would have consumed excessive resources, there is no occasion to condemn the defendant for not having taken them.
>
> If indignation has its roots in inefficiency, we do not have to decide whether regulation, or compensation, or retribution, or some mixture of these best describes the dominant purpose of negligence law. In any case, the judgment of liability depends ultimately on a weighing of costs and benefits.[65]

In this synopsis, Posner advances an economic interpretation of the negligence regime. Then, in an effort to connect this interpretation to the moral dimension of tort law, Posner claims that inefficient actions provoke moral indignation.

Posner may have been following J. S. Mill's lead, suggesting that our usual moral sentiments, which we generally do not consciously consider to be driven by utilitarian or economic concerns, are in fact driven by such concerns.[66] Or, as Posner himself argued in later work, he may have been associating our supposed moral indignation over inefficiency with a quasi-Kantian concern that inefficient social policy interferes with every citizen's autonomy.[67] Posner may even be a latent virtue theorist, claiming that parsimony, possibly a moral virtue, accounts for moral indignation over inefficiency.[68] Posner himself has never satisfactorily related his theory of American negligence law to any moral theory, so he has never delivered an adequate philosophical—or psychological—diagnosis for why we should experience moral indignation when faced with inefficient accidents. Whatever the connection between moral theory and Posner's economic interpretation of the negligence regime, Posner, like Fletcher, never discusses the virtues of prudence and regard for others' safety, traits specifically itemized in negligence law's distinctive standard of care. Posner characterizes his ambition as follows: to "formulate and test... a theory to explain the social function of the negligence concept and of the fault system of accident liability that is built upon it."[69] Along the way, though, Posner overlooks the exact doctrine at the heart of American negligence law.

Other scholars who associated tort law with economics moved even further away from the reasonable person standard. In 1970, Guido Calabresi published a path-breaking book, *The Cost of Accidents: A Legal and Economic Analysis*.[70] Calabresi asserted that "the principle goals of any system of accident law [are that] it must be just or fair [and] it must reduce the costs of accidents."[71] Unlike Posner, Calabresi did not equate or reduce the justness or fairness of tort law to economic efficiency: "An economically optimal system of reducing accident costs... might be totally or partially unacceptable because it strikes us as unfair, and no amount of discussion of the efficiency of the system would do much to save it. Justice must ultimately have its due."[72] But unlike Fletcher, Calabresi chose to set aside questions of distributive justice in pursuit of a prescription for an economically efficient accident law:

> But if the elusiveness of justice cannot justify ignoring the concept, it at least justifies delaying discussion of it.... Apart from the requirements of justice, I take it as axiomatic that the principal function of accident law is to reduce the sum of the costs of accidents and the costs of avoiding accidents.[73]

In somewhat simplified terms, here is Calabresi's view of how to achieve this goal: tort law should assign liability for the cost of an accident to the party who was in the best position to prevent the accident at the least expense, regardless of how carefully or carelessly that party acted at the time of the accident. Now, the reasonable person standard is a measure of care, so it plays no role in Calabresi's theory of accident law. So Calabresi cannot be properly criticized for neglecting to attend to the virtues assigned to the reasonable person in the American negligence regime. But his theory does support my claim that the tort theorists of the 1970s were concerned primarily with distributive justice or economic efficiency, with Calabresi representing the latter concern. In Rawlsian spirit—and like Fletcher—Calabresi conceived of tort law as furthering either economic efficiency or distributive justice. Framing the choice this way invites one to ignore the virtues highlighted in the reasonable person standard.

By the 1980s, some tort theorists—Jules Coleman and Ernest Weinrib in particular—noticed that the previous decade's focus on the distributive justice and economic efficiency of American tort law overlooked one quite distinctive feature of the system: traditional American tort litigation revolves around a particular victim seeking compensation from a particular injurer, a paradigmatic scenario of corrective justice.

Scholars such as Coleman and Weinrib stressed the place of corrective justice in tort law and theory.

Weinrib quite explicitly combines "a Kantian content" with an "Aristotelian corrective justice structure" to develop "[a] moral conception of negligence in tort law."[74] Weinrib's emphasis on a Kantian content aligns him with the previous decade's primary expositor of a moral conception of negligence, George Fletcher, although Weinrib's theory differs from Fletcher's in a number of respects. Fletcher maintained that the reasonable person standard is primarily utilitarian, promoting wealth-maximization at the expense of individual autonomy. Weinrib claims that the reasonableness element in the tort standard should be read as a reference to a Kantian conception of reason, according to which reason itself requires that we treat each other as equals in a kingdom of ends. In this setting, one who injures another disturbs the parity between equals who regard one another as ends in themselves, and this disturbance gives rise to an obligation on the part of the injurer to restore parity by compensating the injured.

Jules Coleman's views on corrective justice and its place in tort law defy easy characterization. Admirably, Coleman has continued to develop and refine his position since he first presented his own affirmative account of American tort law in the 1980s. Through debate and exchange with fellow thinkers such as Posner, Fletcher, and Weinrib, Coleman has continuously sought to improve his own ideas. In this chapter, I take the liberty of freezing Coleman's thoughts, based on his presentation of them in *The Mixed Conception of Corrective Justice*, a chapter in his 1992 book, *Risks and Wrongs*.[75]

Although Coleman differs from Weinrib in that he believes that accident law implements both economic and moral principles and policies, Coleman shares with Weinrib the belief that the structure of tort law embodies corrective justice, a noninstrumental dimension of American tort law. According to Coleman, "Corrective justice imposes on wrongdoers the duty to repair the wrongful losses their conduct occasions, losses for which they are responsible."[76] He explains:

> Corrective justice has two dimensions. First, losses are the concern of corrective justice if they are wrongful. They are wrongful if they result from wrongs or wrongdoings. The wrong grounds the claim that the losses are wrongful (and thus within the ambit of corrective justice). Secondly, the duty to repair those wrongful losses is grounded not in the fact that they are the result of wrongdoing, but in the fact that the losses are the injurer's responsibility, the result of his agency.[77]

As we can see from this passage—and as Coleman himself acknowledges—this theory of corrective justice cannot be complete unless augmented by an account of wrongfulness. In other words, Coleman must explain what makes a loss wrongful. In *Risks and Wrongs*, he pursued this task in the chapter immediately following *The Mixed Conception of Corrective Justice*, in a fascinating chapter titled *Wrongfulness*.[78]

For Coleman, corrective justice poses a problem: if corrective justice is neither a vehicle of distributive justice nor of economic efficiency, it must be grounded in a distinctive conception of wrongfulness, one that differs from the wrongfulness suggested by theories of distributive justice (inequity in distribution) or utilitarian economic theories (inefficiency in utility production).[79] To count as a distinct and legitimate form of justice, corrective justice must influence our substantive theory of wrongfulness; and, furthermore, this influence must differ from that exerted by distributive justice or utilitarianism.

Whereas distributive justice and social efficiency are global aims according to Coleman, corrective justice is justice between private parties, based on local norms.

> [These local norms are] informal conventions [that] typically arise within communities of individuals as ways of giving local expression and content to the prohibition against unreasonable risk taking. These conventions govern the behavior of local communities; members of the communities develop expectations about the behavior of others and internalize constraints regarding their own behavior. These conventions are local, not global. It is failure to comply with them that typically grounds duties in corrective justice.[80]
>
> . . .
>
> *The core idea in the rule of negligence is that of a convention giving expression to a common understanding of reasonable behavior.*[81]

With this statement, Coleman aligns himself with his fellow tort theorists of the 1970s and 1980s. Like them, he focuses on the reasonableness element of the reasonable person standard: to the extent his account of negligence law incorporates a theory of corrective justice, this theory does not examine the place of the virtues of prudence and due care for the safety of others, character traits tort doctrine assigns to the reasonable person whose conduct sets the standard of care required of all members of the community.

Since corrective justice is a concept that originates with Aristotle, whom I have already noted as the central forefather of the virtue ethics tradition, some might conclude that torts scholars who have focused on corrective justice have indeed focused on virtue ethics. Yet Aristotle himself did not seriously connect his theory of corrective justice with his theory of virtue ethics. This perhaps accounts for the fact that modern-day advocates of a place for corrective justice in tort law and theory have not pursued virtue ethics.

In *Nichomachean Ethics*, Aristotle develops a quite complicated relationship between justice and the virtues. The complexity of this relationship is exacerbated by the complexity of Aristotle's conceptions of both justice and virtue. I am not a specialist in Aristotelian philosophy, nor would it be consistent with this chapter's objectives to attempt a full exegesis of Aristotle's account of these matters. Instead, I will provide a more schematic explication in order to clarify my claim that attention to corrective justice does not necessarily coincide with attention to particular virtues or to the virtue ethics tradition.

Aristotle discusses justice in Book V of *Nichomachean Ethics*,[82] after his discussion of flourishing as the highest good for human beings (the subject of Book I) and his discussion of virtues of character (in Books II, III, and IV). When Aristotle turns to the topic of justice, he first distinguishes justice as lawfulness from justice as fairness.[83] He then immediately turns to fairness and claims that an unjust person is greedy, for he will always choose more goods to fewer without regard to equality in distribution.[84] Aristotle proceeds to outline justice as lawfulness, however, he quickly sets aside this sense of justice to return to a discussion of justice as fairness. It is in the course of this extended discussion of justice as fairness that Aristotle distinguishes distributive justice from rectificatory (corrective) justice.

> One species [of justice] is found in the distribution of honours or wealth or anything else that can be divided among members of a community who share in a political system; for here it is possible for one member to have a share equal or unequal to another's.
>
> Another species concerns rectification in transactions. This species has two parts, since one sort of transaction is voluntary, and one involuntary. Voluntary transactions include selling, buying, lending, pledging, renting, depositing, hiring out—these are called voluntary because the origin of these transactions is voluntary. Some involuntary ones are secret, e.g. theft, adultery, poisoning, pimping, slave-deception, murder by treachery, false witness; others are forcible, e.g. assault, imprisonment, murder, plunder, mutilation, slander, insult.[85]

After these passages, Aristotle elaborates on his views concerning distributive justice, and then turns to an explication of rectificatory justice.

The most central difference, according to Aristotle, between distributive justice and rectificatory justice is that the just distribution of common assets should accord with each individual's proportion of virtue, whereas rectificatory justice does not depend upon total character assessment.

> For here [in rectificatory justice] it does not matter if a decent person has taken from a base person, or a base person from a decent person, or if a decent or a base person has committed adultery. Rather, the law looks only at differences in the harm [inflicted], and treats the people involved as equals, when one does injustice while the other suffers it, and one has done the harm while the other has suffered it. Hence the judge tries to restore this unjust situation to equality, since it is unequal.[86]

This passage simultaneously sets the tone for the remainder of Aristotle's account of rectificatory justice and connects this account to his overall view of justice as a type of equality. He notes that rectificatory justice redresses not only theft but also other types of unfair taking, such as "when one is wounded and the other wounds him, or one kills and the other is killed."[87] In these situations "the action and the suffering are unequally divided [with profit for the offender and loss for the victim]; and the judge tries to restore the [profit and] loss to a position of equality, by subtraction from [the offender's] profit."[88] Aristotle himself notes that "profit" is not always "the proper word" to describe the wrongdoer's gain in situations calling for rectificatory justice, but he explains that he is using the term in a somewhat expansive sense: "At any rate, when what was suffered has been measured, one part is called the [victim's] loss, and the other the [offender's] profit."[89] The judge charged with accomplishing rectificatory justice must ensure that both the victim and the offender—or injurer, to use modern parlance—have the same amount of loss and gain, in relation to one another, that each had prior to the incident that created the rectificatory injustice. Rectificatory justice requires a return to the mean between the victim and the offender—a restoration in equality between the two. This equality is to be measured according to the bilateral status quo ante between victim and injurer, regardless of their specific character traits. Modern tort theorists who have concentrated on corrective justice have followed Aristotle's lead here. Ernest Weinrib and Jules Coleman have each assigned corrective justice a prominent role in tort theory. But, like Aristotle himself, neither has incorporated attention to the virtues into their accounts of the role of corrective justice in tort law.

6. Conclusion: judges, juries, and negligence

Ever since the substantive law of negligence emerged from the old common law forms of action, particularly trespass and trespass on the case, commentators have tried to make sense of the respective role of the judge and the jury in deciding negligence.[90] The current usual assignment of duties at trial, according to which the judge decides questions of law and the jury decides questions of fact,[91] does not fit neatly with the inquiry involved in assessing negligence. Usually, when we think of the jury as fact finder, we think of the jury deciding plain old facts—nonnormative empirical questions, such as whether the light was red or green when the defendant drove through the intersection, or whether or not a technological innovation was available to a product manufacturer when she or he created his or her product's design. The inquiry into negligence seems more pervasively evaluative because it requires the jury to apply a standard to facts, to use the standard to evaluate conduct as negligent or nonnegligent, and thereby decide whether the conduct is lawful or unlawful. On a model of division of labor in the legal system that reserves normative questions to the lawgiver—judge or legislature—assigning the question of defendant's negligence to the jury can seem anomalous at best and an evasion of official responsibility at worst.[92]

The virtue-ethical interpretation of the negligence standard conceives of jurors as executing a thought experiment and thereby seeing—or even discovering—how a certain sort of person would behave in a certain situation. The jury's performance of the relevant thought experiment yields a hypothetical but testable result. If we had available an actual person whose sole traits were reasonableness, prudence, and carefulness, we could, in principle, recreate the circumstances that the defendant faced to find out how this person acts in them. So, the jury's verdict has an empirical dimension, which may alleviate some of the concern that courts and legislatures abdicate their law-giving role by allowing juries to decide the question of negligence.

But the thought experiment performed by the jury essentially involves taking up an evaluative perspective. To the extent that taking up such a perspective involves interpreting the traits that define it—in this case reasonableness, prudence, and carefulness—the thought experiment in a negligence action differs from a more strictly scientific experiment, whether actually performed or performed only in thought.[93] Thus, there remains the issue of the appropriateness of the jury's normative power in a negligence action. An older generation of scholars regarded this assignment of power as an abdication of the lawmaking function of the courts,[94] itself a threat to the rule of law.[95]

If we accept the basic principle of democratic self-governance, however, this worry seems rather peculiar. Ordinarily, the idea that responses to nonconstitutional normative questions are political and subject to revision through political processes in which citizens participate raises few eyebrows. If the people have ultimate authority over the law, and law is fundamentally normative, then a process in which ordinary citizens have normative authority seems both commonsensical and easily justifiable. Indeed, in other legal settings, scholars have wrestled to justify judicial lawmaking in light of concerns that it is fundamentally antidemocratic.[96]

In the contemporary academy, many who deride the reasonable person standard criticize it for its supposed indeterminacy, its failure to provide a sufficiently formulaic guide to conduct. These critics tend to prefer an economic interpretation of negligence on the assumption that cost-benefit analyses or social welfare functions are more determinate than the reasonable person standard and therefore can guide conduct more specifically and concretely. Those who make this sort of argument tend to use it to justify dispensing with the jury as the legal decision maker on the issue of negligence.[97] In this chapter, I have attempted to show that, if we emphasize the virtues specified in the negligence standard, we can see that, through repeated applications, jury verdicts provide actors with guideposts to the sort of conduct to be expected from reasonable persons who possess the traits of prudence and due carefulness for the safety of others. One way somebody might anticipate whether his or her actions conform to this standard is for him or her to cultivate the relevant traits. Another would be for an actor to at least learn how to take up the evaluative perspective defined by them. In other words, actors who seek to conform to the standard may attempt to do so by cultivating the virtues of prudence and carefulness or by exercising their own capacity to perform ex ante the sort of thought experiment a jury judging their conduct would perform ex post.

Interestingly, the entities perhaps least well-positioned to use these methods to conform their conduct to the negligence standard are corporate persons, who, some might argue, lack the sort of personhood necessary to cultivate character traits or learn to adopt an evaluative perspective informed by certain sentimental responses. For the sake of my final argument here, I will make two assumptions, each of which merit further investigation: first, that corporations as currently structured can readily perform accurate cost-benefit analyses that take into account social costs and benefits as well as private ones; second, that corporations would have to institute different internal procedures and arrangements to conform their conduct to that called for by the evaluative perspective delineated by the negligence standard. Neither individually nor taken together do these premises command a shift from a negligence standard based on the evaluative perspective of natural persons to one based on the evaluative perspective of a corporate one. The law grants corporate persons their existence; the law also governs their actions. If democratic principles warrant the jury's authority to decide what behavior accords with the requirements of prudence and care, then the jury has the authority to demand that corporate persons conform their conduct to that of a reasonable, prudent, careful natural person. This may mean that in effect juries require corporate persons to set aside the objective of welfare maximization in the name of other values—as the Ford Pinto or McDonald's hot coffee juries arguably concluded those corporate defendants should have done. Unless one is precommitted to the view that the only legitimate way to define an appropriate balance between freedom and safety is to strike the balance that maximizes preference satisfaction or social utility, this possibility should seem entirely unthreatening. The law and the citizens who apply it may rightly expect corporate persons to adopt whatever internal procedures are necessary to ensure that their conduct matches the conduct we expect from the reasonable person of ordinary prudence who acts with due regard for the safety of others.

Notes

1. See 57A Am. Jur. 2D *Negligence* § 7 (1989).
2. I postpone the complete articulation of the evaluative perspective designated by the negligence standard to Heidi Li Feldman, Care, Character, and American Tort Law (forthcoming 2001), a book-length work-in-progress.
3. As I explain further in Section III, I attribute this lapse to tort scholars' preoccupation with justice and efficiency, and correlatively with moral and economic theories related to these subjects.
4. In my view, tort law both does and should involve a naturalistic understanding of reasonableness. On this view, reasonableness is a cognitive trait of human beings, an evolved adaptation we employ to reason about risks

and benefits. To fully understand reasonableness as it figures in tort law, then, we need to take into account both evolutionary and social psychological research into how human beings approach risk and gain. See Heidi Li Feldman, *Science, Reason, and Tort Law: Looking for the Reasonable Person* in Law and Science 35 (Helen Reece ed., 1998); Heidi Li Feldman, Negligence Law and Human Psychology (June 29, 1999) (unpublished manuscript, on file with author).

5. See Robin West, *The Other Utilitarians* in Analyzing Law: New Essays in Legal Theory (Brian Bix ed., 1998), pp. 197, 206.
6. The most prominent classical virtue ethicist was Aristotle. During medieval times, St. Thomas Aquinas developed a Christian virtue ethics. In the eighteenth century, Scottish philosophers such as Francis Hutcheson, David Hume, and Adam Smith connected virtue ethics to emotion and its role in moral judgment. In the mid-twentieth century, English philosophers such as Philippa Foot and Iris Murdoch championed a secular virtue ethics as a rival to Kantianism. Late twentieth-century virtue ethicists such as Martha Nussbaum and Rosalind Hursthouse develop virtue ethics against a background reality of liberal political systems that diverge greatly from the political setting assumed by Aristotle. Contemporary virtue ethicists such as John McDowell, David Wiggins, and Simon Blackburn fall into the category because of their emphasis on how character and specific sentimental responses to the world figure in moral judgment.
7. Aristotle argues for the identity of human flourishing, happiness, and "the soul's activity that expresses virtue." Aristotle, *Nicomachean Ethics* 17 (lines 1098a10–1098a15) (Terence Irwin trans., 1985). He maintains that the end of human life is a "sort of living well and doing well in action" and that "the happy person lives well and does well," thus confirming the identity between the end for humans, happiness, and action in accord with virtue. *Id.* at 19 (line 1098b25); see also Philippa Foot, Virtues and Vices and Other Essays in Moral Philosophy 3 (1978) ("[V]irtues are in general beneficial characteristics, and indeed ones that a human being needs to have, for his own sake and that of his fellows"); Iris Murdoch, The Sovereignty of Good 78 (1971) ("Ethics should not be merely an analysis of ordinary mediocre conduct, it should be a hypothesis about good conduct and about how this can be achieved. How can we make ourselves better? is a question moral philosophers should attempt to answer"); Adam Smith, The Theory of Moral Sentiments (D. D. Raphael and A. L. Macfie eds, 1976), p. 212 ("When we consider the character of any individual, we naturally view it under two different aspects; first, as it may affect his own happiness; and secondly, as it may affect that of other people").
8. See Murdoch, *supra* note 7, at 78 ("Moral philosophy is the examination of the most important of all human activities.... The examination should be realistic. Human nature, as opposed to the natures of other hypothetical spiritual beings, has certain discoverable attributes, and these should be suitably considered in any discussion of morality").
9. Immanuel Kant, Grounding for the Metaphysics of Morals (James W. Ellington trans., 3rd edn, 1993), p. 46. Kant describes actions as heteronymous and therefore nonmoral if they rest on principles "drawn from... happiness."

Id. Kant regards these as empirical or contingent and therefore not derived from principles of pure reason, the proper basis for moral actions:

> Empirical principles are wholly unsuited to serve as the foundation for moral laws. For the universality with which such laws ought to hold for all rational beings without exception (the unconditioned practical necessity imposed by moral laws upon such beings) is lost if the basis of these laws is taken from the particular constitution of human nature or from the accidental circumstances in which such nature is place.

10. *Id.* at 22–23, 34.
11. *Id.* at 30.
12. *Id.* at 13. According to Kant, such purposive action lacks moral worth because it aims to fulfill desire rather than spring from duty arising from respect for moral law. *Id.* at 12–13.
13. The contemporary ethicists John McDowell and David Wiggins both discuss the relationship between our characters, how the world strikes us, and how we respond to those features of the world we find striking. Both authors argue that the possession of certain traits and attitudes leads us to appreciate features of the world that might otherwise be unavailable to our perception, and that some of those features present themselves as inescapable reasons for acting. See David Wiggins, *A Sensible Subjectivism?* in Needs, Values, Truth (3rd edn, 1998), pp. 185, 194–202.

> If a property and an attitude are made for one another, it will be strange for one to use the term for the property if he is in no way party to the attitude and there is simply no chance of his finding that the item in question has the property. But if he is no stranger to the attitude and the attitude is favourable [sic], it will be the most natural thing in the world if he regards it as a matter of keen argument what it takes for a thing to count as having the property that the attitude is paired with.

Id. at 199; see also John McDowell, Are Moral Requirements Hypothetical Imperatives? Part I in 52 The Aristotelian Society, Supplementary Volume 13, 14 (1978) ("To a virtuous person, certain actions are presented as practically necessary . . . by his view of certain situations in which he finds himself").

14. Aristotle, The Basic Works of Aristotle 1026 (Richard McKeon ed., 1941).
15. Aristotle, *supra* note 7, at 155.
16. Aristotle, *supra* note 15, at 1026 (lines 1140a25–1140a30). In the Irwin translation, this passage reads: "It seems proper, then, to an intelligent person to be able to deliberate finely about what is good and beneficial for himself, not about some restricted area—e.g. about what promotes health or strength—but about what promotes living well in general." Aristotle, *supra* note 7, at 153 (lines 1140a25–1140a30).
17. Aristotle, *supra* note 15, at 1026 (lines 1140b4–1140b6). Irwin translates this passage as follows. "[I]ntelligence is a state grasping the truth, involving reason, concerned with action about what is good or bad for a human being." Aristotle, *supra* note 7, at 154 (lines 1140b4–1140b6).

18. 2 Saint Thomas Aquinas, The Summa Theologica 38 (Fathers of the English Dominican Province trans., 1952).
19. Smith, *supra* note 7, at 213.
20. *Id.*
21. Foot, *supra* note 7, at 5.
22. Aristotle, *supra* note 7, at 21 (line 1099b1).
23. See *id.* at 153 (line 1140a28).
24. 1 Saint Thomas Aquinas, The Summa Theologica 632 (Fathers of the English Dominican Province trans., 1952).
25. *Id.* at 635.
26. The concept of tortious negligence is a relatively young one, not really solidified doctrinally until the middle to late nineteenth century. See Roscoe Pound, *Foreword,* in Selected Essays On the Law of Torts iii (1924). Pound explains that the first efforts by treatise and textbook authors to cover tort law, undertaken between 1859 and 1874, tended to be itemized surveys of specific causes of action. Not until Wigmore's *Cases on Torts,* published in 1911, does a commentator provide a completely "generalized systematic treatment" of negligence law. Pound, *supra,* at iii.
27. Henry T. Terry, *Negligence,* in Selected Essays on the Law of Torts, *supra* note 26, at 261, 263–264.
28. See, for example, Richard A. Epstein, Cases and Materials on Torts (6th edn, 1995), pp. 193–195. Epstein includes Terry's list in a section with cases on the "Calculus of Risk." *Id.* at 189–210. This section leads up to the presentation of *United States v. Carroll Towing Co.,* 159 F.2d 169 (2nd. Cir. 1947), the case in which Judge Learned Hand described negligence in "algebraic terms" and claimed that the defendant's actions constituted negligence if the burden of taking adequate precautions against an accident was less than the probability of injury without taking those precautions. *Id.* at 172. Richard Posner famously claimed that in *Carroll Towing* "Hand was adumbrating, perhaps unwittingly, an economic meaning of negligence." Richard A. Posner, *A Theory of Negligence,* 1 J. Legal Stud. 29, 32 (1972).
29. Warren A. Seavey, *Principles of Torts,* 56 Harv. L. Rev. 72, 89 (1942).
30. *Id.* at 88.
31. Aristotle delineated other-regarding virtues (generosity, magnificence, mildness, friendliness, truthfulness, and wit), but apparently did not recognize a disposition to care about humankind in general. Aristotelian other-regarding virtues pertain to dispositions relevant to the treatment of acquaintances and friends, those with whom one comes into direct contact. Aquinas identifies a virtue of beneficence, a disposition to affirmatively bestow benefits on others. Aquinas, *supra* note 19, at 538. Although Aquinas held that beneficence sometimes calls for "succour[ing]" a stranger, *id.,* he thought beneficence is usually directed toward those with whom one is connected, by ties of family, citizenship, or faith. *Id.* Aquinas seems to hold that under certain circumstances beneficence disposes us to affirmatively give to or aid strangers, but that these circumstances are rare. "[B]eneficence follows on love….[B]eneficence also should extend to all, but according as time and place require; for all acts of virtue must be modified with a view to their due circumstances." *Id.* at 537.

32. David Hume, A Treatise of Human Nature (L. A. Selby-Bigge and P. H. Nidditch eds, 2nd edn, 1978) (1888), p. 316.
33. Smith, *supra* note 8, at 9.
34. *Id.*
35. *Id.* at 12.
36. *Id.* at 22.
37. *Id.* at 235.
38. *Id.*
39. Stephen Gilles has explored the significance of the divergence between commentators' commitment to a Learned Hand cost-benefit approach to negligence and the actual instructions given to jurors in negligence cases. Stephen G. Gilles, *The Invisible Hand Formula*, 80 Va. L. Rev. 1015 (1994). Gilles argues that, if courts are committed to a cost-benefit approach to evaluating negligence, they should modify jury instructions to explicitly direct the jury to perform this sort of analysis, calling the Hand Formula "an unjustifiably underenforced norm." *Id.* at 1020. I reject this conclusion since I take the persistence of jury instructions such as those quoted in the text as evidence that the Hand Formula is not the norm that governs negligence law.
40. 1A Committee on Pattern Jury Instructions Ass'n of Supreme Court Justices, New York Pattern Jury Instructions—Civil No. 2:10 (3rd edn, 1999).
41. 1 California Jury Instructions Civil No. 3.10 (8th edn, 1994)
42. Federal Jury Practice and Instruction § 80.03 (5th edn, forthcoming 2000).
43. See, for example, Pattern Civil Jury Instruction Comm., Alaska Pattern Civil Jury Instructions 3.03A (1988) ("Negligence may consist of doing something which a reasonably prudent person would not do, or it may consist of failing to do something which a reasonably prudent person would do"); Arkansas Supreme Court Comm on Jury Instructions—Civil, Arkansas Model Jury Instructions: Civil No. 301 (4th edn, 1999) ("[Negligence is] the failure to do something which a reasonably careful person would do, or the doing of something which a reasonably careful person would not do…"); Illinois Supreme Court Comm on Jury Instructions in Civil Cases, Illinois Pattern Jury Instructions No. 10.01, at 10-17 (3rd edn, 1993) (Negligence is failing to do what "a reasonably careful person would do," or doing what such a person would not do); 1 Special Comm on Uniform Court Instructions, Iowa Uniform Jury Instructions No. 2.1 (1970) (Negligence is "the failure to do something which a reasonably prudent person, guided by those considerations which ordinarily regulate the conduct of human affairs, under the circumstances would do; or the doing of something which such a person, under such circumstances, would not do."); Washington Supreme Court Comm on Jury Instructions, Washington Pattern Jury Instructions: Civil No. 10.01 (3rd edn, 1989) (Negligence is "the doing of some act which a reasonably careful person would not do under the same or similar circumstances or the failure to do something which a reasonably careful person would have done under the same or similar circumstances").
44. For the moment I set aside the matter of a corporate defendant, which would be neither a he nor a she but an it.
45. See Henry Plotkin, Evolution in Mind: An Introduction to Evolutionary Psychology 200–206 (1998) (discussing our skills as "natural psychologists"

and advancing an evolutionary explanation for the emergence of such a talent in humans); Stephen P. Stich, Deconstructing the Mind 115131 (1996) (explaining the conventional, philosophical account of folk psychology).

46. For good discussions of simulation theory, see Alvin I. Goldman, *Empathy, Mind, and Morals* in Mental Simulation: Evaluations and Applications (Martin Davies and Tony Stone eds, 1995), pp. 185, 185–199 and Robert M. Gordon, *Folk Psychology as Simulation* in Folk Psychology: The Theory of Mind Debate (Martin Davies and Tony Stone eds, 1995), p. 60.
47. Gary Klein and his associates have researched the role of mental simulation in predicting events other than human actions. Gary Klein, Sources of Power: How People make Decisions (1998), pp. 45–109. Klein argues that in crises, successful decision makers rely on mental simulation to predict the different outcomes that would follow from different decisions. *Id.* at 45, 51, 89. He also argues that mental simulation results in better decisions than following rational choice strategies, at least for experienced decision makers. *Id.* at 96, 102–103.
48. Psychological research may confirm one or the other models advanced by philosophers of the mind, or it may inspire them to devise new models. See Plotkin, *supra* note 45, at 214 (concluding that contemporary research in developmental psychology tends to confirm that we have a "theory of mind mechanism," a domain-specific module for understanding and predicting the actions of other human beings). Note that such a mechanism could involve the attribution of intentional attitudes to others, simulation, or a combination of the two.
49. See, for example, Robert L. Rabin, *The Historical Development of the Fault Principle: A Reinterpretation*, 15 Ga. L. Rev. 925, 930–931 (1981) (rejecting either an exclusively economic or exclusively moral interpretation of tort law's "fault" principle); Gary T. Schwartz, *Mixed Theories of Tort Law: Affirming Both Deterrence and Corrective Justice*, 75 Tex. L. Rev. 1801, 1819–1824 (1997) (arguing that both economic and ethical considerations underwrite tort law's liability standards); Gary T. Schwartz, *The Beginning and the Possible End of the Rise of Modern American Tort Law*, 26 Ga. L. Rev. 601, 607 (1992) ("In light of all the tensions that are possible between ethical and economic approaches to tort law, what is distinctive about the negligence standard is that it achieves a certain synthesis of fairness and deterrence values").
50. See, for example, Guido Calabresi, The Costs of Accidents: A Legal and Economic Analysis (1970), pp. 24–26 (claiming that accident law should serve both justice and economic efficiency, but delaying discussion of justice in favor of focusing on the reduction of the costs of accidents); Jules L. Coleman, Risks and Wrongs (1992), p. 198 (claiming that corrective justice is the core purpose of tort law, although not its only purpose).
51. See Richard A. Posner, The Economics of Justice (1983). In chapters three and four, Posner argues that the traditional concerns animating justice, such as autonomy and equality, can best be vindicated by law that aims for wealth-maximization. *Id.* at 48–115. Posner relies on a theory of hypothetical consent to support this claim, arguing that uninjured people would agree to law that maximizes wealth and that negligence law achieves this aim. Therefore, Posner concludes that those who are actually injured do not suffer

a loss of autonomy if they go uncompensated under a negligence regime. *Id.* at 88–101, 103–106.

52. Richard Epstein's early tort scholarship provides a counterexample. There, Epstein attempted a tort theory premised on formal ideas of Aristotelian corrective justice. Richard A. Epstein, *A Theory of Strict Liability*, 2 J. Legal Stud. 151 (1973). In his later work, however, he has been increasingly influenced by the idea of tort law as a tool for efficient welfare maximization. Richard A. Epstein, Simple Rules for a Complex World (1995), p. 97 ("Efforts to refine and apply strong moral intuitions often lead to inquiries with a distinct economic cast...."). According to Epstein, economic welfare militates in favor of strict liability in tort. *Id.*
53. John Rawls, A Theory of Justice (1971). *A Theory of Justice* exerted influence over legal theorists outside of tort scholarship. See, for example, Ronald Dworkin, Taking Rights Seriously (1977), pp. 151–183; Ronald Dworkin, *The Original Position*, 40 U. Chi. L. Rev. 500 (1973); Frank I. Michelman, *In Pursuit of Constitutional Welfare Rights: One View of Rawls' Theory of Justice*, 121 U. Pa. L. Rev. 962 (1973).
54. These are well-known, and I will simply restate them here. The first, lexically prior principle is the equality principle, which requires equality in the assignment of basic rights and duties. The second is the difference principle, which allows social and economic inequalities only if they improve the situation of the least well-off. Justice as fairness, Rawls' substantive theory of justice, requires that the basic structure of society conforms to these principles. See John Rawls, Political Liberalism 273 (1993).
55. See Heidi Li Feldman, *Rawls' Political Constructivism as a Judicial Heuristic: A Response to Professor Allen*, 51 Fla. L. Rev. 67, 76–78 (1999) (analyzing when, if ever, common law falls within the basic structure of society on a Rawlsian view of the basic structure).
56. George P. Fletcher, *Fairness and Utility in Tort Theory*, 85 Harv. L. Rev. 537 (1972).
57. *Id.* at 543.
58. *Id.* at 550.
59. *Id.* at 550–551.
60. *Id.* at 556–557.
61. *Id.* at 560.
62. I have argued this point elsewhere. See Heidi Li Feldman, *Harm and Money: Against the Insurance Theory of Tort Compensation*, 75 Tex. L. Rev. 1567 (1997). Many philosophers and some economists have criticized the neoclassical economic conception of rationality. See, for example, Elizabeth Anderson, Value in Ethics and Economics 201–202 (1993); Amartya K. Sen, *Rational Fools: A Critique of the Behavioral Foundations of Economic Theory* in Beyond Self-Interest (Jane J. Mansbridge ed., 1990), pp. 25, 42–43. Legal scholars have also offered critiques. See Cass R. Sunstein, *Legal Interference with Private Preferences*, 53 U. Chi. L. Rev. 1129 (1986).
63. Posner, *supra* note 29.
64. *Id.* at 33.
65. *Id.* at 33–34.
66. In chapter five of *Utilitarianism*, Mill addresses our feelings of justice and injustice, and argues that, despite appearance and intuitions to the contrary,

these feelings spring from the utility of just action and the disutility of unjust ones. See John Stuart Mill, Utilitarianism 42 (Samuel Gorovitz ed., 1971) (1861).

67. Richard A. Posner, *The Ethical and Political Basis of the Efficiency Norm in Common Law Adjudication*, 8 Hofstra L. Rev. 487 (1980).
68. Posner's commitment to virtue ethics may not be so latent. When defending wealth-maximization, an ethical goal, he writes, "[T]he wealth-maximization principle encourages and rewards the traditional 'Calvinist' or 'Protestant' virtues and capacities associated with economic progress." Posner, *supra* note 52, at 68. Ultimately, however, Posner seems to maintain wealth-maximization as a moral good justifiable on grounds independent of any major philosophical tradition, including virtue ethics, Kantianism, and utilitarianism. See *id.* at 115 ("I have tried to develop a moral theory that goes beyond classical utilitarianism and holds that the criterion for judging whether acts and institutions are just or good is whether they maximize the wealth of society. This approach allows a reconciliation among utility, liberty, and even equality as competing ethical principles").
69. Posner, *supra* note 28, at 29.
70. Calabresi, *supra* note 50.
71. *Id.* at 24.
72. *Id.* at 25–26.
73. *Id.* at 26.
74. Ernest J. Weinrib, *Toward a Moral Theory of Negligence Law*, 2 Law & Phil. 37, 37 (1983).
75. Coleman, *supra* note 50, at 303–328.
76. *Id.* at 325.
77. *Id.* at 326.
78. *Id.* at 329–360.
79. *Id.* at 350.
80. *Id.* at 358.
81. *Id.* at 359 (emphasis added).
82. Aristotle, *supra* note 7, at 116–147 (lines 1129a–1138b10).
83. *Id.* at 117 (line 1129b).
84. *Id.* at 118 (line 1129b10).
85. *Id.* at 122 (lines 1131a1–1131a10).
86. *Id.* at 125 (lines 1132a3–1132a8).
87. *Id.* at 125–126 (lines 1132a8–1132a9).
88. *Id.* at 126 (lines 1132a9–1132a11).
89. *Id.*
90. See, for example, Oliver Wendell Holmes, The Common Law (Mark DeWolfe Howe ed., 1963) (1881); Leon Green, Judge and Jury (1930), pp. 395–417; Fleming James, Jr., *Functions of Judge and Jury in Negligence Cases*, 58 Yale L. J. 667 (1949); Mark P. Gergen, *The Jury's Role in Deciding Normative Issues in the American Common Law*, 68 Fordham L. Rev. 407, 424–439 (1999).
91. See Martin A. Kotler, *Reappraising the Jury's Role as Finder of Fact*, 20 Ga. L. Rev. 123, 126 (1985) ("Following the American Revolution, the view of the jury as finder of law gave way to the more contemporary view of the jury as finder of fact with the lawmaking function vested in the legislature, and, to a lesser extent, the judiciary").

92. Oliver Wendell Holmes, Jr., predicted that gradually judges would supplant juries as the decision maker on the issue of breach of the negligence standard, a development he wholeheartedly endorsed:

> But supposing a state of facts often repeated in practice, is it to be imagined that the court is to go on leaving the standard to the jury forever?... Either the court will find that the fair teaching of experience is that the conduct complained of usually is or is not blameworthy, and therefore, unless explained is or is not a ground of liability; or it will find the jury oscillating to and fro, and will see the necessity of making up its mind for itself.

Holmes, *supra* note 90, at 98.

93. Scientists do use thought experiments as well as actual ones. One of the most famous ones is Galileo's imagined ball and plane apparatus, which he used to prove inertia. Galileo has us begin by picturing a ball rolling up and down in a U-shaped track resting on a level plane in a frictionless world. The Galilean experiment then asks us to mentally manipulate the apparatus. We fold down one side of the U, notch by notch, until it lies flat along the plane, extending into infinity. As we lower the track, we roll the ball from the high side to the low, until the final roll when one side of the track runs along the plane. Finally, we imaginatively observe the state of the device to see if it teaches us anything. We see that a ball rolled in the U will obey the law of equal heights, always reaching the same height from which it started before reversing course. In our final drop, a ball started from the high side of the former U will run along the side of the track that now is level. Since it will never reach the height from which it was initially dropped, it will continue rolling infinitely. The thought experiment has demonstrated the phenomenon of inertia. See Roy A. Sorensen, Thought Experiments (1992), pp. 8–9 (describing Galileo's experiment in detail). Galileo's experiment shows how scientific thought experiments start from a defined situation, have the experimenter mentally manipulate a particular variable, and imaginatively observe what happens to the other parts in the setup. Both the designer of the thought experiment and others who perform it intend cognitive results. They mean to construct a scenario that others can use to gain information about a specific problem that the designer of the experiment also has in mind. I have been arguing that the reasonable person standard as presented to the jury asks them to solve a particular problem using their abilities to reason about how a certain kind of person would behave in a hypothetical situation, just as Galileo's argument asks us to solve a particular problem by reasoning about how a ball on a track would behave in a hypothetical situation.
94. Oliver Wendell Holmes, Jr., argued:

> [T]he featureless generality, that the defendant was bound to use such care as a prudent man would do under the circumstances, ought to be continually giving place to the specific one, that he was bound to use this or that precaution under these or those circumstances....[I]t is obvious that it ought to be possible, sooner or later, to formulate these standards

at least to some extent, and that to do so must at last be the business of the court.

Holmes, *supra* note 90, at 89.

95. See James A. Henderson, Jr., *Expanding the Negligence Concept: Retreat from the Rule of Law*, 51 Ind. L. J. 467, 468–482 (1976). Although Henderson's primary target is not the reasonable person standard, he thinks that this approach to tort law is problematically "polycentric" or open-ended, a difficulty that is hidden by having juries apply the standard.
96. In constitutional law scholarship, resolving the "countermajoritarian" problem—the tension between judicial review and democracy—has been called "the central obsession of modern constitutional scholarship." Barry Friedman, *The History of the Countermajoritarian Difficulty, Part One: The Road to Judicial Supremacy*, 73 N.Y.U. L. Rev. 333, 334 (1998). Alexander M. Bickel seems to have introduced the term "countermajoritarian" and articulated an influential encapsulation of the problem in the context of American law and government. Alexander M. Bickel, The Least Dangerous Branch: The Supreme Court at the Bar of Politics (1962), pp. 16–23. The root difficulty is that judicial review is a countermajoritarian force in our system . . . [that] thwarts the will of representatives of the actual people of the here and now; it exercises control, not on behalf of the prevailing majority, but against it. That, without mystic overtones, is what actually happens. It is an altogether different kettle of fish, and it is the reason the charge can be made that judicial review is undemocratic. *Id.* at 16–17.
97. See Reid Hastie and W. Kip Viscusi, *What Juries Can't Do Well: The Jury's Performance as a Risk Manager*, 40 Ariz. L. Rev. 901 (1998).

    Thus we ask: Can the jury perform in a manner so that it serves as an effective societal risk manager? To avoid any pretense of suspense, we believe that this is an extremely difficult function that is often not performed effectively even by the best informed experts. The jury is ill-informed and poorly equipped to perform this function. In our view, effective risk identification and management often requires the application of technical, statistical, and scientific analytic tools that cannot be effectively communicated to the unschooled layperson through expert testimony in adversarial procedures. Furthermore, although an effective risk management policy is founded on the detailed analysis of individual cases (e.g. accidents and nonaccidents), it requires an omnibus consideration of the distribution of cases, probabilities, benefits, and costs. In contrast, the tort jury trial focuses on a single case, sampled from only one of the four cells of a hypothetical risk-analysis matrix: the too-few-precautions, harmful outcome cell. *Id.* at 902.

3
Judges of Character

*Suzanna Sherry**

1. Introduction

For forty years, legal academics have been lost in a wilderness born of the counter-majoritarian difficulty. Despite a two-century pedigree, we are still arguing about the legitimacy of judicial review and asking whether it is a curse or a blessing. Many of our most prominent constitutional scholars are mired in attempts to constrain judicial review so as to reconcile it with their idealized vision of a constitutional regime grounded in pure majoritarianism. None has succeeded.

The few scholars who have attempted to move beyond the counter-majoritarian difficulty face a different problem. As one scholar has argued, "[i]t takes a theory to beat a theory."[1] Without a theory of constitutional interpretation—whether grounded in majoritarianism or in some other value—there arises the fear that judicial review is, as the legal realists supposed, merely the ad hoc implementation of the judges' own values. Theories of constitutional interpretation are supposed to constrain judicial discretion and ensure that the rule of law will prevail over the rules of men. Unfortunately, no constitutional theory proposed so far is either an accurate description of how judicial review works in practice or a useful prescription for constraining judges. The theories provide, at best, a partial window into the American judicial soul.

The task for post-countermajoritarians, then, is to provide an attractive normative and descriptive picture of successful judicial review. For those of us who are legal pragmatists, this means providing a positive description of how pragmatist judges do or ought to judge. This essay is meant to be a first step in that direction. Judicial review as an institution

*Herman O. Loewenstein Professor of Law, Vanderbilt University.

may be a blessing, but particular instances of judicial review can be less salutary. I try here to identify conditions that make it more or less likely that the exercise of judicial review will be beneficial. The key, I believe, is a very old-fashioned notion: judicial character.

2. Character and judgment

Ironically, Alexander Bickel, who in many ways inspired the late-twentieth-century concern about the legitimacy of judicial review, would likely be at least amused—and perhaps appalled—by much of the last four decades of constitutional scholarship. Bickel firmly aligned himself with what he called the "Whig" tradition of Edmund Burke. That tradition valued existing institutions, eschewing radical change in favor of incremental movement toward unfulfilled aspirations:

> We do well to remain attached to institutions that are often the products more of accident than of design, or that no longer answer to their original plans, but that challenge our resilience and inventiveness in bending old arrangements to present purposes with no outward change.[2]

Despite his coinage of the "counter-majoritarian" terminology, then, his work on judicial review was designed more to preserve the practice from what were at the time very real political threats than to deny its legitimacy.[3]

In addition to their use of Bickel's terminology to support arguments he might not have agreed with, the majoritarian scholars who trace their roots to Bickel are missing the most valuable parts of his philosophy. For Bickel provided more than the nomenclature and modern reinvigoration of the debate over judicial review, and more than a Whiggish caution against radical restructuring of existing institutions. He also, as Anthony Kronman has so eloquently argued, provided a philosophy of judging that can, even now, help us to move beyond the counter-majoritarian difficulty. Kronman describes Bickel's "philosophy of prudence" as both "an intellectual capacity and a temperamental disposition."[4] Prudence, or practical wisdom, in turn depends on what Kronman himself later labeled "traits of character": those habits of mind and spirit that allow an individual to make judgments where intellect runs out.[5]

Life is full of choices, and the life of the law is no exception. American constitutional jurisprudence in particular seems pervaded by opposing dualities that cannot be fully resolved. The Constitution itself provides for both majority rule and minority rights, creating the counter-majoritarian dilemma. When judges must resolve particular cases in the face of this dilemma, judicial review gives rise to what Bickel identified as the "Lincolnian tension" between principle and consent.[6] In interpreting the Constitution over time, judges must also navigate between fidelity to the past and the needs and values of the present, between the general and the particular, and between the abstract and the concrete. As if that were not enough, individual clauses of the Constitution create tensions of their own: between liberty and equality, between religious exercise and religious establishment, and between governmental powers and accountability.

Many constitutional scholars—and some judges—try to resolve these tensions by ignoring, de-emphasizing, or outright rejecting one-half of the dichotomy. Majoritarians allow majority rule to trump rights,[7] moral philosophers privilege rights and principles over majoritarianism and consent,[8] originalists neglect the present in favor of the past.[9] And critical legal scholars, recognizing these inherent tensions (as well as others) as part of a "fundamental contradiction," see them as a fatal flaw and therefore as a reason to abandon objectivity and the rule of law in favor of pure political adjudication.[10]

Even the post-majoritarians who focus on judicial techniques, as, for example, Cass Sunstein does, get caught in the problem of dualities. Sunstein is right to notice that judicial minimalism can foster both democracy and the beneficial use of judicial review (thus moving beyond the counter-majoritarian dilemma). But, as he also notes, "the minimalist path *usually—not always, but usually*—makes a good deal of sense" in certain circumstances.[11] "Maximalist" invalidations, he argues, should be avoided "*unless* there is a good argument for invalidation on democratic grounds, or unless the Court has considerable confidence in its judgment."[12] The rub lies in his justifiable refusal to adopt an absolutist stance. If minimalism is only a presumption, how are judges to know when to depart from it? Sometimes what Sunstein calls a wide and deep, or maximalist, decision is warranted, as with *Brown v. Board of Education*[13] or *Loving v. Virginia*.[14] And one conspicuously minimalist opinion, written a year after Sunstein's book was published, has drawn fire from none other than Sunstein himself. Discussing *Bush v. Gore*,[15] notorious for both its narrowness[16] and its shallowness,[17] Sunstein noted that "the majority's opinion has some of the most severe vices of minimalism."[18]

I do not mean to single out Sunstein. Indeed, he is one of a few prominent constitutional scholars who have left the narrow path marked out by the debate over the counter-majoritarian dilemma and sought instead to specify guidelines for the exercise of judicial review. But his thoughtful—and to a large extent useful—guidelines nevertheless founder on the same shoals that any constitutional *theory* does: if it is to be practical, it has to have nuances and exceptions, and if it has nuances and exceptions, then it cannot satisfactorily account for every possible case. In other words, the devil is in the details—specifically, in the practice: knowing when the theory applies and when it does not. And that is where judges, judgment, and judicial character come in.

Purportedly simple techniques and intricate theories of interpretation may dazzle temporarily, but ultimately they cannot disguise the need to make choices among conflicting and often incommensurate values. Intellectual ability and abstract reason may help us identify the values and the conflicts and give us some insight into the consequences of our choices, but cannot alone lead us to sound results. Only good judgment can mediate between constitutional dualities. As Walter Murphy pointed out long ago, "[n]o method can reduce the art of judgment, whether legal, political, or ethical, to an IBM punch-card system."[19] Whether one calls it prudence, practical wisdom, practical reason,[20] pragmatism,[21] or situation-sense,[22] in the end it comes down to an exercise of judgment. That, after all, is why we call them judges.

But judges, like all of us, can judge poorly or well. Here is where Bickel's "temperamental disposition" and Kronman's "traits of character" can help. Judges—like any person officially entrusted with making decisions that affect others—should exhibit certain character traits, such as honesty, impartiality, and integrity. The wise exercise of the power of judicial review, however, requires more. It is my purpose in this essay to sketch briefly two of the most important of these additional character traits: humility and courage.

Note that in discussing the necessary character traits of good judges, I am indifferent to *personal* character: it is *judicial* temperament that matters.[23] Because I am focusing on judicial character, moreover, "courage" takes on a more limited meaning than it might in other contexts. Judges rarely face the sort of physical threat that most often separates the courageous from the cowardly. Nevertheless, courage—in the sense of confronting one's fears and acting despite them—has a role to play in judging. A good judge, because he/she is humble about his/her own role and abilities, is especially likely to fear being wrong. In the face of such a fear, it is easier not to act than to act: sins of omission never seem as frightening when the alternative is to take a bold step that might be mistaken. Thus, judicial courage entails acting despite the uncertainty, born of humility, about the correctness of one's actions.[24]

Finally, a caveat: I do not mean to suggest that humility and courage are the only character traits relevant to good judging, nor that character alone defines the good judge. Judges also need empathy, imagination, candor, and self-awareness, among other traits. Moreover, it is certainly possible to imagine a judge who is simultaneously humble and courageous...and utterly, undeniably wrong on the merits. Good character is but one of many restraints on judicial error. Nor will a focus on character save us from the necessity of making—and evaluating—hard decisions about value choices. Character is not a substitute for judgment, but merely facilitates it.

3. Humility and arrogance

The proposition that judges should be humble rather than arrogant hardly needs stating. The need for judicial humility was most famously recognized by Learned Hand, who described "the spirit of liberty" as "the spirit which is not too sure it is right."[25] Felix Frankfurter similarly urged on judges "humility and an understanding of...their own inadequacy in dealing with" the broad range of problems they confront.[26] Stephen Breyer has recently reiterated Hand's caution, suggesting that judges should "consider the constitutionality of statutes with a certain modesty."[27] Scholars have also frequently called for judicial humility.[28] One scholar has specifically linked humility with the exercise of Kronman's practical wisdom, arguing that humility helps to "synthesize or mediate...competing claims" similar to the dualities I described earlier.[29]

My contribution to this tradition is a pragmatic one: I want to illustrate the need for judicial humility by showing how its absence produces bad constitutional decisions. I focus on two Supreme Court decisions, a century-and-a-half apart, that exhibit a particularly seductive type of judicial arrogance.

Arrogance, of course, comes in many forms. The most common judicial variant is, as Hand, Frankfurter, and Breyer recognized, a misleading certitude in the correctness of one's own decisions. This type of arrogance is perhaps an occupational hazard for judges, whose decisions, even when they are not infallible, are often final.[30] It may be exacerbated by the recent tendency to accept judicial supremacy unquestioningly. Several aspects of our judicial system moderate its pernicious effect, however. First, it is such a well-known danger that conscientious judges—like those quoted earlier—work hard to combat it in themselves. Second, the hierarchical nature of the federal courts means that all federal judges (with only nine exceptions) face the possibility of reversal by a higher court, tempering their temptation to consider themselves infallible. The common law method, which encourages a simultaneously respectful but open-minded attitude toward precedent, tends to rein in the most radically arrogant.[31] Finally, the existence of multimember courts appointed over time reduces the tendency toward arrogance by producing differences of opinion: it is more difficult to maintain absolute faith in one's own beliefs in the face of equal but opposite certitude by one's respected colleagues. Self-aggrandizing arrogance is therefore not as dangerous in practice as it might appear in theory.

A more dangerous manifestation of judicial arrogance, however, stems not from too much self-esteem but from a kind of selfless devotion to the public good. The most troubling lack of humility comes from the judge who takes it upon himself/herself to save a nation in crisis. Two of the greatest misuses of the power of judicial review stem, at least in part, from this sort of arrogance: *Dred Scott v. Sandford*[32] and *Bush v. Gore*.[33] While history has yet to judge the latter case as it has the former, the cases have much in common. Arguably driven by a desire to avert a constitutional crisis, a divided Court in each case produced a result that was both controversial and inadequately supported by precedent or reasoning.

It is almost an article of faith in American jurisprudence that the decision in *Dred Scott* was flawed as well as disastrous, exemplifying "judicial review at its worst."[34] The analytical weakness of the majority and concurring opinions in *Bush v. Gore* is more contested, but even the decision's supporters tend to be lukewarm in their endorsements. Michael McConnell gives it "two-and-a-half cheers," and criticizes the Court's halting of the recount.[35] Richard Epstein roundly criticizes both the rationale and the remedy of the majority opinion, finding only the reasoning of the three-Justice concurrence sound.[36] Richard Posner calls the result "rough justice" and can only conclude that "it *may* have been legal justice as well."[37] Posner and John Yoo defend the decision primarily for its success in averting a constitutional crisis.[38] Most academic commentary has been highly critical.[39] Almost no one defends the reasoning of the two lead opinions. It is thus fair to characterize *Bush v. Gore* as not one of judicial review's most shining moments.

For purposes of this essay, however, the weakness of the opinions in *Dred Scott* and *Bush v. Gore* is less important than the motivation behind the decisions. In both cases, the Court acted—at least in part—out of a genuine sense of responsibility for the fate of the nation. As Robert McCloskey described the context of *Dred Scott*: "The nation was in deadly jeopardy. It would be tragic for the Court to withhold its hand, if that hand might save the Union."[40] Don Fehrenbacher, the preeminent *Dred Scott* scholar, talks about "the Court's own sense of strategic responsibility in the American constitutional system" and describes the case as "[Chief Justice] Taney's attempt to end the slavery controversy by judicial fiat."[41]

The motives for the Supreme Court's intervention in the 2000 presidential election are murkier, but the most plausible explanation attributes to the Justices in the majority the same sense of obligation toward the nation's constitutional well-being. Justice O'Connor's majority opinion speaks of the Court's "unsought responsibility."[42] Justice Breyer, in dissent, attributes to his brethren an intent "to bring this agonizingly long election process to a definitive conclusion."[43] Defenders of the decision describe the Court's motivation similarly. John Yoo argues that "the Supreme Court believed that it could finally bring an end to the destructive partisan struggle over the presidential election."[44] Richard Posner suggests that "without the Court's intervention the deadlock would have mushroomed into a genuine crisis" and defends the Court's willingness to act even at the risk of endangering its own legitimacy: "Judges unwilling to sacrifice some of their prestige for the greater good of the nation might be thought selfish."[45]

This sort of institutional arrogance does not necessarily depend on certitude. Sometimes it springs instead from a belief that regardless of the "right" answer, the judiciary is the only branch that can supply a practical solution. The *Dred Scott* Court tried—unsuccessfully—to prevent the nation from being torn apart by the political stalemate on slavery. The *Bush v. Gore* Court turned out to be more successful (although no less arrogant) in its belief that an immediate judicial solution was more conducive to constitutional stability than a drawn-out political battle, even if both would have ended in the election of George W. Bush. Note that the lack of humility that characterizes this type of institutional arrogance rests more on a belief in judicial omnipotence than on any notion of judicial supremacy, although a judicial solution is unlikely to succeed in the absence of popular acceptance of judicial supremacy.

Institutional arrogance is both more alluring and more difficult to guard against than the garden-variety delusion of infallibility. As Posner's comment demonstrates, this type of arrogance masquerades as selflessness or heroism, verging on martyrdom. The Court is asking not what judges can do for themselves but what they can do for their country. This seems, superficially, to be a beneficial character trait, not a dangerous one; judges—and the public—are less likely to be vigilant in cabining it. And, of course, there is a disarming kernel of truth in the attitude of institutional arrogance: in cases from *McCulloch*[46] to *Brown*[47] to the *Nixon* tapes case,[48] the Supreme Court's intervention was necessary to combat the paralysis of, or resolve a conflict between, the political branches. The civil rights movement would have been severely handicapped—if not stillborn—but for the courageous acts of lower court judges.[49]

This last insight—that institutional judicial arrogance has its advantages—leads to a second, and perhaps more important, point. While judges must guard against arrogance, they should also be wary of the opposite flaw: timidity.

4. Courage and timidity

While many have urged judicial humility, few have focused on judicial courage. Bickel himself emphasized the caution that comes with prudence more than the action that comes with courage. This has led some modern scholars to reject Bickel as intolerably conservative.[50] Whether or not this is an accurate reading of Bickel, it is wrongheaded insofar as it demands a choice between humility and courage rather than an attempt to accommodate both.

A few pragmatist scholars have recognized the need for accommodation: Kronman argues that a prudent judge needs what he calls "deliberative imagination."[51] Richard Posner describes good judgment as "some ineffable compound of caution, detachment, and imagination."[52] Although each of these scholars means something slightly different, both recognize that a necessary part of good judgment (or practical wisdom) is an ability to know when it is more appropriate to act than to abstain from acting.

A few scholars and judges have similarly recognized that too much humility can prevent judges from acting when they ought to. Describing Hand's humility, for example, Ronald Dworkin says that it stemmed from "a *disabling uncertainty* that he—or anyone else—could discover which convictions were true."[53] Steven Burton, in defending and defining law as practical reason, eloquently notes that "[t]he life of the law has not been logic or experience: it has been imagination and courage in action."[54] Judge John Noonan praises Marshall, Brandeis, Holmes, and Cardozo for their "fortitude," quoting Brandeis on "the virtues... of truth, of courage, of willingness to risk positions, of the willingness to risk criticisms, of the willingness to risk the misunderstandings that so often come when people do the heroic thing."[55] At least three Justices on the current Supreme Court similarly recognize the potentially disabling effects of self-doubt: "Liberty finds no refuge in a jurisprudence of doubt."[56]

In general, however, the vices of humility are less well known than its virtues. And the character trait that counters the vices of too much humility and inclines one toward acting—even in the face of self-doubt—is courage; its opposite is timidity.

The widespread recognition of the need for humility makes it especially important to stress the need for judicial courage. The problem is that one common response to humility and doubt is to privilege humility: to urge a system of pure self-restraint rather than an attempt to live with both humility and courage. The modern turn toward grand theory in constitutional law typifies this reaction. The scholars (and a few judges) who urge courts to tether themselves to a single method of interpretation—whether originalism, textualism, intra-textualism, or constitutional dualism—are, in effect, privileging humility over courage.[57] Afraid that judges might make mistakes, they seek refuge in a constraining methodology designed to produce right answers without the exercise of judgment. As I have argued elsewhere, this mechanical certitude is an impossible goal: no theory applies itself, and there is always room for judgment and discretion.[58]

But responding to humility with timidity is not only self-defeating but also pernicious. Some of the most successful instances of judicial review have been acts of courage, and a cowardly failure to act can be as damaging as arrogance. I have already mentioned briefly a few of the cases in which courageous judges stepped into the breach and accomplished much good; readers can undoubtedly provide additional examples. Here, I want to focus instead on the dangers of timidity. I hope that in doing so, I will both demonstrate the need for judicial courage and show how it balances humility.

Three very different examples may serve to illustrate the harms that can arise when judges are too diffident. First, judges who are overly awed by the political branches, and overly humble about their own role, may allow shameful events to occur or continue. In 1937, after a momentous struggle over the role of the judiciary in our constitutional democracy, a Court acutely aware of its own shortcomings vowed eternal humility. That vow produced many good decisions, but it also produced two reminiscent of *Dred Scott*: in the early 1940s, the Supreme Court decided *Hirabayashi v. United States*[59] and *Korematsu v. United States*,[60] approving racially based curfews and relocation orders. *Korematsu* has been called "a case that has come to live in infamy,"[61] and "one of the Court's most embarrassing moments."[62] The two cases are also an example of a Court with an overly humble attitude toward its own role:

> Where, as they did here, conditions call for the exercise of judgment and discretion and for the choice of means by those branches of the Government on which the Constitution has placed the responsibility of war-making, it is not for any court to sit in review of the wisdom of their action or substitute its judgment for theirs.[63]

The dissenting opinions in *Korematsu*, which history has vindicated, achieved a better balance between humility and courage. Justice Murphy, after noting that judgments of military necessity "ought not to be overruled lightly by those whose training and duties ill-equip them to deal intelligently with matters so vital to the physical security of the nation,"[64] nevertheless found the relocation order unconstitutional. Justice Jackson—who ten years later would describe so humbly the Court's fallibility—struck a similar balance, voting to invalidate the relocation order despite his recognition that "[i]n the very nature of things military decisions are not susceptible of intelligent judicial appraisal."[65] Jackson also recognized the peculiar dangers of a *court* unwilling to stand up for principle: "[A] judicial construction of the due process clause that will sustain this order is a far more subtle blow to liberty than the promulgation of the order itself."[66]

Korematsu thus illustrates that judicial humility is not always a good thing. Note that in this it differs from another infamous discrimination case, *Plessy v. Ferguson*.[67] In *Plessy*, the Court failed to invalidate racially discriminatory laws in large part because the Justices shared the underlying belief in the appropriateness of racial segregation.[68] In *Korematsu*, while judicial racism may have played some minor part in the decision, the Court's humble deference to the military and the political branches was much more apparent.[69] Only the dissenters were courageous enough to risk being mistaken. (That the risk seems small in hindsight does not diminish their courage.)

The case of *Poe v. Ullman*[70] provides a different sort of illustration of the dangers of responding to humility with timidity. *Poe*, decided four years before *Griswold v. Connecticut*,[71] refused to reach the merits of a challenge to the constitutionality of Connecticut's ban on the sale or use of contraceptives.

In *Poe*, the majority drew on a long tradition of justiciability, described by Justice Frankfurter as flowing from the "restricted" role of the federal courts.[72] These rules operated to cabin the judicial tendency toward arrogance. But in this case, the caution was misplaced. Justice Harlan's eloquent dissent tore to shreds the majority's reasoning and demonstrated its misuse of precedent. And Harlan offers another example of courage in the face of doubt. Like Jackson before him, Harlan recognized that the Court should "exercise limited and sharply restrained judgment," and should "hesitate long before concluding that the Constitution precluded Connecticut from choosing as it has among [the] various views" on the morality of contraceptives.[73] Nevertheless, Harlan thought the Court was required not only to confront the merits of the case but to invalidate the Connecticut statute on constitutional grounds. History has vindicated Harlan as well. Not only did the Supreme Court ultimately invalidate the Connecticut statute in *Griswold,* but *Griswold* itself—when separated from its extension in *Roe v. Wade*[74]—has become so enshrined in the American pantheon of rightly decided cases that Robert Bork's nomination foundered in large part on his rejection of it.[75]

Poe differs from *Korematsu* in two respects. It is not as bad, symbolically, as *Korematsu*—pace Gunther—because in *Poe* the Court refused to act at all rather than giving its imprimatur to unconstitutional government action. But the Court's timidity in *Poe* is worse than *Korematsu* in another respect. In *Korematsu,* the lapse of time and the change of the fortunes of war meant that the relocation and internment programs were ending even as the Court validated them; aside from its symbolic or expressive effect, then, the decision in *Korematsu* affected relatively few people. *Korematsu* did not, ultimately, perpetuate an ongoing constitutional violation. But during the four-year gap between the Court's abdication in *Poe* and its decision in *Griswold,* birth control remained unavailable to poor women in Connecticut and other states.[76] We have no way of knowing how many women died—of childbirth, of suicide born of desperation, or of illegal abortions—or how many unwanted children were born during those four years. Those deaths and births are all the more painful because the Supreme Court ultimately found the statute unconstitutional. That *Korematsu* has never been formally reversed—or completely repudiated—by the Supreme Court may be a blot on our history, but it means that the Court's timidity was not merely the postponement of the inevitable. (Indeed, I would not be at all surprised if *Korematsu* ends up being cited with approval by the Supreme Court some time during the current war on terrorism.) *Poe,* by contrast, was a futile effort to stave off the need to act courageously.

My third example involves an ongoing Supreme Court effort to postpone deciding a difficult constitutional question. The first constitutional challenge to affirmative action in educational institutions reached the Supreme Court in 1973.[77] The Court ducked the issue then and for the last thirty years has refused to provide a definitive answer to a question that continues to divide Americans. The Court's only discussion on the merits, in *Regents of the University of California v. Bakke*,[78] produced such a quagmire that lower courts cannot even agree on what it stands for. The Court has since steadfastly denied certiorari in all cases raising questions about educational affirmative action.[79] Regardless of one's views on the merits, the current uncertainty increases friction and resentment on both sides and encourages litigation. The situation also discourages both sides from focusing on additional or alternative remedies for the poor performance of African-Americans on the standardized tests used in college admissions. A definitive ruling on the constitutionality of affirmative action (and, if constitutional, its legal contours) would allow us to move on.

The history of antiabortion laws provides an illuminating contrast to affirmative action. With the change in personnel in the 1980s came a change in the Court's ideological outlook. The reach of *Roe v. Wade* was incrementally narrowed, leading opponents to believe that it might soon be overruled. During this period, then, the constitutional status of antiabortion laws was uncertain, similar to the state of affirmative action today. In response, state legislatures enacted a steady stream of restrictions on abortion, moving increasingly closer to outright bans—and resulting in almost constant litigation. For a time the Court wavered, upholding many of the restrictions without overruling *Roe*. But the courageous decision in *Planned Parenthood of Southeastern Pennsylvania v. Casey*[80] made clear that the core of *Roe*—although not its broadest implications—was still good law and put an end to legislative flirtation with unconstitutionality. Subsequent state restrictions on abortion were much narrower, and the enactment of new antiabortion laws slowed to a trickle. Both sides have since moved on. Proponents of choice have turned to state courts and state constitutions for protection where *Casey* left off, and opponents have turned to methods other than legislation to discourage abortion. Had the Court in *Casey* instead overruled *Roe*, that course, too, would have provided a clear answer and allowed both sides to focus on more effective strategies than constant litigation.

The affirmative action and abortion situations illustrate an important point about judicial courage. In both cases, my critique focuses not on the result but on the mere need for a clear decision. What if the Court had reached (or did or would reach) the wrong result? It is exactly that possibility that makes the Court's action in *Casey* courageous and the Court's inaction in the affirmative action context overly timid. Judicial courage entails acting in the face of justifiable humility and risking the very real possibility of making a mistake.

5. Conclusion

Readers may complain that rather than describing *how* pragmatist judging might be accomplished, I have focused only on *who* might make a good pragmatist judge. That is because, in one sense, pragmatist judging is like good writing: you cannot teach someone to do it by laying down rules, or even guidelines. Indeed, rules tend to diminish rather than improve the quality of writing. (Look at any example of good writing and see how many times it violates the "rules" you were taught in school.) Experience, particularly under the careful tutelage of a good writer, is the best teacher. And so it is with pragmatism: at best, we can provide exemplars, we can rely on experience to guide judges, and we can look for character traits—akin to an inborn ear for language in good writers—that lend themselves to good judgment.

In the end, humility and courage are like other constitutional dualities: there is no mechanical device that can mediate between them. But judges who are inclined *both* to doubt themselves *and* to risk being wrong are more likely to reach a happy medium than are judges who are too strongly inclined toward arrogance or timidity. I can point to no better example of the happy amalgam of courage and humility than Justice Jackson's concurrence in *McGrath v. Christensen*.[81] Having concluded in 1940, when he was Attorney General, that the Selective Service Act allowed the United States to draft visiting foreigners who, for reasons beyond their control, were temporarily unable to return home, Jackson faced exactly the same question in 1950 as a Justice. Joining the Court's opinion holding that the Act did *not* apply to such foreign nationals, he concurred to explain the inconsistency:

> Baron Bramwell extricated himself from a somewhat similar embarrassment by saying, "The matter does not appear to me now as it appears to have appeared to me then." And Mr. Justice Story, accounting for his contradiction of his own former opinion, quite properly put the matter: "My own error, however, can furnish no ground for its being adopted by this Court." ... If there are other ways of gracefully and good naturedly surrendering former views to a better considered position, I invoke them all.[82]

His courage in 1940 and his humility (and courage in admitting error) in 1950, as well as his openness to persuasion, exemplify the character traits of a good judge.

Justice Jackson is not alone. Justice Blackmun displayed the same combination of courage and humility—albeit without Jackson's humor—when, in *Garcia v. San Antonio Metropolitan Transit Authority*,[83] he provided the fifth vote to overrule an earlier case in which he had joined the majority. Justice Stevens was persuaded to change his views on affirmative action,[84] and Justices Black and Douglas rethought the constitutionality of requiring students to salute the flag.[85] Chief Justice Rehnquist, having once believed that *Miranda v. Arizona*[86] was not a constitutionally based decision, later changed his mind and voted to invalidate Congress's attempt to overrule it.[87] Willingness to change one's mind—to be persuaded—is one hallmark of a judge who is both humble and courageous.

How we identify other such judges I leave for another day, noting only that there are no mechanical tests for good judgment. As former Attorney General Nicholas Katzenbach told the Senate Judiciary Committee deliberating on the nomination of Robert Bork to the United States Supreme Court:

> Were I in your position... the central question I would be asking is this. Is Judge Bork a man of judgment? Not intellect, not reasoning, not lawyering skills, not ideology, not philosophy—simply judgment. Is he a wise person?[88]

However daunting the task may seem, in the end describing (and finding) individuals well suited to the task of judging is likely to prove more useful than seeking artificial mechanisms to constrain poor judgment, or debating once again whether modern American judicial review is a curse or a blessing.

Notes

1. Randy E. Barnett, *An Originalism for Nonoriginalists,* 45 Loy. L. Rev. 611, 617 (1999).
2. Alexander M. Bickel, Reform and Continuity: The Electoral College, the Convention, and the Party System 3 (1971); see also Alexander M. Bickel, *Constitutionalism and the Political Process* in The Morality of Consent 3,11–25 (1975).
3. Bickel, of course, was not alone in urging caution in the face of political threats. Walter Murphy suggested that judges needed courage—but he meant

the courage to pursue the prudent course, "even when it means risking some political dangers and enduring bitter criticism from contemporaries as well as from historians for refusing to risk other dangers." Walter F. Murphy, Elements of Judicial Strategy 210 (1964).

4. Anthony T. Kronman, *Alexander Bickel's Philosophy of Prudence*, 94 Yale L. J. 1567, 1569 (1985).
5. Anthony Kronman, *Practical Wisdom and Professional Character* in Philosophy and Law, 203, 208 (Jules Coleman and Ellen Frankel Paul eds, 1987) ("*Practical Wisdom*"); see also Anthony T. Kronman, The Lost Lawyer: Failing Ideals of the Legal Profession (1993) ("*Lost Lawyer*"). Another nice description of character—and why it is important for judges—may be found in Mark Tushnet, *Constitutional Interpretation, Character, and Experience*, 72 B.U. L. Rev. 747, 762–763 (1993).
6. Alexander M. Bickel, The Least Dangerous Branch: The Supreme Court at the Bar of Politics, 65–72 (1962).
7. Examples include Akhil Amar and Bruce Ackerman. For further discussion, see Daniel A. Farber and Suzanna Sherry, Desperately Seeking Certainty: The Misguided Quest for Constitutional Foundations, 75–121 (2002).
8. The most prominent scholars of this type are Ronald Dworkin and Richard Epstein. For elaboration, see *id.* at 55–74, 122–139.
9. Frank Easterbrook, Robert Bork, and Antonin Scalia are among those who often favor originalist approaches. For further discussion, see *id.* at 10–54.
10. For a critique of the postmodern abandonment of objectivity and the rule of law, see Daniel A. Farber and Suzanna Sherry, Beyond All Reason: The Radical Assault on Truth in American Law (1997).
11. Cass R. Sunstein, One Case at a Time: Judicial Minimalism on the Supreme Court 5 (1999) (emphasis added).
12. *Id.* at 30 (emphasis added).
13. 347 U.S. 483 (1954).
14. 388 U.S. 1 (1967).
15. 531 U.S. 98 (2000).
16. In noting that "[o]ur consideration is limited to the present circumstances, for the problem of equal protection in election processes generally presents many complexities," *id.* at 109, the Court made clear that the equal protection arguments were a ticket for one train only.
17. As many other scholars have noted, the equal protection reasoning does not support the remedy, and the remedy-supportive reasoning of the concurrence did not command a majority. See articles cited in note 39, *infra*.
18. Cass R. Sunstein, *Order Without Law*, 68 U. Chi. L. Rev. 757, 767 (2001).
19. Murphy, *supra* note 3, at 208. Ironically, Murphy's insight has outlasted computer punch-cards.
20. See, e.g. Richard A. Posner, The Problems of Jurisprudence (1990); Steven J. Burton, *Law as Practical Reason*, 62 S. Cal. L. Rev. 747 (1989).
21. See, e.g. Daniel A. Farber, *Reinventing Brandeis: Legal Pragmatism for the Twenty-First Century*, U. Ill. L. Rev. 163 (1995).
22. See Karl N. Llewellyn, The Common Law Tradition: Deciding Appeals (1960).
23. While it may be more usual for personal and judicial character to align, it is not necessary. Holmes and Frankfurter, for example, both of whom are known for their humility about the judicial role, were hardly humble

personally. Cardozo, on the other hand, might be seen as a courageous judge but a rather timid individual.

24. I mean to distinguish this fear of error from a different type of fear that some have recently attributed to federal judges, especially Supreme Court Justices: fear of public opinion. Lawrence Solum calls this "civic cowardice." See Lawrence B. Solum, *Virtue Jurisprudence: A Virtue-Centred Theory of Judging*, 34 Metaphilosophy 178, 183 (2003).
25. Learned Hand, *The Spirit of Liberty* (1944) in The Spirit of Liberty: Papers and Addresses of Learned Hand, 189, 190 (Irving Dillard ed., 3rd edn 1960).
26. Felix Frankfurter, *Chief Justices I have Known*, 39 Va. L. Rev. 883, 905 (1953); see also Felix Frankfurter, *Mr. Justice Roberts*, 104 U. Pa. L. Rev. 311, 312–313 (1955) (praising Justice Roberts for his "humility engendered by consciousness of limitations").
27. Stephen Breyer, *Our Democratic Constitution*, 77 N.Y.U. L. Rev. 245, 250 (2002).
28. See, e.g. Paul Gewirtz, *On "I Know It When I See It,"* 105 Yale L. J. 1023, 1034–1035 (1996); Lawrence Lessig, *Fidelity and Constraint*, 65 Fordham L. Rev. 1365, 1372 (1997); Cass R. Sunstein, *Incompletely Theorized Agreements*, 108 Harv. L. Rev. 1733, 1749 (1995).
29. Brett Scharffs, *The Role of Humility in Exercising Practical Wisdom*, 32 U.C. Davis L. Rev. 127, 157 (1998).
30. See *Brown v. Allen*, 344 U.S. 433, 540 (1953) (Jackson, J., concurring) ("We are not final because we are infallible, but we are infallible only because we are final").
31. It is therefore no surprise that judges who express radical views in their scholarship often do not implement those views in their judicial decisions. See Farber and Sherry, *supra* note 7, at 29–54 (discussing Scalia); Daniel A. Farber, *Do Theories of Statutory Interpretation Matter? A Case Study*, 94 Nw. U. L. Rev. 1409 (2000); Tushnet, *supra* note 5.
32. 60 U.S. (19 How.) 393 (1857).
33. 531 U.S. 98 (2000).
34. Malcolm M. Feeley and Samuel Krislov, Constitutional Law 34 (2nd edn. 1990); see also Alexander M. Bickel, The Supreme Court and the Idea of Progress 41 (1970) (a "ghastly error"); Robert H. Bork, The Tempting of America: The Political Seduction of the Law 28 (1990) ("the worst constitutional decision of the nineteenth century"); David P. Currie, The Constitution in the Supreme Court: The First Hundred Years 1789–1888, at 264 (1985) ("bad policy," "bad judicial politics," and "bad law"); Gary J. Jacobsohn, The Supreme Court and the Decline of Constitutional Aspiration 44 (1986) ("the most odious action ever taken by a branch of the federal government"); Robert G. McCloskey, The American Supreme Court 94 (1960) ("the most disastrous opinion the Supreme Court has ever issued"); Christopher L. Eisgruber, Dred *Again: Originalism's Forgotten Past*, 10 Const. Comment. 37, 41 (1993) ("the worst atrocity in the Supreme Court's history").
35. Michael W. McConnell, *Two-and-a-Half Cheers for Bush v. Gore*, 68 U. Chi. L. Rev. 657 (2001).
36. Richard A. Epstein, *"In such Manner as the Legislature Thereof May Direct": The Outcome in Bush v. Gore Defended*, 68 U. Chi. L. Rev. 613 (2001).

37. Richard A. Posner, *Florida 2000: A Legal and Statistical Analysis of the Election Deadlock and Ensuing Litigation*, Sup. Ct. Rev. 1, 60 (2000) (emphasis added).
38. Richard A. Posner, Breaking the Deadlock: The 2000 Election, the Constitution, and the Courts (2001); John C. Yoo, *In Defense of the Court's Legitimacy*, 68 U. Chi. L. Rev. 775 (2001).
39. For a sampling of the voluminous criticism, see, e.g. Alan M. Dershowitz, Supreme Injustice: How the High Court Hijacked Election 2000 (2001); Howard Gillman, The Votes That Counted: How the Court Decided the 2000 Presidential Election (2001); Erwin Chemerinsky, *Bush v. Gore Was not Justiciable*, 76 Notre Dame L. Rev. 1093 (2001); Elizabeth Garrett, *Institutional Lessons from the 2000 Presidential Election*, 29 Fla. St. U. L. Rev. 975 (2001); Stephen Holmes, *Afterword: Can A Coin-Toss Election Trigger a Constitutional Earthquake?* in The Unfinished Election of 2000, pp. 235–250 (Jack N. Rakove ed., 2001); Samuel Issacharoff, *Political Judgments*, 68 U. Chi. L. Rev. 637 (2001); Pamela S. Karlan, *Equal Protection: Bush v. Gore and the Making of a Precedent* in The Unfinished Election of 2000, *supra*, at 159; Larry D. Kramer, *The Supreme Court in Politics* in The Unfinished Election of 2000, *supra*, at 105; Frank I. Michelman, *Suspicion, or the New Prince*, 68 U. Chi. L. Rev. 679 (2001); Peter M. Shane, *Disappearing Democracy: How Bush v. Gore Undermined the Federal Right to Vote for Presidential Electors*, 29 Fla. St. U. L. Rev. 535 (2001); David A. Strauss, *Bush v. Gore: What Were They Thinking?*, 68 U. Chi. L. Rev. 737 (2001); Sunstein, *supra* note 18; Vikram Amar and Alan Brownstein, *Bush v. Gore and Article II: Pressured Judgment Makes Dubious Law*, 48 Fed. Law. 27 (March/April 2001).
40. McCloskey, *supra* note 34, at 93.
41. Don E. Fehrenbacher, The Dred Scott Case: Its Significance in American Law and Politics 209, 573 (1978).
42. *Bush v. Gore*, 531 U.S. 98, 111 (2000).
43. *Id.* at 158 (Breyer, J., dissenting).
44. Yoo, *supra* note 38, at 789.
45. Posner, *supra* note 38, at 161.
46. *McCulloch v. Maryland*, 17 U.S. (4 Wheat.) 316 (1819).
47. *Brown v. Bd. of Educ.*, 347 U.S. 483 (1954).
48. *United States v. Nixon*, 418 U.S. 683 (1974).
49. See Jack Bass, Unlikely Heroes (1981).
50. Gerald Gunther was the first scholar—and perhaps the most sophisticated—but not the last, to criticize Bickel on these grounds. See Gerald Gunther, *The Subtle Vices of the "Passive Virtues"—A Comment on Principle and Expediency in Judicial Review*, 64 Colum. L. Rev. 1 (1964). For a more elaborate argument about Bickel's lack of followers, see Kronman, *supra* note 4, at 1571–1573.
51. Kronman, *Lost Lawyer*, *supra* note 5, at 325–328.
52. Richard A. Posner, *The Jurisprudence of Skepticism*, 86 Mich. L. Rev. 827, 854 (1988).
53. Ronald Dworkin, Freedom's Law: The Moral Reading of the American Constitution 342 (1996) (emphasis added). Dworkin himself suffers from no such uncertainty. And Hand, despite his purported disability, could be courageous on occasion. See *Masses Publishing Co. v. Patten*, 244 F. 535 (S.D.N.Y.), *rev'd*, 246 F. 24 (2d Cir. 1917).
54. Burton, *supra* note 20, at 792.

55. John T. Noonan, Jr., *Education, Intelligence, and Character in Judges*, 71 Minn. L. Rev. 1119, 1130–1321 (1987) (quoting Alpheus Thomas Mason, Brandeis: A Free Man's Life 281 (1956)).
56. *Planned Parenthood of Southeastern Pa. v. Casey*, 505 U.S. 833, 844 (1992).
57. For descriptions, scholarly adherents, and critiques of some of these methods of interpretation, see Farber and Sherry, *supra* note 7.
58. *Id.*
59. 320 U.S. 81 (1943).
60. 323 U.S. 214 (1944).
61. Kathleen Sullivan and Gerald Gunther, Constitutional Law 631 n. 4 (14th edn, 2001).
62. David Cole and William N. Eskridge, Jr., *From Hand-Holding to Sodomy: First Amendment Protections of Homosexual (Expressive) Conduct*, 29 Harv. C.R.-C.L. L.R. 319, 343 (1994).
63. *Hirabayashi*, 320 U.S. at 93.
64. *Korematsu*, 323 U.S. at 234 (Murphy, J., dissenting).
65. *Id.* at 245 (Jackson, J., dissenting).
66. *Id.* at 245–246.
67. 163 U.S. 537 (1896).
68. See, e.g. Michael J. Klarman, *The Plessy Era*, 1998 Sup. Ct. Rev. 303.
69. Historian (and lawyer) Peter Irons concludes that the military orders culminating in internment "resulted from racism, war hysteria, and the failure of leadership at the highest levels of government," but that the legal cases simply "reflected the failure of the legal system." Peter Irons, Justice At War 365 (1983). His discussion of the Supreme Court's treatment of the cases does not indicate that racial prejudice played much role in the decisions. See *id.* at 227–250, 319–345. And his overarching conclusion is that political actors and government lawyers lied to the courts, eliminating any hope that they might reach correct results. See, e.g. *id.* at viii ("Never before has evidence emerged that shows a deliberate campaign to present tainted records to the Supreme Court").
70. 367 U.S. 497 (1961).
71. 381 U.S. 479 (1965).
72. *Id.* at 503.
73. *Id.* at 544, 547 (Harlan, J., dissenting).
74. 410 U.S. 113 (1973).
75. Michael Klarman includes *Griswold* in his list of cases in which the Supreme Court's decision reflected national majority views and suppressed "outlier state practices." Michael J. Klarman, *Rethinking the History of American Freedom*, 42 Wm. Mary L. Rev. 265, 279 (2000).
76. The effect is made worse if one considers that the Supreme Court first refused to confront the merits of the Connecticut birth control statute almost twenty years before *Poe*. In *Tileston v. Ullman*, 318 U.S. 44 (1943), the Court rejected a constitutional challenge to the law on standing grounds.
77. *DeFunis v. Odegaard*, 416 U.S. 312 (1974) (finding the challenge moot, on somewhat weak reasoning exposed by the dissent).
78. 438 U.S. 265 (1978).
79. See, e.g. *Smith v. Univ. of Wash. Law Sch.*, 233 F.3d 1188 (9th Cir. 2000), *cert. denied*, 532 U.S. 1051 (2001); *Eisenberg v. Montgomery County Pub. Sch.*, 197

F.3d 123 (4th Cir. 1999), *cert. denied,* 529 U.S. 1019 (2000); *Tuttle v. Arlington County Sch. Bd.,* 195 F.3d 698 (4th Cir. 1999), *cert. denied,* 529 U.S. 1050 (2000); *Hunter v. Regents of the Univ. of Cal.,* 190 F.3d 1061 (9th Cir. 1999), *cert. denied,* 531 U.S. 877 (2000); *Hopwood v. Texas,* 78 F.3d 932 (5th Cir.), *cert. denied,* 518 U.S. 1033 (1996). Since this article was first published, the Supreme Court has decided a pair of cases on affirmative action, striking down one program and upholding another. *Gratz v. Bollinger,* 539 U.S. 244 (2003); *Grutter v. Bollinger,* 539 U.S. 306 (2003). It is fair to say that taken together, the cases provide little guidance. As the dissenters note, there was in fact very little difference between the two programs.

80. 505 U.S. 833, 845–846 (1992).
81. 340 U.S. 162 (1950).
82. *Id.* at 178 (Jackson, J., concurring) (citations and some ellipses omitted).
83. 469 U.S. 528 (1985), *overruling National League of Cities v. Usery,* 426 U.S. 833 (1976).
84. *Compare Regents of the Univ. of Cal. v. Bakke,* 438 U.S. 265, 408 (1978) (Stevens, J., concurring in part and dissenting in part) with *Adarand Constructors, Inc. v. Pena,* 515 U.S. 200, 242 (1995) (Stevens, J., dissenting).
85. *Compare Minersville Sch. Dist. v. Gobitis,* 310 U.S. 586 (1940) with *W. Va. State Bd. of Educ. v. Barnette,* 319 U.S. 624 (1943).
86. 384 U.S. 436 (1966).
87. *Dickerson v. United States,* 530 U.S. 428 (2000). Justice Rehnquist's earlier views may be found in *Michigan v. Tucker,* 417 U.S. 433, 444 (1974) and *New York v. Quarles,* 467 U.S. 649, 654 (1984).
88. Anthony Lewis, *Abroad at Home; Question of Judgment,* N.Y. Times, September 27, 1987, at D23.

4
Civic Liberalism and the "Dialogical Model" of Judicial Review*

Colin Farrelly

> In a world that is inherently indeterminate, a suitable theory of distributive justice must perhaps itself be indeterminate, and its indeterminacies must accommodate those of the world where relevant.
>
> Russell Hardin, *Indeterminacy and Society*[1]

1. Introduction

Consider the following scenarios which could occur in any affluent, liberal democratic society:

Scenario 1: Intelligence gathering operatives believe that there is a good chance that the country will be the target of a terrorist attack within the next 48 hours. The exact nature of the attack is unknown, but there is good reason to believe that the risk of attack is significant. Military personnel and equipment have been stationed at airports and some airlines have cancelled flights. Much debate takes place in the media concerning how much is being done to guard against this possible attack. Critics of the existing government claim that more should be done. One prominent critic complains that "citizens should not have to be fearful of such attacks in their own homes, schools or airports; the government needs to do more to eliminate these threats!"

Scenario 2: Leroy has been diagnosed with bowl cancer and is not expected to live until the end of the year. A new expensive drug therapy could, however, extend Leroy's survival by 5 months. This would permit

*For their helpful comments on earlier drafts of this paper, I am grateful to the members of the democracy reading group at Waterloo University (especially my colleague Jan Narveson) and two anonymous referees for this journal.

him to spend one last Christmas with his family and friends. However, the drug is only available to sufferers with private health care, which Leroy could not afford. Leroy's family find this predicament unacceptable. They write to their local politician complaining about the state of the publicly funded health care system. They believe we have a collective responsibility to ensure that patients like Leroy have the chance to experience one last Christmas with their loved ones.

Scenario 3: Tragedy hits a small rural community. A young child has been abducted from her home. The local community is mounting pressure on the media and government to commit more resources to the search for the child and the kidnapper. Details about the abduction are sketchy, but one eyewitness did see a suspicious vehicle in the neighbourhood shortly before the abduction. The community demands that more investigators should be assigned to this case. Furthermore, the community demands that more be done to ensure that such crimes do not occur again in the future. More police officers are needed and they should be equipped with the most modern and effective crime-fighting equipment.

Scenario 4: The beef industry in the country is reeling from the repercussions of a recent report that the tests done on a dead calf confirm that it had BSE (commonly known as mad cow disease). Other countries have since banned imports of beef from our country. Much debate now takes place concerning not only the issue of how to improve existing procedures so further cases of BSE do not occur but also about what the government should do to help the crippled beef industry.

Scenario 5: The economy is rapidly moving towards a *knowledge-based economy*, an economy built on technology and innovation. Long-term projections suggest that stable economic growth will require a much-needed investment in the education sector. More skilled educators are needed, better research facilities are required and some concerted effort must be made to keep the current "knowledge workers" in this country. Reports suggest that a significant number of such workers have left the country for work in a neighboring country.

Scenario 6: Beth is a single mother of three and juggles two part-time jobs. Her family lives in low-income housing. The government and Beth's local parish help her to provide for her family by providing various forms of social assistance (e.g. affordable housing, clothes for her children). Despite this assistance, Beth feels that she is fighting a losing battle. She barely scrapes enough money together to make ends meet but is unable to save anything for the future. There is a chance she might loose one of her part-time jobs. Given the high unemployment rate and Beth's limited skills, she knows that losing that job will have dire consequences for her family and will extinguish any remaining hopes she has of helping her family escape life in poverty.

As human beings we are all *vulnerable*. We are vulnerable to innumerable misfortunes—disease, malnutrition, illiteracy, murder, theft, assault, unemployment, injury at work, terrorist attack, etc. One of the primary functions of government is to reduce, as far as is reasonable, our vulnerability to these various misfortunes. Each of the scenarios described above are ones that occur in real, affluent, liberal, democratic countries. In each of the scenarios, we see different demands being placed on society. These include the following:

We should do more to *protect ourselves from terrorist attack*.
We should do more to *provide the necessary medical treatment to those in need*.
We should do more to *prevent and solve crimes*.
We should do more to *protect industries vital to our economy*.
We should do more to *improve our education system*.
We should do more to *reduce poverty*.

Behind each of these different demands are claims of *distributive justice*. Distributive justice concerns the fair division of the benefits and burdens of social cooperation. But what "terms of agreement" would constitute fair terms of social cooperation among members of large, pluralistic, unequal liberal democracies that exist in an era of rapid globalization? Consider, for example, the country that I am from—Canada. Canada is made up of approximately 32,000,000 people. These people are from diverse ethnic, religious and cultural backgrounds. They also greatly differ in their level of skills and abilities, their income and wealth and their work habits. They also have different preferences ranging from the kinds of automobiles they prefer to drive to the food they enjoy eating and the habits and values they wish to instill in their children.

All Canadians have certain legal rights and freedoms that are enshrined in the *Charter of Rights and Freedoms*. These include the right not to be arbitrarily detained or imprisoned, the right to move and to take up residence in any province, freedom of expression and freedom of association. Canada is also a democratic country. We hold regular elections, have a secret ballot and there is much competition between political parties and leaders for securing political office. The resources of the country are diverse, and this influences our industry and commerce. Our economy is subject to the pressures of a global market. The fate of our prosperity is not completely in our own hands, but there are steps we can take to better position ourselves so that we prevent capital flight and encourage investment so that we are, and can remain, a competitive country in an era of rapid globalization. As I write these words, the current national debt of my country is $510,576 million.[2] By the time you read these words that figure will no doubt have changed. And the factors that influence these changes will be a mix of things within our collective control and things beyond our control.

Every year, many of my compatriots suffer misfortunes ranging from losing their job to being the victim of a crime (e.g. property crimes, sexual assault) and premature death (e.g. caused by disease, traffic accidents). We have some influence over how vigorously we can pursue mitigating these diverse misfortunes, but we cannot prevent all of these misfortunes from occurring. And our efforts to mitigate these misfortunes will be influenced by a variety of factors, ranging from budget constraints and dietary habits to the level of our medical expertise and the threat of international insecurity. By what *metric* can one measure the justness of such a society? The dominant metric invoked by contemporary political theorists is that of the *fulfillment of principles* (or serially ordered principles) *of justice*. I aim to displace this metric with one that focuses instead on the *exercise of the virtues of fair social cooperation*. These two distinct approaches can be represented as follows:

Principle-oriented approach: The justness of a society is measured by the extent to which it satisfies the *principles of justice*.

Virtue-oriented (non-perfectionist)[3] *approach*: The justness of a society is measured by the extent to which it *exercises the virtues of fair social cooperation*.

Contemporary political theory is dominated by "principle-oriented" theories of distributive justice. Since the publication of John Rawls's influential book *A Theory of Justice* (1971), much of the work of Anglo-American political theorists has been preoccupied with the project of searching for, and defending, the principles of justice. The details of these principles will vary from theorist to theorist, but a partial list of some of the main contemporary contenders includes the following:

1. Principle of *equal basic liberties*.[4]
2. Principles of *entitlement*.[5]
3. Principle of *state neutrality*.[6]
4. Principle of *need*.[7]

5. Principle of *desert*.[8]
6. Principle of *equality of ___X___*.[9]
7. Principle of *sufficitarianism*.[10]
8. Principle of *democratic equality*.[11]
9. Principle of *minimax relative concession*.[12]
10. The *difference principle*.[13]

In this paper, I aim to help lessen the stranglehold the principle-oriented approach to justice has on political theorists. These principles are of limited practical guidance. This is not to say that the appeal to principles of justice is never appropriate or useful. Of course principles have a role to play, but the real challenge is knowing when the appeal to principles is appropriate and when it is not, as well as who these principles apply to. Does the principle of equality of opportunity, for example, apply to every conceivable advantage—such as health, health care, education, security, procreation, companionship, attractiveness, friendship, employment, height? Why does it apply only to some of these goods and not to others? And whose responsibility is it to fulfil the requirements of this principle (e.g. legislators, judges, citizens)? Furthermore, if we think that *quality* education, health care and security matter, and not only equal opportunity for these things,[14] what do we do when we cannot have it all, when we are forced to make trade-offs between these competing demands? What guidance does the appeal to equality of opportunity provide in such a scenario? The search for principles of justice should not be the main preoccupation of a theory of distributive justice that seeks to take the complexities of real life seriously. Taking real life seriously means taking seriously a diverse range of pressing concerns, like those raised in the six scenarios described in the introduction. These concerns range from the facts of scarcity, non-compliance and indeterminacy to human fallibility, pervasive disadvantage and disagreement. To have practical import, a theory of justice should provide some guidance in terms of helping us transform the current (non-ideal) state of affairs into one that is more just.

I aim to revive the transformative potential of liberal democratic theory by endorsing a "virtue-oriented" conception of justice entitled *civic liberalism*.[15] Unlike principle-oriented theories of distributive justice, which seek to protect the vulnerable in society by endorsing a version of either *judicial* or *legislative supremacy*, civic liberalism inspires a public philosophy that seeks to take seriously the moral and pragmatic demands of toleration, civility and fairness. Such a public philosophy, I argue, ought to embrace a "dialogical model" of judicial review.[16]

Such a model currently informs Canadian Constitutional law and I draw upon the Canadian experience in order to develop a virtue-oriented political theory that takes seriously what Robert Bork calls the "Madisonian dilemma."[17] Civic liberalism interprets the Madisonian dilemma as the dilemma between the moral demands of the virtues of toleration and civility. Respect for toleration leads us in the direction of limited government, government that does not unjustly interfere with individual liberty. This concern for individual rights provides the normative basis for constitutionalism. This can be contrasted with the moral demands of civility, demands that lead us to majority rule and the idea of self-government.

If we take only the moral dimensions of these two virtues into account, it seems that we cannot resolve the Madisonian dilemma. For we have two contradictory prescriptions—limited government and self-government. But civic liberalism inspires a public philosophy that gives due attention to both the moral and *pragmatic* dimensions of these virtues. It does not seek to give an absolute priority to any of the moral demands of toleration or civility. Instead, it seeks to reconcile the diverse demands of toleration, civility and fairness. Civic liberalism does not see the Madisonian dilemma as paradoxical. Rather, this dilemma reinforces the need for a virtue-oriented approach rather than a principle-oriented approach to political theory. Civic liberalism defends a virtue-oriented conception of liberal democracy that takes both sides of the Madisonian dilemma seriously.

In Section 2 of this paper, I outline some of the main deficiencies of the principle-oriented approach to distributive justice. In Section 3, I develop a virtue-oriented theory that is premised on the virtues of toleration, civility and fairness. I then bring to the fore the institutional implications of this account of justice in Section 4 when I consider the design of Canada's *Charter of Rights and Freedoms* and the dialogical model of judicial review that has emerged since the adoption of the *Charter* in 1982. I argue that civic liberalism instructs us to seek a middle ground between judicial and legislative supremacy.

2. The domination of "principle-oriented" theories of justice

A virtue-oriented conception of distributive justice may appear to many as a more limited and indeterminate theory than a principle-oriented theory. But this perception stems from the fact that most principle-oriented theories function at the level of ideal theory and thus gloss over or simply ignore many of the complexities that arise in non-ideal theory. The distinction between ideal and non-ideal theory is not given rigorous classification in the existing literature. As Andrew Mason[18] notes, this distinction is employed by John Rawls in *The Law of Peoples*. An account of justice in ideal theory must recognize "some moderately strong feasibility constraints which require it to be realistic in the best of foreseeable conditions."[19] Rawls describes ideal theory as being *realistically utopian*. Political philosophy is realistically utopian "when it extends what are ordinarily thought of as limits of practical political possibility."[20] This contrasts with non-ideal theory, which is concerned with problems of non-compliance or unfavourable (historical, social or economic) conditions. Non-ideal theory is much more *fact sensitive* than ideal theory. As such, it is not surprising that a virtue-oriented account of justice, which attempts to track the complexities of non-ideal considerations, yields indeterminate prescriptions.

Principled approaches to ideal theory construe the justness of an action or policy as follows:

> *Principle-oriented approach*: An action or policy is right if and only if it is in accordance with a moral rule or principle.

Two examples[21] of specific instantiations of the above premise include

(i) The relevant principle is self-ownership (Nozick, 1974);
(ii) The relevant principles are the serially ordered principles chosen in the original position (Rawls, 1971).

It is not possible, in a paper of this size, to survey the main principle-oriented theories of justice and their specific shortcomings. So I shall limit my criticism to the most prominent principle-oriented philosopher—John Rawls. Rawls is a good example of a political philosopher who invokes a number of "simplifying assumptions" to help clarify what the principles of justice are. These include the assumption that society is a *closed system* and a society of *normal, fully cooperating* members. Rawls invokes the assumption[22] that everyone has physical needs and psychological capacities within the normal range, for example, when he attempts to identify who the least advantaged are. Rawls's difference principle requires the basic structure of society to be organized so that social and economic inequalities are to the greatest benefit of the least advantaged. But if all citizens are within the normal range of functioning then we would not need to worry about health care concerns like those raised in scenario 2. With the money freed up from providing health care, we would have more to invest in education, policing and eliminating poverty. But of course no society in the world is like this. The fact that we are vulnerable to illness and disease complicates the story of justice in a variety of important ways.[23]

The idea that we can derive the principles of justice by simply ignoring or postponing non-ideal considerations (like human vulnerability) is severely misguided. Rawls claims that addressing such non-ideal considerations should be dealt with "at the legislative stage when the prevalence and kinds of these misfortunes are known and the costs of treating them can be ascertained and balanced along with total government expenditure."[24] But once Rawls's legislators have the information about the prevalence of these misfortunes and the costs of treating them, they will need some *criteria* by which to make a judgement about how much should be spent on health care. If the fundamental principles of justice that are supposed to help guide their deliberations are ones that are derived for societies that do not have people in need of medical treatment, then such a theory will be of no use to them. The principles of justice will be ineffective in helping them determine how much they should spend on health care.

The concerns I raised in scenarios 1, 4 and 5 would not arise in a society that is what Rawls calls *a closed system*. If our society were closed, then we would not have to worry about threats of international terrorism, bans on exports or the migration of knowledge workers. In the introduction to the paperback edition of *Political Liberalism*, there is a brief section where Rawls makes some policy prescriptions concerning what the essential prerequisites are for a just basic structure.[25] One of these prescriptions is that society should take the role as employer of last resort through general or local government, or other social and economic policies. This prescription might sound like a good idea when we assume that society is a closed society that is comprised solely of normal functioning people. But the case for such a prescription is much harder to make in a society that does not have Rawls's idealizing assumptions. Beth's concerns in scenario 6 are pressing ones, but ones we must also balance against the concerns expressed in the other five scenarios. The clash between these interests is avoided if one invokes the idealizing assumptions that Rawls suggests theorists should make. It is a lot easier to make the kind of policy prescriptions Rawls does when one imposes such artificial constraints on a theory of justice.

If everyone in society was fully *cooperative*, as Rawls *also* assumes, we could ignore demands like those raised in scenario 3. We would not have to worry about things like crime and crime prevention if our society did not contain immoral people who would willfully injure others. Once we invoke all of Rawls's "simplifying assumptions," we see that he has basically reduced all the main concerns of justice to the kinds of concerns raised in scenario 6. I admit that it is much easier for a political theorist to construct a theory of justice that only takes concerns about poverty seriously. But I introduced the six different scenarios above because all of them are pressing ones that cannot be bracketed or ignored. How we respond to combating poverty cannot be answered in the abstract, detached from the question of how we also address the other various concerns that arise in the real world, concerns like those raised in the other five scenarios. Rawls makes things easier on himself by functioning at the level of ideal theory, but I think the result is a normative theory that is deeply deficient and simplistic.[26] Starting at the level of non-ideal theory makes things much tougher for the political theorist. But the reward, if executed successfully, is worth it. For we shall have a theory that takes seriously the complexities of real life.

One of the consequences of endorsing a principle-oriented theory of justice is that many justice theorists tend to downplay the importance of democracy and endorse instead an optimistic vision of *judicial supremacy*. This follows because principle-oriented theories tend to be *rights-based theories*. And the constitution and judicial branch of government are taken to be the primary rights-protecting institutions. If the demands of justice can be established by simply invoking the principles chosen in the original position (Rawls), the principles of entitlement (Nozick), or equality of ___X____ (insert any name from the very long list of contemporary political philosophers who espouse this position), then what is the role of democratic politics? If we can arrive at the correct answer to what laws and policies are legitimate *independently* of any real democratic process, then it seems that the later is *superfluous*. All we need to do is bring into existence a constitutional framework that protects those rights we believe justice requires. This is in fact the line of argument recently advanced by Cécil Fabre in *Social Rights Under the Constitution*. Fabre argues in favour of granting social rights constitutional protection. These social rights include rights to adequate minimum income, education, housing and health care. Such rights are necessary, argues Fabre, for protecting autonomy and well-being.

Numerous criticisms have been levied against constitutionalism from scholars on both the left and the right. Much of these debates concern American Constitutionalism which has a long history of judicial activism. Left-wing critics of constitutionalism point to the *Lochner* era (1885–1930) in America. "During the *Lochner* era in the United States, the Supreme Court constitutionalized laissez-faire economics, and advantaged interests such as corporations could easily go to court to oppose the regulatory and redistributive activities of the state."[27] Jeremy Waldron, a prominent critic of judicial activism, points out that during this time period, state and federal courts struck down some 150 pieces of legislation concerning labour relations, labour conditions and working hours.[28] These concerns might be alleviated if one adopts, as Fabre suggests, a specific list of social rights that should be given constitutional protection. Though if such a proposal is to be adopted in a democratic society, it will need the support of democratically elected and accountable legislators in order to make it law. So justice theorists need to emphasize *legislative activism* as well as judicial activism. But the problem with a proposal like Fabre's is that it fails to take the complexities of non-ideal theory seriously enough. In particular, by insulating itself from the dilemmas posed by scarcity, such a proposal compromises the demands of civility.[29]

In *The Cost of Rights: Why Liberty Depends on Taxes*, Stephen Holmes and Cass Sunstein effectively illustrate how all rights (both the so-called negative and positive) cost money and that "nothing that costs money can be absolute."[30] Appeals to constitutionalizing social rights are thus problematic, not because the aims of such a proposal (e.g. eliminating poverty) are objectionable but because such a *cost-blind* approach to rights presupposes that the judicial branch of government is well placed to resolve rights enforcement issues. But "courts are not well positioned to oversee the tricky process of efficient resource allocation conducted, with more or less skill, by executive agencies, nor are they readily able to rectify past misallocations."[31] All of the demands being made in the six scenarios in the introduction to this paper are pressing demands, but the judicial branch of government is not the institution we would (or *should*) turn to for remedying such concerns. What rights-based justice theorists overlook is the fact that "the entire range of legal rights must be drawn from the same inevitably limited budgets."[32] Rights enforcement does not depend on the courts alone. Trade-offs in rights enforcement must and will be made and this raises fundamental questions of both distributive justice and democratic accountability. Civility requires us to take seriously the question of *who* decides how much we should spend on the protection of the different rights we believe should be protected. Fabre's endorsement of judicial supremacy compromises the demands of civility as the fate of resource allocations is now taken out of the hands of democratically accountable officials and placed in the hands of *politically insulated* judges. Public officials that are not well positioned to make such important decisions. Appeals to judicial supremacy might be appropriate in a society that did not have to struggle with the dilemmas imposed by scarcity or with the problem of partisan or fallible judges. But no society is like that.

By focusing exclusively at the level of ideal theory, many principle-oriented justice theorists fail to give due consideration to our *democratic* commitments. The relation between justice and democracy is a much-debated topic in the history of political thought. In *The Republic*, for example, Plato argued that democracy was unjust. One can perhaps be sympathetic to some of Plato's criticisms when one bears in mind the fact that Athenians condemned Plato's mentor—Socrates—to death for corrupting the minds of young Athenians. But the emergence of liberalism as a political theory, starting with John Locke's emphasis on natural rights and limited authority in the seventeenth century, has witnessed a concerted effort to defend a form of self-government that would guard against the "tyranny of the majority." From the founders of the American Constitution like James Madison to utilitarians like John Stuart Mill, liberals have tried to reconcile their liberal convictions with their democratic commitments. Two of John Stuart Mill's greatest political writings—*On Liberty* (1859) and *Essay on Representative Government* (1861)—capture the tension of the so-called Madisonian dilemma that liberals have tried to resolve. How can Mill argue for representative government and also endorse the constrained view of government entailed by his liberty principle? This is the seemingly paradoxical nature of liberal democracy.[33]

The supposed paradox of liberal democracy stems from the principle-oriented tendency to reduce our moral and political convictions to principles of justice that then lead us to endorse the ideals of either constitutionalism or democracy. For example, the moral values of toleration, autonomy and impartiality may lead us in the direction of judicial supremacy. The Court should be given the power to limit legislatures so that individual rights cannot be overridden or compromised. Judges should be given this power because, unlike legislatures, the judiciary is *politically insulated*. It is thus insulated from the temptation to infringe upon individual rights for spurious reasons (e.g. to win re-election). As such, judges can make decisions based solely on reasons that follow from the appeal to principles. This position is endorsed by Ronald Dworkin when he claims the following:

> My own view is that the Court should make decisions of principle rather than policy—decisions about what rights people have under our constitutional system rather than decisions about how the general welfare is best promoted—and that it should make these decisions by elaborating and applying the substantive theory of representation taken from the root principle that government must treat people as equals.[34]

While Dworkin sees the institution of judicial review as essential to treating all as equals, democrats may view constitutionalism as an affront to the ideals of self-government. Self-government requires that we place power in the hands of democratically elected and accountable officials, rather than politically insulated and unaccountable judges. The "will of the people" stands a better chance of being implemented if the organs of government are attuned to the expansive range of reasons (both principled and pragmatic) that may arise in the course of the deliberations and accommodations typical of democratic institutions and practices.

If one functions at the level of non-ideal theory, rather than ideal theory, one quickly sees that there are dangers with both judicial and legislative supremacy. Judges might make decisions based on a limited range of political principles or they may base their decisions on reasons that stem from judicial *vice* (e.g. corruption or concerns about career advancement) rather than virtues of impartiality. Legislatures may also act in ways that threaten the requirements of justice. They may act hastily and thus bring about unnecessary harms. This can occur, for example, when legislation is overbroad. Or legislatures may even intentionally seek to inflict such harms for licentious reasons (e.g. to simply win re-election). Once we highlight these non-ideal considerations, we recognize that the danger of tyranny can come from either Courts or legislatures. What we want is to reap the benefits these institutions can provide in terms of bringing attention to the moral and pragmatic concerns facing real, non-ideal societies, while at the same time minimizing the potential dangers of the distinct branches of government. We can do this, I argue in Section 4, by aspiring to satisfy the dialogical model of judicial review.

The aspiration to take seriously the task of resolving the Madisonian dilemma has been marginalized by the dominance of principle-oriented theories of distributive justice. I now turn to the task of outlining a rival conception of distributive justice. One that is premised on the virtues of toleration, civility and fairness. Such a normative framework, I shall argue, resolves the Madisonian dilemma and inspires a public philosophy that seeks to avoid the extremes of both legislative and judicial supremacy.

3. Towards a "virtue-oriented" theory of justice

I turn now to the virtue-oriented theory I wish to defend—*civic liberalism*. I cannot provide a complete account of that theory here,[35] but I will provide the basics of the theoretical foundation for the theory and then, in the next section, illustrate how this theory can be applied to the issue of judicial review.

Recall, as I mentioned above, that principle oriented accounts of justice maintain the following:

Principle-oriented approach: An action or policy is right if and only if it is in accordance with a moral rule or principle.

This can be contrasted with the foundational premises of the virtue-oriented theory I wish to defend. Civic liberalism is premised on the following three premises.

Premise 1. An action or policy is right if and only if it is what a virtuous agent (e.g. parent, spouse, country, legislature, judiciary) would do in the circumstances.

Premise 2. A virtuous agent is one who acts in accordance with *reasons* no one could reasonably reject.

Premise 3. A virtue is a character trait that an agent needs in order to demonstrate *respect* for both herself and others (e.g. family, compatriots, humanity).

There are a number of ways in which civic liberalism is distinct from principled accounts of justice. Firstly, as an account of virtue that applies to both individual persons (e.g. parents, spouses, citizens) and institutions (e.g. legislatures, Courts), civic liberalism is what Rawls calls a "partially comprehensive theory."[36] A virtue-oriented account of justice must be at least partially comprehensive as it takes seriously the complexities of non-ideal theory. This means that it starts from where we currently are and seeks to help shed light on what we could do to enhance the exercise of the virtues of fair social cooperation to create a more humane social existence. Thus, civic liberalism can be contrasted with the "state-centric" conception of justice advocated by Rawls in

Political Liberalism. For Rawls, a political conception of justice (unlike a comprehensive doctrine) adopts a restrained posture towards questions concerning how individuals are to live their daily lives.

As a *transformative* public philosophy, civic liberalism must be at least partially comprehensive because our personal conduct will influence the range of possible institutional reforms open to us as a society. But this does not make civic liberalism a *perfectionist* doctrine. Civic liberalism is not premised on a particular conception of the good life (e.g. Kantianism, Catholicism, Aristotelianism). To premise a theory of justice on dubious metaphysics would be to limit its appeal as a motive for our collective action. The moral demands of the virtues of fair social cooperation do invoke core sentiments embedded in what Rawls calls the "public political culture" of liberal democracies, such as the aspiration to treat others as equals (i.e. respect them). But the pragmatic dimension of these virtues seek to balance these sentiments with an appreciation of the history of one's society and the complexities that we face, both collectively and as individuals, in the non-ideal modern era of rapid globalization.

This leads me to a second distinctive feature of a virtue-oriented theory, namely that the *scope* of reasons that it accommodates is more expansive than that typically permitted by principle-oriented accounts of justice. The latter limits the scope of reasons to those of rational self-interest (as in the case of Hobbesian contractarainism) or the maximization of happiness (as in the case of utilitarianism) or those required by impartiality (as in the case of Rawlsian justice). Civic liberalism expands the scope of reasons entailed by the contractualist account of morality advanced by Thomas Scanlon (1998).[37] According to Scanlon's contractualism, the only reasons that can be invoked are those that can be derived from *principles* no one can reasonably reject. Civic liberalism does not limit the range of defensible reasons to those that can only be derived from principles of justice. Exercising the civic virtues requires that we give due attention not only to reasons that can be derived from principles but also to reasons that arise from the non-ideal constraints of the human condition and world (e.g. the facts of scarcity, pervasive disadvantage, human nature, indeterminacy, disagreement). Many of these non-ideal facts impose constraints on our actions, and these constraints raise pragmatic considerations no one could reasonably reject.[38]

Civic liberalism thus interprets the virtues of fair social cooperation (e.g. toleration, civility and fairness) as *multi-track dispositions*. Judicial supremacy impedes the exercise of the virtues of fair social cooperation for it only permits room for consideration of the reasons that can be derived from principles. To exercise the virtues of toleration, civility and fairness, we must balance the concerns that arise with respect to principles with those concerns that arise, given the history of the culture, people, political institutions, economy, etc. of the society in question. So civic liberalism seeks to accommodate the moral and *pragmatic* dimensions of the virtues of fair social cooperation. The moral dimension is derived from the reasons that follow from idealized principles, while the pragmatic dimension is derived from the non-ideal considerations that arise, given the actual history of a society. Thus, it is important to emphasize that the reasons identified in Premise 2 above—A virtuous agent is one who acts in accordance with *reasons* no one could reasonably reject—go beyond those entailed by principles no one could reasonably reject. Though one cannot, in the abstract, provide an exhaustive account of what such reasons will be as they will be contingent upon the history of a particular society.

In this paper, I shall limit my discussion of civic liberalism to two of our most fundamental political convictions—liberalism and democracy. Liberals believe that individual rights are important and that government should respect citizens as autonomous individuals who are capable of determining for themselves how they wish to live their lives. Democrats believe that the authorization to exercise the use of state power should arise from a collective decision-making process that includes all those who are affected by the use of such power.

One can point to recent political developments to illustrate the strength we, collectively as a society, have for these two convictions. In the wake of the terrorist attacks on September 11, 2001, many believed that it was both necessary and perfectly reasonable to rethink the balance between liberty and security. Liberal democracies like Canada, England and America increased domestic security in an attempt to reduce the risk of such attacks. But the efforts to protect the public potentially threaten those values we cherish in liberal societies. Critics of the *USA Patriot Act*, for example, complain that the *Act* jeopardizes the constitutional rights of Americans. The American Civil Liberties Union (ACLU) has created a website dedicated to reforming the Act called "Reform the Patriot Act."[39] On this website, the ACLU charge that the *Act* allows the government to:

- Search your home and not tell you for weeks, months or indefinitely (s. 213)
- Collect information about what you read, what you buy, your hotel visits and your medical records (s. 215)

- Seize business and financial records (s. 505)
- Track your email activity and web usage (s. 216).

Our liberal commitments instruct us to be cautious in our zeal to mitigate the threat posed by terrorism. If we compromise our liberal values in the interests of protecting ourselves from terrorist attack then the terrorists have already won. They have succeeded in destroying the way of life we currently value. This is not to say that rights cannot be limited. As shall become evident later on, the version of liberalism I defend does not take the view that rights are absolute. But the concerns being raised against legislation like the *USA Patriot Act* are premised on the conviction that rights should be taken seriously, even if they are not absolute. And thus we must be conscious of the potential danger of democracy. It would be inappropriate for critics of the *USA Patriot Act* to describe such legislation as an example of the "tyranny of the majority." Rather, it is an example of how legislators can perhaps be overambitious or inattentive in their desire to secure certain admirable ends. Justice not only requires that we pursue just aims (e.g. public safety) but that we pursue them via *just means*. The function of a constitution is to help ensure that democracies do not forget this important insight. And so constitutions and judicial review do have an important role to play in ensuring that we, collectively, exercise the virtues of fair social cooperation.

A number of recent political developments illustrate the collective importance we place on our democratic ideals. For example, at the end of the 2000 American Presidential campaign, the nation was riveted to the developments of the count of the final votes as the judicial branch of government was brought in to resolve the issue. Many expressed concerns that if the decision of such an important issue was partisan this would be a gross violation of our commitment to self-government. The people, *not judges*, should determine who shall govern our society.

Another feature of the 2000 American election that threatens our democratic ideals was its reliance on rich contributors. According to the Federal Election Commission,[40] the total amount of campaign contributions the 2000 American Presidential candidates George Bush and Al Gore received was, respectively, $94,466,341 and $49,202,745.[41] Running an effective political campaign, whether it be a national or a local campaign, requires vast amounts of wealth, and this reliance on rich contributors threatens to undermine our ideals of self-government and political equality. "The more money politicians need to be elected, the more they need rich contributors, and the more influence such contributors then have over their political decisions once elected."[42] There is something wrong with democracy when the main preoccupation of political parties is fund-raising rather than solutions to society's many problems.

If one believes, as I do, that these different political convictions are *reasonable* convictions for us to have, the real difficult and challenging project is to explore what the implications are for a public philosophy that seeks to give due consideration to each of them. Concerns for the priority we ought to place on toleration and rights, for example, lead many liberals to *constitutionalism*. Constitutionalism means "a system that establishes individual legal rights that the dominant legislature does not have the power to override or compromise."[43] But constitutionalism is often thought to be contrary to, or at least in tension with, our democratic aspirations. When we appeal to unelected and unaccountable officials (i.e. judges) to resolve contentious and important issues, we violate the norm of inclusion entailed by our commitment to democracy. How can we reconcile these apparently contradictory convictions?

Part of the reason why liberalism and democracy appear somewhat in tension with each other (if indeed not contradictory) stems from the fact that many theorists found their justification for either political arrangement on *principles* of justice which thus give an absolute priority to either individual rights or to democratic practices. But such an approach overlooks the fact that each of these convictions has *limits*. While there are times when invoking the concern for individual rights or democracy is appropriate, similarly there are times when such appeals are at best unhelpful, and at worst unjust. For example, the rights liberals champion (e.g. security of the person, freedom of expression) often conflict with each other. The developments since September 11, 2001, clearly illustrate how the goals of liberty and security are often in tension with each other. In such cases, we must find a reasonable balance between the interests behind these different rights. Invoking the slogan "rights are trumps" in such situations is unhelpful. Imagine someone raises this slogan against the *Patriot Act*. Perhaps they feel, as the ACLU does, that rights of privacy are being unjustly compromised by the provisions entailed in the *Act*. But someone who defends the *Act* could invoke the very same motto in *defence* of the *Act*. The right they want to defend is the right to security of the person. So they may invoke the slogan "rights are trumps" as a way of buttressing support for the *Patriot Act*. In such a scenario, invoking the slogan will not do justice to the stakes at risk in the *Patriot Act*. Justice requires that we find a reasonable balance between liberty and security. Appealing to the inviolability of rights gets us nowhere when the fact is that rights often conflict with each other. Such a slogan may actually be harmful as it may detract from a full appreciation of the stakes at risk in the trade-offs between rights protection.

Appeals to self-government can also be misplaced. Take for instance a referendum. Democracies should, for a variety of reasons, use referendums sparingly. One reason for this is that referendums are very *costly*. To strive for some sort of direct democracy would mean that society would be less efficient and that many complex policy issues would be decided by people who lack the expertise needed to make an informed judgement. Imagine, for example, if we decided to resolve policy issues related to just public safety through direct democracy. So we ask the general public if we should permit medical procedure X or new drug Y. Such a course of action would be very dangerous, as the average person will not know what constitutes a reasonable degree of risk in different, complex contexts. We want people with the relevant expertise to play an important role in determining such issues. Democracy is important but it is equally important to recognize that certain conditions must be met before it can be considered an appropriate form of resolving disagreements.

How just any particular society is depends not on whether all citizens enjoy the fundamental rights and freedoms we believe are paramount, or that all pass the minimum threshold of some goods/capabilities, or have an equal voice in the political process, etc. Rather it depends on the degree to which we collectively and individually exercise the virtues of fair social cooperation. Thinking about justice in this way will obviously mean that answering the question—how just is my society?—will be indeterminate. There is no simple formula for measuring how tolerant, civil or fair a particular society is. But rather than striving to provide a normative theory that will allow us to make blanket judgements about society as a whole, civic liberalism seeks instead to be a normative theory that can help us deliberate about, and work towards resolving, particular issues and policies that we face at any given time. In particular, the focus of this paper is resolving the Madisonian dilemma. Rather than beginning with a shortlist of the principles of justice, civic liberalism forces us instead to consider the more complex questions that arise in non-ideal theory. Civic liberalism instructs us to begin from where we are and seeks to inspire a public philosophy which finds a *reasonable balance* between the moral and pragmatic dimensions of the virtues of fair social cooperation.

Civic liberalism emphasizes three moral and political virtues—*toleration, civility and fairness*. Given the nature of what virtues are—character traits that are multi-track—they will be elusive and indeterminate. One cannot completely describe, in the abstract, what the demands of these virtues are. It is only when we consider the context of a particular situation that one can begin to give some concrete life to these elusive virtues. Furthermore, the three virtues I identify are not conceptually distinct. Fairness and civility, for example, are closely related, and in certain contexts appealing to just one of these virtues may be sufficient. Adding the point that X is "fair" as well as "civil" may not necessarily tell us anything new. The ambiguous nature of virtues means that a theoretical examination of a virtue-oriented account of justice will be limited. Despite the elusive and interdependent nature of the virtues of fair social cooperation, I shall attempt, nonetheless, to give some precision to these virtues.

The moral dimension of the virtue of toleration requires us to respect others as autonomous agents. As a political virtue, toleration requires us to refrain from prohibiting or seriously interfering with conduct we find objectionable. Citizens may find, for example, the religious and sexual practices of their fellow citizens to be morally repugnant, but this does not motivate them to try to criminalize such behaviour. To be tolerant entails appreciating the fact of reasonable pluralism and the importance of individual autonomy. Toleration thus leads us to endorse *constitutionalism*, a vision of *limited* government.

But the moral demands of toleration go beyond simply respect for individual autonomy. Toleration also promotes other important values—such as truth and democracy. John Stuart Mill, for example, argued that censorship inhibited the search for truth.[44] Knowledge progresses through a forum of open debate, a marketplace of ideas, where competing ideas can be freely challenged and scrutinized. Censorship not only mistakenly presupposes the censor's infallibility, argued Mill, but also undermines the conditions necessary for us to gain a better understanding of the truth. Other liberals emphasize the importance freedom of expression has for democracy. Alexander Meiklejohn[45] argued that the exercise of self-government requires the citizenry to have the opportunity to freely and openly question and debate ideas and information concerning public issues. So toleration leads us in the direction of *liberal democracy* as the most appropriate form of government. The virtue of toleration overlaps with, and is dependent upon, the virtues of civility and fairness.

Toleration also has a *pragmatic* dimension. Toleration is often a matter of degree and its virtue has limits. If taken too far, toleration becomes a vice rather than a virtue. Clearly there are times when society should not tolerate conduct we find objectionable. For example, when such conduct harms other people. Furthermore, toleration is often a matter of degree. To what degree should we infringe on such practices and conduct when we have decided that intervention is justified? This is a very important concern for the exercise of toleration as a political virtue.[46] The pragmatic dimension of toleration is essential as there exists a large category of practices, beliefs, etc. that occupy the grey area between being harmful to others and being harmless. The risk of harm and severity of harm occur along a spectrum from the trivial to the serious, and toleration helps us to determine where along these various spectrums we should draw the line. How are we to balance the competing interests that arise when there are harms with both tolerating X and not tolerating X? Who decides which interests it would be fair to sacrifice when we cannot avoid sacrificing someone's interests? Appeals to the motto that "rights are trumps" is of little use when the reality is that rights can conflict with each other.

The pragmatic dimension of toleration raises concerns related to the virtues of civility and fairness. Citizens of liberal democracies face many different kinds of harms. Some of these may be imposed by our own governments (e.g. suppression of our rights like free speech), but other harms will be imposed upon us by scarcity, natural disasters, disease, accidents, crime, etc. Redressing this diversity of disadvantage will require decisions to be made concerning how public funds should be spent on mitigating these diverse disadvantages and possible disadvantages. So appeals to some form of judicial supremacy that many might be tempted to endorse when focusing exclusively on the moral demands of toleration (or fairness as in the case of Fabre's argument) are misguided as they fail to recognize both the pragmatic demands of toleration and the moral and pragmatic demands of civility and fairness.

Like toleration, the virtue of civility has a moral and pragmatic dimension. Civility is a willingness to listen to others, a commitment to resolve our disagreements via deliberation and a democratic process rather than through deception, manipulation or the appeal to violence. As a political virtue, the moral dimension of civility invokes the ideals of active popular sovereignty. For example, it endorses Iris Young's norm of inclusion, which states that "all those who are affected by a decision should be included in the decision-making process and have the opportunity to influence the outcome."[47] The virtue of civility prescribes a form of self-government. Democracy is thus a virtue-enhancing political arrangement as it is the form of government most conducive to the moral demands of civility. But there are different kinds of democracies (e.g. direct democracy, representative democracy, social democracy) and different levels of democratic politics (e.g. national, sub-national). The particular kind of democratic government appropriate for any one society cannot be determined in the abstract. Much will depend on a number of complex factors dealing with the historical situation of any given society.

Civic liberalism seeks to provide a justificatory framework for a particular vision of democratic politics—*liberal democracy*. Every democracy must temper the moral demands of civility with the concerns raised by the *pragmatic dimension* of civility. The pragmatic dimension of civility instructs us to recognize the limitations and potential dangers of the recourse to the ethics of civility. Firstly, there may be times where more debate hinders progress, a time when decisive action must be taken despite the fact that there is no consensus on an issue. Given the size and diversity of modern democracies, we shall face a number of obstacles (some surmountable others insurmountable) in trying to strive towards the moral demands of civility. These pragmatic considerations lead us away from the overly stringent requirement that equates democratic legitimacy with unanimity towards an appropriate form of majoritarianism.

Furthermore, many of the policy issues facing advanced industrial capitalist societies will be too complex and complicated for the average citizen to comprehend and too costly for them to be informed about. Given such considerations, it is prudent to defer judgement to elected representatives who can make informed decisions about the relevant policy issues. These representatives are accountable to the general public. Such considerations lead us to refine our democratic commitments so that an appropriate form of *representative democracy* is established rather than a form of direct democracy. And finally, as all humans are fallible, it is possible for even democratically elected majorities who have admirable intentions (e.g. to promote the common good) to act in irrational or arbitrary ways. We thus want to ensure that appropriate checks are placed on democracy so that groups and individuals who are not well positioned to influence the political process have their voices heard. This leads us to a form of constitutionalism. Taking the pragmatic demands of civility seriously will lead us to reject a form of legislative supremacy. But civility will also require us to be cautious in our endorsement of judicial review. Judicial supremacy also contravenes the demands of civility as it gives the last word on resolving our social and economic conflicts to public officials who are unelected and unaccountable.

Finally, the virtue of fairness is perhaps the most elusive of the three virtues. The moral dimension of fairness appeals to a broad range of values. In some situations fairness requires us to be impartial. This is perhaps captured most clearly in our commitment to fair procedures in criminal justice. Consider, for example, the jury system. We can dispense with potential jury members if we think they will fail to be impartial because it is only fair for such decisions to be resolved impartially. In other situations, fairness requires us to give greater consideration to the interests of those most in need (e.g. when allocating health care provisions). In some scenarios, fairness requires us to hold people responsible for their actions and take seriously concerns of desert (e.g. when punishing criminals).

The pragmatic dimension of fairness helps us to see when appeals to fairness are and are not appropriate and also guides us to find a reasonable compromise between competing demands of fairness. For example, the moral dimension of fairness may instruct us to give more weight to the interests of the least advantaged. But what if scarcity prevents us from helping everyone who needs help? This occurs, for example, in the case of health care provisions. What should we do in such a situation? The pragmatic dimension of fairness instructs us to give consideration to other factors that must be balanced against the moral demands of fairness. Such considerations might be concerns of utility (e.g. severity and pervasiveness of the disadvantage), efficiency (e.g. the cost of various medical treatments) or civility. Reconciling these competing demands is what the struggle for justice is all about. Like the virtues of toleration and civility, determining what fairness requires in any given situation will require us to also exercise the other virtues of fair social cooperation. One cannot determine what fairness requires in the abstract.

As a virtue, fairness goes beyond demands for impartiality and priority; indeed it often requires us to constrain these demands. Fairness requires us to accommodate considerations that stem from bonds of affection and love. Permitting room for such partiality is neither irrational nor immoral. Much of course depends on the amount of extra weight that might be at issue in any particular circumstance. The virtue of fairness requires us to recognize a diverse array of motives (beyond rational conviction) that move humans to act. In certain situations, it is fair for people to act out of love and affection (e.g. caring more for their family than for strangers) and in other situations appeals to such partial considerations are unfair (e.g. when public officials decide how to allocate scarce medical resources). The account of human motivation which civic liberalism endorses thus recognizes the fact that we are *social* beings and not unencumbered selves.[48]

Virtue ethicists are often criticized for failing to give some precise prescriptions, and above I stated that this criticism is due, in part, to the bias that many principle-oriented theorists take to moral and political philosophy. Anything short of a shortlist of the principles of justice that can be directly linked to some specific policy prescription will be unsatisfactory for such theorists. But this criticism is unfair as a virtue-oriented theory takes seriously the complexities of non-ideal theory, and this often makes it difficult, if not impossible, to formulate general rules or prescriptions that can be followed in all situations. A virtue-oriented account of justice will be indeterminate as much depends on the historical, cultural, economic and political situation of any given society. This indeterminacy of the theory is not a shortcoming. Despite the limitations of a virtue-oriented theory of justice, I do believe that such a theory can yield some general prescriptions and I shall argue in the next section that one such prescription of civic liberalism is that we ought to strive for a middle ground between judicial and legislative supremacy. One such middle ground is the "dialogical model" of judicial review. This model of judicial review does not give courts the final say on matters of public policy, rather it necessitates the possibility that judicial decisions to strike down a law can be reversed, modified or avoided by the legislative process. But in such cases, the democratic process will itself be influenced by the reviewing court. Civic liberalism instructs legislators to engage in a self-conscious dialogue with the judiciary. I now turn to a discussion of the model of judicial review that informs Canadian Constitutional law to illustrate the virtue-enhancing potential of constitutions and judicial review.

4. The "dialogical model" of judicial review

The Canadian *Charter of Rights and Freedoms* was adopted as the Supreme Law of Canada in 1982. The *Charter* protects a range of rights (freedom of expression, the right to vote, the right to life, liberty and security of the person, etc.) and gives unelected and unaccountable judges the power to strike down laws that have been authorized by democratically elected and accountable legislators. While there are many differences between the American *Bill of Rights* and Canada's *Charter*, I would like to emphasize two distinctive and important features of Canada's *Charter* that make it a good example of how constitutions and judicial review can be *virtue-enhancing*[49]: firstly, section 1 of the *Charter* which allows for "reasonable limits" on *Charter* rights. And, secondly, section 33 of the *Charter* known as the "power of legislative override."

Section 1 of the *Charter* states that the *Charter* guarantees the rights and freedoms set out in it "subject only to such reasonable limits prescribed by law as can be demonstrably justified in a free and democratic society." When interpreting this section of the *Charter*, the Canadian courts have taken a *purposeful, contextual* approach to rights and freedoms. In *Oakes* (1986), C. J. Dickson noted that section 1 of the *Charter* has two functions: "first, it constitutionally guarantees the rights and freedoms set out in the provisions which follow; and secondly, it states explicitly the exclusive justificatory criteria (outside of s. 33 of the Charter) against which limitations on those rights and freedoms must be measured."[50] Elaborating on the latter, C. J. Dickson claimed,

> A second contextual element of interpretation of s. 1 is provided by the words "free and democratic society." Inclusion of these words as the final standard of justification for limits on rights and freedoms refers the court to the very purpose for which the Charter was originally entrenched in the Constitution: Canadian society is to be free and democratic. The court must be guided by the values and principles essential to a free and democratic society which I believe embody, to name but a few, respect for the inherent dignity of the human person, commitment to social justice and equality, accommodation of a wide variety of beliefs, respect for cultural and group identity, and faith in social and political institutions which enhance the participation of individuals and groups in society. The underlying values and principles of a free and democratic society are the genesis of the rights and freedoms guaranteed by the Charter and the ultimate standard against which a limit on a right or freedom must be shown, despite its effect, to be reasonable and demonstrably justified.[51]

Section 1 of the Canadian *Charter*, with its exclusive justificatory criteria, does not place any one particular value (e.g. autonomy) at the heart of the diverse rights and freedoms which the *Charter* seeks to protect and promote. It recognizes a plurality of values. This is very much in line with the prescriptions of a virtue-oriented rather than principle-oriented approach to justice. The latter takes an uncompromising approach to rights. This is evident in American free speech jurisprudence, for example, where the American courts take an absolutist approach to free speech (entailed by the First Amendment) that rules out restrictions on the content of speech (e.g. hate speech). But such an absolutist approach places too much weight on the moral dimension of toleration, to the detriment of the demands of civility and fairness. By adopting a principle of *view-point neutrality*,[52] the American courts have ruled out the possibility of taking a purposeful, contextual approach to rights like free speech.

The *Charter* establishes a two-step process for the adjudication of rights claims. The first step is to establish whether a *Charter* right has been breached by a state act. The second stage focuses on the justification of the limits on *Charter* rights. As noted above, section 1 of the *Charter* stipulates that the protected rights and freedoms can be limited, provided the limits are "prescribed by law," "reasonable" and "demonstrably justified in a free and democratic society." At this stage in the process, the burden of proof lies with the party seeking to uphold the limitation. The court has interpreted "reasonable and demonstrably justified" as involving a balancing exercise. Each of the following requirements must be fulfilled in order for a limitation to be deemed "reasonable and demonstrably justified":

1. The objective of the impugned legislation must relate to concerns which are "pressing and substantial in a free and democratic society."
2. The means must be rationally connected to the objective. They must not be arbitrary, unfair or based on irrational considerations.
3. Even if rationally connected to the objective in this first sense, should "impair as little as possible" the right or freedom in question.
4. There must be a proportionality between the effects of the measure which are responsible for limiting the *Charter* right or freedom, and the objective which has been identified as of sufficient importance.

Adopting something like the section 1 limitation clause is one way of ensuring that legislators and judges exercise the virtues of fair social cooperation. The first component of the section 1 test gives due attention to the moral demands of civility. It permits legislators to limit *Charter* rights when the stakes are deemed high enough. Of course legislators will have to convince the judiciary that the aims of the legislation in question are indeed "pressing and substantial in a free and democratic society." So a pressing rationale for the legislation will have to be presented to the judiciary, a branch of government that is *politically insulated*. Because the judiciary is politically insulated, judges will not be subject to the same pressures (e.g. the need to be re-elected) that face legislators. This feature of the judicial branch of government makes its involvement in rights adjudication vital for a virtue-oriented theory of justice.

Even when the courts have found that a limitation of a *Charter* right is premised on pursuing an aim that is "pressing and substantial," this is not sufficient for limiting a *Charter* right. The means chosen to pursue this aim must also be justified. The requirement (2) that the means be rationally connected to the objective imposes an obligation on legislators to *demonstrate* that the legislation is necessary to secure the pressing aim. So legislators must take a responsible approach to limiting rights. This is further emphasized by the minimal impairment requirement (3). And finally, concerns of fairness require that there be a proportionality between the harmful and beneficial aspects of the law in question (4).

Most *Charter* challenges arise because of concerns related to (3). In such cases, the initial law did not pursue its objective through means that were deemed by the courts to be the least restrictive of the right or freedom in question. When this occurs, courts will provide an explanation of why the legislation was struck down, "which will involve explaining the less restrictive alternative law that would have satisfied the section 1 standard."[53] So legislators then have another opportunity to draft more careful legislation that secures the desired aim in a more responsible way. In such cases, judges do not have the "final word" on disputes about rights. Rather, they play an important role in helping legislatures negotiate the difficult task of balancing the competing demands of toleration, civility and fairness.

In their comprehensive examination of *Charter* judicial nullification cases between 1984–1997, Peter Hogg and Allison Bushell[54] conclude that in the sixty-five cases where legislation was invalidated for a breach of the *Charter*, the competent legislative body amended the impugned law in forty-four cases (two-thirds). In most cases, minor amendments were all that were required and the objective of the original legislation was not compromised.[55] Their study of judicial review in Canada suggests that the *Charter* rarely blocks a legislative objective; rather, it *influences* the design of implementing legislation. Such an account of judicial review coheres with the demands of civic liberalism which rejects the extremes of judicial or legislative supremacy. All branches of government have limitations. The dialogical model of judicial review is thus appealing, from a virtue-oriented approach to justice, because it does not entrust the task of upholding justice to any one particular institution or branch of government. Rather, it recognizes that a diverse institutional structure is required to enhance the exercise of the virtues of toleration, civility and fairness.

The purposeful approach to rights exemplified by section 1 of the *Charter* opens the door to the possibility of adopting a proposal like that put forth by Fabre in a way that does not lead to the problems associated with judicial supremacy. In *The Supreme Court on Trial: Judicial Activism or Democratic Dialogue*, Kent Roach argues that "the ability of the legislature to justify limits on rights also opens the possibility that social and economic rights might be entrenched without giving unelected courts a final say on the complex budgetary priorities of government."[56] In fact, this approach to social rights has been adopted in South Africa.[57] Fabre actually commends the South African approach,[58] but she seems to believe that either her proposal would not seriously contravene the government's control of public expenditures or that if it does, this contravening is not objectionable. Much of course depends on how robust and expansive one's list of social rights are as well as the affluence of the country in question.

While civic liberalism does not rule out the idea of including social rights in a constitution, it does caution against placing too much optimism in the ability of judges (or political philosophers) to make informed decisions concerning the allocation of scarce public resources. The viability of such a proposal depends not just on the reasons derived from principles (e.g. autonomy) but also on the reasons that stem from the pragmatic considerations of societies in the non-ideal world. The legislative and executive branches of government are better placed to make judgements about such matters. This is so because these two branches of government *are* publicly accountable and elected and thus more informed about the competing demands being placed on the government at any given time. Recall the six scenarios outlined in the introduction. The diverse dimensions of disadvantage in society, coupled with the facts of scarcity and indeterminacy, necessitate that any desire to fulfil the moral demands of fairness must take seriously the demands of civility. Civic liberalism does not necessarily rule out the proposal that we constitutionalize social rights (nor does it require that this be done) but any such proposal would have to place, at a minimum, a "reasonable limitation" clause on these social rights and courts should be willing to defer judgement to legislatures on such limitations as courts will not be well placed to make such decisions. Furthermore, such a proposal would also have to be coupled with a second distinctive feature of Canada's *Charter*—a legislative override.

Section 33 of the Canadian *Charter* permits Parliament or a legislature to insert a "notwithstanding" clause into a statute as a way of overcoming a judicial decision invalidating the law as unconstitutional. Such an override coheres with the moral demands of civility which grant legislatures with the power to re-assert the democratic will over the judicial branch of government. But it is important to note that section 33 establishes "manner and form" requirements for its use, which *fine-tune* the exercise of the virtue of civility. These include the requirement that the override be enacted by legislatures (not executives), they must pertain to statutes rather than regulations and they expire after five years.[59]

Section 33 promotes the virtue of civility and is premised on a confidence in the political process. Such a process should not be construed as one of the "tyranny of the majority." This is not to suggest that Canada's experience with section 33 has been unproblematic. The first instances of section 33 being invoked reveal the possible dangers of having a legislative override. The provinces of Quebec and Saskatchewan invoked the notwithstanding clause to pre-empt a constitutional challenge, respectively, to a ban on English external signs and back-to-work legislation. But the five-year expiration limits the dangers of abusing section 33 in such a pre-emptive fashion. The political climate of provinces change, as do governing political parties, and thus legislative overrides typically expire without being reapplied. So concerns that a legislative override will lead to tyranny of the majority has not come to fruition in Canada. In fact, legislators are very reluctant to apply section 33. The political climate in Canada is one of resistance to its use.[60] And such a climate is evidence of a *democratic* commitment to dialogical judicial review rather than legislative supremacy. Legislators exercise the virtues of fair social cooperation when they refuse to apply section 33 pre-emptively. The resistance to using the legislative override pre-emptively is virtuous because fair social cooperation requires us to be aware of our own fallibility and pre-emptively using a legislative override assumes an arrogance of infallibility that contravenes the demands of toleration, civility and fairness. Thus, it is appropriate for citizens to impose *hefty political costs* to using the legislative override arbitrarily.

The legislative override is a vital component of the dialogical model of judicial review because it creates a situation of *equality* between legislatures and courts. Judges do not have the final word on rights, nor do legislators. Legislators that wish to end the dialogue by invoking the notwithstanding clause can temporarily suspend the debate with the judiciary, but in order to do so they will have to make a compelling case to citizens who view it as a last resort to be used in exceptional circumstances. So a larger, political debate will ensue when section 33 is invoked. And even when this override is utilized, in five years the legislature must again undertake this demanding process if it wishes to continue to override the *Charter*. So section 33 does not end the debate about rights; it does not give legislatures or courts the final word.

The Canadian example is one that illustrates a central insight of civic liberalism, namely that the appropriate response to judicial activism is *legislative activism*. The fact that the great majority of *Charter* disputes in Canada are resolved by dialogue between legislatures and courts, rather than through the legislative override, demonstrates the sincere commitment legislatures and citizens have to the rights and freedoms enshrined in the *Charter*. Proponents of judicial supremacy are likely to object to placing the fate of rights in the hands of the majority. But what champions of judicial supremacy fail to realize is that a polity that seeks to resolve issues solely in the judicial arena is one that will fail to exercise the virtues of fair social cooperation. Advocates of judicial supremacy should pay due heed to Mill's insight that if you let a person have nothing to do for their country, they will not care for it.[61]

The conception of dialogue civic liberalism endorses is more substantive than that envisioned by advocates of judicial supremacy like Ronald Dworkin. In *Freedom's Law: The Moral Reading of the American Constitution*, Dworkin argues that in some circumstances judicial review does not conflict with democracy but it actually enhances it.[62] Dworkin believes that constitutional adjudication actually improves the quality of public debate on important issues.

> When an issue is seen as constitutional . . . and as one that will ultimately be resolved by courts applying general constitutional principles, the quality of public argument is often improved, because the argument concentrates from the start on questions of public morality . . . When a constitutional issue has been decided by the Supreme Court, and is important enough so that it can be expected to be elaborated, expanded, contracted, or even reversed by future decisions, a sustained national debate begins, in newspapers and other media, in law schools and classrooms, in public meetings and around dinner tables.[63]

Jeremy Waldron rejects Dworkin's argument and appeals to empirical evidence to substantiate this. If Dworkin is correct, argues Waldron, then we would expect to find national debates about issues that are not constitutionalized in other countries to be less robust and well informed. But this is not so. In fact, the quality of public debate on issues like abortion might be even better in countries like the United Kingdom and New Zealand where such issues are not constitutionalized. Such debates do not have to be framed around how to interpret a document that is over two hundred years old. Waldron also points to the issue of capital punishment. The public does not need this issue to be an interpretative debate about the constitution before it can become a moral debate. Reducing it to the former results in excluding important considerations relating to the broader aims of penal policy.[64]

In *Sovereign Virtue*, Dworkin defends what he calls the "partnership conception of democracy." The partnership conception of democracy has three dimensions. These are the following:

1. *Popular sovereignty*. This sovereignty is defined as a relation between the public as a whole and the various officials who make up its government. Partnership democracy demands that the people, and not officials, be masters.
2. *Equality*. Citizen equality demands that they participate as equals.
3. *Democratic discourse*. Citizens must deliberate together as individuals before they act collectively and this deliberation must focus on the reasons for and against that collective action.[65]

Dworkin's commitment to judicial supremacy contradicts all three dimensions of his partnership conception of democracy. When judges make the final decisions on fundamental moral and political questions, the officials, and not citizens, are masters. So judicial supremacy threatens popular sovereignty. Citizen equality demands that citizens participate as equals but the important role Dworkin ascribes to the courts threatens this equality. Citizens may be equals in the democratic process, but if this process is subordinate to the decisions of unelected and unaccountable officials, citizens will feel that the political process offers little hope of lasting and effective change. It thus robs liberal democracy of its *transformative* potential. Finally, when judges are given the final say on resolving important moral and political controversies, this may detract, not enhance, the quality of public debate. The important issue becomes "is X constitutional?" and thus other important issues may be ignored.

Civic liberalism embraces Dworkin's partnership conception of democracy but rejects his defence of judicial supremacy. Invoking something like the section 33 legislative override, as civic liberalism prescribes, makes constitutionalism and judicial review more congenial to the partnership conception of democracy. The dialogical model of judicial review endorsed by civic liberalism requires that neither judges nor legislators be given the final word on interpreting what constitutes a reasonable balance between competing rights. Sections 1 and 33 of the Canadian *Charter* help ensure that a meaningful and substantive dialogue occurs not only between legislatures and courts but in society more generally. A legislative override can "have a positive impact by encouraging a more politically vital discourse on the meaning of rights and their relationship to competing constitutional visions than what emanates from the judicial monologue that results from a regime of judicial supremacy."[66]

5. Conclusion

I began this paper with a number of scenarios which illustrated the various dimensions of misfortune that citizens of liberal democracies face. Principle-oriented theories of justice are ill-suited for helping us grapple with the complexities that arise in non-ideal theory. The facts of scarcity, natural disasters, disease, accidents, crime, globalisation, etc. mean that countless indeterminacies must be accounted for in a viable account of distributive justice that takes non-ideal theory seriously. Such a theory will thus itself inevitably be *indeterminate*. But this does not mean that political theorists have no contribution to make in helping us tackle the issue of what justice entails in non-ideal theory. In this paper, I have outlined a virtue-oriented conception of distributive justice entitled "civic liberalism". Civic liberalism provides some normative guidance in terms of helping us deliberate about what fair terms of social cooperation are. Instead of searching for the principles of justice that parties in a hypothetical original position would endorse, civic liberalism seeks to inspire a public philosophy that searches for a reasonable balance between the moral and pragmatic dimensions of the virtues of fair social cooperation—toleration, civility and fairness. Such a public philosophy endorses a dialogical model of judicial review and emphasizes the potential dangers of both judicial and legislative supremacy. I hope the argument advanced in this paper will stimulate more debate on the viability of invoking a *virtue-based metric* for measuring the justness of a system of social cooperation.

Notes

1. Russell Hardin, *Indeterminacy and Society* (Princeton, NJ: Princeton University Press, 2003), p. 103.
2. Access online at http://canadianeconomy.gc.ca/english/economy/index.cfm.
3. The virtue-oriented political theory advanced in this paper is a non-perfectionist account. Thus, it is distinct from the dominant virtue-ethics tradition which is premised upon Aristotle's account of *eudaimonia* (human flourshing). Given space limitations, I cannot fully elaborate on the differences between civic liberalism and neo-Aristotelianism (or other accounts of virtue-ethic theories). For such an examination see my (forthcoming) book *Justice, Democracy and Reasonable Agreement.*
4. See John Rawls, *A Theory of Justice* (Cambridge, MA: Harvard University Press, 1971) and *Political Liberalism* (New York: Columbia University Press, 1993).
5. See Robert Nozick, *Anarchy, State and Utopia* (New York: Basic Books, 1974).
6. The literature on state neutrality is extensive. A partial list of its main proponents include Rawls, *A Theory of Justice* and *Political Liberalism*; Nozick, *Anarchy, State and Utopia*; Bruce Ackerman, *Social Justice and the Liberal State* (New Haven: Yale University Press, 1980); Ronald Dworkin, *A Matter of Principle* (Cambridge, MA: Harvard University Press, 1985); Brian Barry, *Justice as Impartiality* (Oxford: Oxford University Press, 1995).
7. See Michael Walzer, *Spheres of Justice* (New York: Basic Books, 1983); David Miller, *Principles of Social Justice* (Cambridge, MA: Harvard University Press, 1999).
8. See Walzer, *Spheres of Justice*; Miller, *Principles of Social Justice*; Serena Olsaretti (ed.), *Desert and Justice* (Oxford: Oxford University Press, 2003).
9. This includes a long list (too long to even cite briefly) of more specific egalitarian principles, including equal opportunity, equality of resources, equality of capabilities, equality of opportunity for welfare. This "equality of what?" debate currently dominates much of normative political theory, and the main proponents of this debate include Richard Arneson, G. A. Cohen, Ronald Dworkin and Amartya Sen.
10. See Cécil Fabre, *Social Rights Under the Constitution* (Oxford: Oxford University Press, 2000); Martha Nussbaum, *Women and Human Development: The Capabilities Approach* (Cambridge: Cambridge University Press, 2000); Stuart White, *The Civic Minimum* (Oxford: Oxford University Press, 2003).
11. There is an ever-growing literature on *deliberative democracy* which emphasizes the importance of the principle of democratic equality. For a critical theory interpretation of this principle, see Iris Marion Young, Inclusion and Democracy (Oxford: Oxford University Press, 2000).
12. David Gauthier, *Morals by Agreement* (New York: Oxford University Press, 1986).
13. See Rawls, *A Theory of Justice* and *Political Liberalism.*
14. A society that lacked adequate education, health care and security could conceivably be one that satisfied "equality of opportunity" for these various deficient provisions, but I suspect no one would want to describe such a society as a *desirable* state of affairs.

15. Civic liberalism appropriates a number of concerns and ideas from the *republican* political theory tradition, as well as from the *virtue-ethics* tradition in moral philosophy. In this paper, I do not examine the historical or contemporary influences of the version of distributive justice I defend here. Such a project would deflect from my central concern which is to bring to the fore the complexities of justice in non-ideal theory and to emphasize the practical significance of a virtue-oriented theory of justice.
16. Proponents of the dialogical model of judicial review include Peter Hogg and Allison Bushell, "The Charter *Dialogue* Between Courts and Legislatures", 35(1) *Osgoode Hall Law J.* 75–124 (1997); and Kent Roach, *The Supreme Court on Trial: Judicial Activism or Democratic Dialogue* (Toronto: Irwin Law, 2001).
17. See Bork, *The Tempting of America: The Political Seduction of the Law* (New York: Simon and Schuster, 1990), pp. 139–143.
18. Andrew Mason, "Just Constraints", 34 *Br. J. Political Sci.* 251–268 (2004).
19. Mason (2004), p. 265.
20. Rawls, *The Law of Peoples* (Cambridge, MA: Harvard University Press, 1999), p. 6.
21. See Hursthouse, "Virtue Theory and Abortion", 20(3) *Philos. Public Affairs* 223–246 (1991) for an elaboration of deontological and consequentialist accounts of this premise.
22. Rawls, *A Theory of Justice* (2nd edn) (Oxford: Oxford University Press, 1999), p. 83.
23. Some have tried to remedy this deficiency in Rawls's account by adding health care to the list of things governed by the principle of fair equality of opportunity. See, for example, Norman Daniels's *Just Health Care* (Cambridge, MA: Cambridge University Press, 1985). Rawls actually endorses Daniels's strategy in *Political Liberalism*. However, such a strategy is rife with problems as such a cost-blind approach to health care is ill-equipped to deal with the problem of prioritizing limited resources in health care. For a discussion of these concerns, see Dan Brock, "Broadening the Bioethics Agenda", 10 *Kennedy Inst. Ethics J.* 21–38 (2000).
24. Rawls, *Political Liberalism*, p. 184.
25. See *Political Liberalism*, pp. lviii–lix.
26. Rawls in fact acknowledges these shortcomings of his theory. In *Political Liberalism*, he claims that "the idea of political justice does not cover everything, nor should we expect it to... Political justice needs always to be complemented by other virtues" (p. 21). Rawls's statement that political justice needs always to be complemented by other virtues is in fact a recognition of the need for a virtue-oriented approach to justice.
27. Roach, *The Supreme Court on Trial*, p. 127.
28. Jeremy Waldron, "Judicial Review and the Conditions of Democracy", 6(4) J. Pol. Phil. 337–338 (1998). Also see Waldron's *Law and Disagreement* (Oxford: Oxford University Press, 1999).
29. I expand on what the requirements of this virtue are in the next section.
30. Stephen Holmes and Cass Sunstein, *The Costs of Rights: Why Liberty Depends on Taxes* (New York: W.W. Norton & Company, 1999), p. 97.
31. Holmes and Sunstein, *The Costs of Rights*, p. 94.
32. *Ibid.*, p. 96.
33. Mill's answer of course lies with the principle of utility.

34. Dworkin, *A Matter of Principle* (Cambridge, MA: Harvard University Press, 1985), p. 69.
35. See my forthcoming book *Justice, Democracy and Reasonable Agreement*.
36. A doctrine is comprehensive "when it includes conceptions of what is of value in human life, and ideals of personal character, as well as ideals of friendship and of familial and associational relationships, and much else that is to inform our conduct, and in the limit to our life as a whole. A conception is fully comprehensive if it covers all recognized values and virtues within one rather precisely articulated system; whereas a conception is only partially comprehensive when it comprises a number of, but by no means all, nonpolitical values and virtues and is rather loosely articulated" (Rawls, 1993, p. 13).
37. See Scanlon, *What We Owe to Each Other* (Cambridge, MA: Harvard University Press, 1998). Scanlon describes the subject matter of judgments of right and wrong as:

    > ...judgments about what would be permitted by principles that could not reasonably be rejected, by people who were moved to find principles for the regulation of behavior that others, similarly motivated, could not reasonably reject. In particular, an act is wrong if and only if any principle that permitted it would be one that could reasonably be rejected by people with the motivation just described (or, equivalently, if and only if it would be disallowed by any principle that such people could not reasonably reject).
    >
    > (Scanlon, 1998, 4)

38. The emphasis on pragmatic reasons does not mean that civic liberalism takes *all* existing constraints as a given. As a transformative public philosophy, civic liberalism is open to the possibility that many existing constraints might be imposed by things we could reasonably expect to transcend. By striving for a reconciliation between the moral and pragmatic dimensions of the virtues of fair social cooperation, civic liberalism guards against what Mason (2004, pp. 253–254) calls "adaptive preference formation." This occurs when a political theory takes the current circumstances as the best possible circumstances.
39. http://action.aclu.org/reformthepatriotact/
40. Available on web at http://www.fec.gov/finance_reports.html.
41. This number rose drastically in the 2004 Presidential campaign, with President George W. Bush raising just over $272,000,000 and John Kerry approximately $250,000,000. See http://edition.cnn.com/ELECTION/2004/special/president/fec/total.raise.html.
42. Ronald Dworkin, *Sovereign Virtue* (Cambridge, MA: Harvard University Press, 2000), p. 351.
43. Ronald Dworkin, "Constitutionalism and Democracy", 3(1) *Eur. J. Philos.* 2 (1995).
44. See J. S. Mill, *On Liberty* (Harmondsworth: Penguin, 1982).
45. See A. Meiklejohn, Political Freedom (New York: Oxford University Press, 1965) and "The First Amendment is an Absolute" in *Free Speech and Association*:

The Supreme Court and the First Amendment (P. B. Kurland ed., Chicago: University of Chicago Press, 1975).

46. See, for example, my paper "Neutrality, Toleration and Reasonable Agreement" in *Toleration, Neutrality and Democracy* (D. Castiglioni and C. Mackinnon eds, Amsterdam: Kluwer, 2003).
47. Iris Marion Young, *Inclusion and Democracy*, p. 5.
48. This vision of the self is endorsed, for example, by Michel Sandel in *Democracy's Discontent* and by David Miller in *On Nationality* (Oxford: Oxford University Press, 1995).
49. These two features of Canada's *Charter* have prevented Canada from going down the same path that America has gone (i.e. to a system of judicial supremacy).
50. *Regina v. Oakes* (1986), 26 D.L.R. (4th) at pp. 224–225.
51. *Ibid.* at p. 225.
52. See Sandel's *Democracy's Discontent* for a discussion of how this principle became embedded in American Constitutional law and the costly consequences it has had for democracy.
53. Hogg and Bushell, "The Charter *Dialogue* Between Courts and Legislatures", p. 85.
54. *Ibid.*
55. *Ibid.*, pp. 80–81.
56. Roach, *The Supreme Court on Trial*, p. 61.
57. "In South Africa, rights to housing, healthcare, and social assistance are all protected, but subject to the qualification that the state must take reasonable legislative measures within its available resources, to achieve the progressive realization of these rights" (*ibid.*, p. 61).
58. Fabre, *Social Rights Under the Constitution*, p. 166.
59. Peter Hogg, *Constitutional Law of Canada* (Toronto: Carswell, 1985), pp. 690–692.
60. Andrew Heard argues that a binding constitutional convention is emerging in Canada (at least outside Quebec) against the notwithstanding clause. See *Canadian Constitutional Conventions: The Marriage of Law and Politics* (Toronto: Oxford University Press, 1991), p. 147.
61. John Stuart Mill, *Representative Government*, in Utilitarianism (H. B. Acton ed., London: Dent, 1972), p. 204.
62. The following three paragraphs are taken from my more detailed discussion of Dworkin's stance on judicial review in Farrelly, *An Introduction to Contemporary Political Theory* (London: Sage Publications, 2004), Section 4.4.
63. Ronald Dworkin, *Freedom's Law: The Moral Reading of the American Constitution* (Cambridge, MA: Harvard University Press, 1996), p. 345.
64. Waldron, *"Judicial Review and the Conditions of Democracy"*, p. 339.
65. Ronald Dworkin, *Sovereign Virtue*, pp. 363–364.
66. Christopher Manfredi, *Judicial Power and the Charter* (Toronto: McClelland & Stewart Inc.), pp. 207–208.

5
A Virtue-Centered Account of Equity and the Rule of Law*

*Lawrence B. Solum***

> *The rule of law, it is argued, is preferable to that of any individual.*
> *Aristotle, Politics*[1]

This essay explores the relationship between two notions, the *rule of law* and *equity*. One important ideal of western legal systems is captured by the phrase, "the rule of law," and one interpretation of that ideal can be expressed in the proposition that the rule of law requires a law of rules.[2] A second legal ideal is sometimes called "equity," and a common interpretation of the notion of equity is that legal decision makers sometimes ought to depart from the rules in order to do justice in particular cases. Given these interpretations of equity and the rule of law, the two ideals seem to be in tension. The resolution of that tension at the level of theory is one of the classic projects of jurisprudence or legal philosophy.

I propose a partial resolution to the seeming tension between equity and the rule of law. My claim will be that properly understood, the practice of equity—of doing justice in particular cases under appropriate circumstances—is broadly consistent with the ideal of the rule of law. My argument is Aristotelian and virtue-centered. Departure from the rules in order to achieve particularized justice is not always (or even usually) inconsistent with the rule of law when legal decision makers possess certain judicial virtues—characteristics of mind and will that

---

 An earlier version of this essay was delivered at the annual meeting of the American Society for Political and Legal Philosophy, January 2, 1991, San Antonio, Texas and published as *Equity and the Rule of Law*, Nomos XXXVI: The Rule of Law 120 (1994).

**John E. Cribbet Professor of Law, University of Illinois College of Law, USA.

produce excellence in judging. One of the virtues of a good judge is judicial wisdom, the particularly adjudicatory form of the intellectual virtue of *phronesis* or practical wisdom. Because an excellent judge is a *phronimos*, a person of wisdom, she or he can discern those situations in which a departure from the letter of the law is consistent with its spirit and hence with the rule of law. As will become clear, my claim, although ambitious, is not unqualified; even if guided by judicial wisdom, doing justice in particular cases will sometimes conflict with the values of generality and publicity that underlie the rule of law.

1. The rule of law

The ideal of the rule of law, which can be traced back at least as far as Aristotle,[3] is deeply embedded in the public political cultures of most modern democratic societies. For example, the Universal Declaration of Human Rights of 1948 declared that "it is essential if man is not to have recourse as a last resort, to rebellion against tyranny and oppression, that human rights should be protected by the Rule of Law."[4] Although the ideal of the rule of law has been criticized on the ground that it is an ideological construct that masks power relationships, even Marxist critics may acknowledge that observance of the ideal may curb abuses by the ruling class.[5]

What is the ideal of the rule of law?[6] An initial observation is that there are several different conceptions of the meaning of the rule of law.[7] Indeed, the rule of law may not be a single concept at all; rather, it may be more accurate to understand the ideal of the rule of law as a set of ideals connected more by family resemblance than a unifying conceptual structure.[8]

The purposes of this essay require neither a comprehensive survey of conceptions of the rule of law nor a resolution of debates about the contours of the ideal. A brief mapping of the territory will suffice. Historically, the most influential account of the rule of law was offered by A. V. Dicey. His formulation incorporated three ideas: (1) the supremacy of regular law as opposed to arbitrary power; (2) equality before the law of all persons and classes, including government officials; and (3) the incorporation of constitutional law as a binding part of the ordinary law of the land.[9]

A contemporary elaboration of the ideal of the rule of law is provided by John Rawls. He defines the rule of law as "the regular, impartial, and in this sense fair" administration of "public rules."[10] In schematic form and with some alterations, Rawls offered the following conception of the rule of law:[11]

1. *The Requirement that Compliance Be Possible.* The legal system should reflect the precept that ought implies can.
   a. The actions which the rules of law require and forbid should be of a kind which men can reasonably be expected to do and to avoid.
   b. Those who enact the laws and issue legal orders should do so in good faith, in the sense that they believe "a" with respect to the laws and orders they promulgate.
   c. A legal system should recognize impossibility of performance as a defense, or at least a mitigating circumstance.
2. *The Requirement of Regularity.* The legal system should reflect the precept that similar cases should be treated similarly.
   a. Judges must justify the distinctions they make between persons by reference to the relevant legal rules and principles.
   b. The requirement of consistency should hold for the interpretation of all rules.
3. *The Requirement of Publicity.* The legal system should reflect the precept that the laws should be public.
   a. The laws should be known and expressly promulgated.
   b. The meaning of the laws should be clearly defined.
4. *The Requirement of Generality.* Statutes and other legal rules should be general in statement and should not be aimed at particular individuals.
5. *The Requirement of due Process.* The legal system should provide fair and orderly procedures for the determination of cases.
   a. A legal system ought to make provision for orderly and public trials and hearings.
   b. A legal system ought to contain rules of evidence that guarantee rational procedures of inquiry.
   c. A legal system ought to provide a process reasonably designed to ascertain the truth.
   d. Judges should be independent and impartial, and no person should judge his or her own case.

Absent so far is the notion that the rule of law requires that the government and government officials be subject to the law.[12] Thus, a sixth aspect of the rule of law might be added to Rawls' formulation as follows:

6. *The Requirement of Government under Law.* Actions by government and government officials should be subject to general and public rules.
   a. Government officials should not be above the law.
   b. The legality of government action should be subject to test by independent courts of law.

More can be said about the content of the ideal of the rule of law, but this brief exposition provides sufficient clarity for the moment, as we turn our attention to a second topic, the notion of equity.

2. Equity

Equity has acquired a number of distinct meanings in contemporary legal discourse. When used by legal historians, equity may refer to a distinct body of legal rules that were once administered by the Court of Chancery in England and other common law countries.[13] When used by some legal economists, the same term refers to considerations of distributive justice.[14] By using the term "equity," I mean to refer to the practice of doing justice in the particular case, when the just result is either (a) not required by the set of applicable legal rules or (b) contrary to the result required by the set of applicable legal rules.

Some of what modern American lawyers call "equity" fits my definition. For example, Justice Douglas' opinion in the United States Supreme Court's decision of *Hecht v. Bowles* stated, "The essence of equity jurisdiction has been the power of the Chancellor to do equity and to mold each decree to the necessities of the particular case."[15] In the view of conservative critics, some federal judges have (mis)used their injunctive powers to depart from the rule of law and achieve particularized justice.[16] But generally speaking, the modern legal understanding of equity is based solely on pedigree. "Equity" refers to powers and categories of disputes that were within the jurisdiction of the Chancellor. For the most, these powers, such as the injunction, and categories of cases, such as trusts or fraud, do not differ from other powers and categories with respect to the method of decision. Most modern equity, as that term is used by lawyers and judges, is relatively rule bound, and therefore would not fit my definition.

The notion of equity as departure from the rules is rooted in Aristotle, and the best place to begin an exposition is with Aristotle's statement of the problem of equity and justice:

> The same thing, then, is just and equitable, and while both are good, the equitable is superior. What creates the problem is that the equitable is just, but not the legally just but a correction of legal justice. The reason is that all law is universal but about some things it is not possible to make a universal statement which will be correct. In those cases, then, in which it is necessary to speak universally, but not possible to do so correctly, the law takes the usual case, though it is not ignorant of the possibility of error. And it is none the less correct; for the error is not in the law nor in the legislator but in the nature of the thing, since the matter of practical affairs is of this kind from the start. When the law speaks universally, then, and a case arises on it which is not covered by the universal statement, then it is right, when the legislator fails us and has erred by over-simplicity to correct the omission–to say what the legislator himself would have said had he been present, and would have put into his law if he had known.[17]

This is the core of Aristotle's view of *epieikeia*, usually translated as equity or fair-mindedness. As is frequently the case with Aristotle, the text is rich and suggestive, but ambiguous. I will offer an elaboration of Aristotle's text that I believe is consistent with the larger body of Aristotle's work, but my purpose is not to provide an interpretation of Aristotle. Rather, my goal is to sketch a viable theory of the practice of equity. Aristotle and his contemporary expositors inform the sketch, but I do not claim to have discovered Aristotle's own view of the nature of equity.

One characteristic of equity is that equity involves a departure from the rules. Thus, equity corrects the law's generality by filling gaps in the law, by adjusting conflicts and tensions between legal provisions, and by making exceptions in cases in which the rule leads to unanticipated and unjust results. An equitable departure from the rules can relate to the intentions of the legislator in two distinct ways. In some cases, doing equity requires the judge to realize the intention of the legislature, considering "what the legislator would have said himself, had he been present."[18] The familiar example of the statute prohibiting motor vehicles in the park can serve as an illustration: the city council would not have wanted the provision to interfere with an ambulance rescuing a park visitor. In other cases, it may require the judge to correct a defect that the legislator did not or could not have anticipated—for example, in cases in which circumstances have changed or previously unknown facts have come to light.[19]

A second characteristic of equity is its particularism. The point of the practice of equity is to tailor the law to the requirements of the particular case. The fundamental reason for engaging in the practice of equity is the infinite variability of particular fact patterns. As Aristotle put it,

> This is also the reason why everything is guided by law, for about some matters it is impossible to lay down a law, and so a decree is needed. For the standard is indefinite where the subject-matter is itself indefinite, just like the lead rule used in Lesbian building which does not remain rigid but adapts to the shape of the stone; similarly, a decree is adapted to fit the circumstances.[20]

Understanding equity as particularistic allows us to distinguish equity from other practices that involve a departure from legal rules. For example, equity is not the resolution of conflicts between law and morality (or natural justice) in favor of the latter. The judicial nullification of a statute that legalized the practice of human slavery on the basis that slavery is always morally wrong (or contrary to principles of natural justice) would not be an example of the practice of equity, because such a decision would not involve a departure from the rule on the basis of the facts of the *particular* case.

In sum, the practice of equity has two identifying characteristics: first, equity is not decision according to a legal rule, and second, an equitable decision is responsive to the facts of a particular case.

3. The conflict between equity and the rule of law

This section explores the nature of the conflict between equity and the rule of law. On what basis can it be argued that the practice of equity, doing justice in the particular case, undermines the ideal of the rule of law? An intuitive sense of the conflict can be stated simply: the rule of law seems to require judges to follow the rules, whereas the practice of equity seems to require a departure from the rules.

This section considers three approaches to the conflict between the practice of equity and the rule of law. The first approach is conceptual, focusing on the particular aspects of the ideal of the rule of law that seem inconsistent with the practice of equity. The second approach focuses on theories about the nature of law and in particular about the distinction between rules and discretion in adjudication. The third approach explores concerns of principle and policy underlying the seeming conflict between equity and the rule of law—investigating both consequentialist and deontological arguments for the conflict.

3.1 Conceptual conflict

The first approach to the conflict between equity and rule of law is conceptual. An example of such an argument can be found in a 1988 report by the Office of Legal Policy to the Attorney General of the United States: "When this conception of the federal judiciary as courts of conscience is combined with the conception of equity as an ad-hoc unreviewable power of trial judges, the result is a justice without rules, or in other words, *justice without law.*"[21]

We have already explored the basic conceptual structures of the ideal of the rule of law and the practice of equity. Was the Office of Legal Policy correct in contending that the practice of equity vitiates the rule of law? Initially, notice that most conceptual elaborations of the ideal of the rule of law do not state the ideal in a way that makes conflict with equity a matter of definition. The rule of law might be defined as a law of rules, but it usually is not. Rather, several features of the rule of law provide overlapping reasons for adjudicators to follow the rules when they decide cases.

The first of these features is the requirement of regularity—that like cases be treated alike. This feature can cut both for and against the compatibility of the practice of equity with the rule of law. It could be argued that the practice of equity is predicated on the unique features of the particular case as unique—as relevantly different from the cases to which the legal rule properly is applied. Thus, equity could be said to respect the requirement of legal regularity—by treating different cases differently. The difficulty with this argument is that all cases differ in factual particulars. The requirement that like cases be treated alike must be elaborated to specify which similarities and differences count. As Rawls put it, the requirement that like cases be treated alike requires judges, "to justify the distinctions that they make between persons by reference to the relevant legal rules and principles."[22] To the extent that a judge doing equity departs from the rules, she or he could be said to treat differently cases that are similar in the relevant respect—the feature identified by the legal rule. For this reason, the best view (at least provisionally) seems to be that equitable departure from legal rules violates the requirement of regularity.

The second feature is the requirement of publicity. The requirement that "the laws be known and expressly promulgated,"[23] would seem to direct judges to decide the cases that come before them according to legal rules that have been announced in advance. But the practice of equity seems to authorize judges to shape a "new" rule to apply to the facts of the particular case. The practice of equity is post hoc: equity is done after the fact. The result required by equity may not be knowable until after all the parties have acted, but this feature (seemingly) makes it impossible for persons subject to the law to guide their behavior by it.

The third feature is the requirement of generality. The rule of law requires that the laws be framed in general terms, and not be aimed at particular individuals. Equity does not involve the framing of legal rules aimed at particular parties, but a judge doing equity will give reasons for his or her decision that are based on the facts of the particular dispute and will not decide on the basis of rules framed in general terms. The practice of equity is ad hoc: equity is done on particular facts. The reasons given in equity need not be particularistic in the sense that they relate only to named individuals; one can discuss the requirements of justice in particular circumstances in impersonal terms. The requirement of generality, however, is more than a requirement that cases not be decided on the basis of reasons that are specific to individual persons. Decision by general rules requires the judge to fit the case within a category that encompasses a general class of cases. Because equity requires judges to focus on the uniqueness of particular fact patterns, there is tension between the generality requirement and the practice of equity.

Together, these three features provide prima facie reasons to believe that the practice of equity conflicts with the rule of law. For the purposes of the argument so far, the ideal of the rule of law is best realized when cases are decided by treating like cases alike, where the relevant grounds for difference are rules or principles that are public and general. Equity involves treating some cases as unique, relying on the particular features of the case and on reasons that may not have been publicly available until the case was decided. At a conceptual level, equity and the rule of law seem to be in tension.

3.2 Rule and discretion

The conflict between law and equity can be approached from a second direction, by consideration of the relationship between rule and discretion in adjudication.[24] The practice of equity can be conceived—at least as a working hypothesis—as an exercise of discretion by judges.[25] This suggestion is explored by invoking five "pictures" of the relationship between legal rules and discretion in adjudication, with five corresponding views of the nature of equity.

The first picture of the relationship between rule and discretion is provided by what I will call *strong legal formalism*.[26] This formalism holds that outcomes of legal disputes are determined by the legal rules, that is, by the complete set of authoritative legal materials, including cases, regulations, statutes, and constitutional provisions. Strong legal formalism, as I define it, is the view that the complete outcomes of all possible legal disputes can and ought to be determined by the existing legal rule set, and hence, that there is no legally sanctioned judicial discretion. For the strong legal formalist, equity is inherently problematic: the practice of equity would be judicial lawlessness, an usurpation of legislative or executive power. If the adjudication proceeds as it should, there is no equity.

A second picture of the relationship between rule and discretion is suggested by the work of the legal realists.[27] The legal realist movement was complex and multifaceted; the position that I will describe as realist is simply one of many "legal realisms." Let me stipulate that there is a picture of the relationship between rule and discretion in law called "strong instrumental legal realism." For the strong instrumental legal realist, the outcome of a particular case is never determined by the legal rules. Instead, judges decide particular cases in order to achieve policy goals and accommodate social interests; law is instrumental rather than formal in nature. For these realists, all adjudication is (or should be) equitable in nature.[28] The possibility of the rule of law as a law of rules is illusory. To the extent that judges believe themselves constrained by legal rules, they are mistaken, and their mistake may well result in bad legal decision making.

A third picture of the relationship between rule and discretion is provided by H. L. A. Hart's picture of the core and penumbra.[29] On Hart's familiar picture, the outcomes of some cases are determined by the rules. These are easy cases, cases within the core of a legal rule. Other cases are more difficult; the legal rule does not point clearly in one direction or another. In this zone, the penumbra, decisions are governed by the discretion of the judge. How does the practice of equity fit into Hart's scheme? Two classes of cases should be distinguished. Consider the first class: equity might operate in the penumbra of a legal rule (including, I think, cases in which the conjunction of two or more rules casts a shadow, where either rule alone would have been clear). Doing equity in the penumbra of the rules is simply the exercise of discretion—a normal event in Hart's picture.

Equity is more problematic, however, in a second class of cases; equity might operate in the core of a rule, to produce a result that is contrary to that sanctioned by the rule. At first blush, this seems to be inconsistent with Hart's scheme.

> At any given moment judges, even those of a supreme court, are parts of a system the rules of which are determinate enough at the centre to supply standards of correct judicial decision. These are regarded by the courts as something they are not free to disregard in exercise of the authority which cannot be challenged within the system.... Such standards could not continue to exist unless most of the judges of the time adhered to them, for their existence at any given time consists simply in the acceptance and use of them as standards of correct adjudication.[30]

Hart's theory can explain how equitable decisions are legal decisions. He can posit a secondary rule (a power-conferring rule) that authorizes the practice of equity. Nonetheless, when the practice of equity operates in the core of a rule, it undermines the very basis for the predictability and certainty of judicial practice that is constitutive of the core. For Hart, the rules have a core of determinate meaning because judicial practice in the core is consistent. Equity undermines that practice and hence undermines the rule of law.

A fourth picture of the relationship between rule and discretion is contained in Ronald Dworkin's theory of law as integrity, framed partly in response to Hart.[31] Dworkin rejects the notion that judges have discretion, even in the penumbra of a legal rule.[32] Dworkin argues that the phenomenology of legal practice is that judges feel obligated to arrive at the "right answer," even when rules conflict or contain gaps:

> Law as integrity asks judges to assume, so far as this is possible, that the law is structured by a coherent set of principles about justice and fairness and procedural due process and it asks them to enforce these in fresh cases so that each person's situation is fair and just according to the same standards.[33]

Although particular legal rules may be ambiguous or contain gaps or conflict, the judge can still determine the right answer in a particular case by appealing to the set of principles that best fits and justifies the law as a whole. This procedure provides the judge with a "metarule" that enables him or her to decide each case in accordance with the law without directly resorting to discretion or personal preference.

How would Dworkin view the practice of equity?[34] The question is difficult to answer, because Dworkin's picture of the relationship between rules and discretion does not quite fit our idea of equity. On one hand, one might say that Dworkin's picture reconciles equity with the rule of law. Doing equity is simply following the metarule specified by law as integrity. The appearance that equity is inconsistent with the rule of law is generated by a misconception—that the law can be reduced to legal rules, when in fact it includes principles as well. Dworkinian "equity" is not focused on the unique facts of the particular case; rather Dworkin's mythical judge, Hercules, has the task of generating a set of "principles that fit, not only the particular precedent to which some litigant directs his attention, but all other judicial decisions within his general jurisdiction and, indeed, statutes as well."[35] Hercules must be very good at the construction of big theories, but nothing in Dworkin's theory demands that he be particularly sensitive to the facts of particular cases. Thus, one could argue that Dworkin reconciles the practice of equity with the rule of law by explaining equity as the application of general legal principles which justify decisions that are not sanctioned by the more specific legal rules.

On the other hand, one could say that Dworkin has simply eliminated the idea of equity altogether, by arguing for an expansive concept of the complete set of legal rules in which every case should be decided according to the rules and principles. Dworkin emphasizes coherence in the law as a whole as the basis for decision in particular cases. This emphasis suggests that our second interpretation, that Dworkin's theory does not allow for equity, is in accord with the conception of equity specified in this essay. This conception of equity makes sensitivity to the facts of the particular case constitutive of the practice of equity. In a limited sense, Dworkin agrees with the formalist that law is all a matter of rules (broadly understood to include a coherence metarule) and that all discretion (and hence equity) is illegitimate.

What are the lessons from these four views of the relationship between rule and discretion for the question whether the practice of equity conflicts with the ideal of the rule of law? Two theories reduce all law to legal rules (and principles). Strong legal formalism views the line between rules and discretion as demarcating the line between lawful decision and judicial lawlessness; the irreconcilable conflict between the rule of law and equity should be resolved in favor of the rule of law. Dworkin's theory is more subtle; all adjudication should be guided by the metarule specified by the theory of law as integrity. On the interpretation that best fits Dworkin's theory as a whole, if equity is really distinct from rule application broadly understood, then equity is illegitimate.

One theory reduces all law to discretion (and policy or political preference). Strong instrumentalist realism sees all law application as involving discretion guided by policy concerns; the rule of law should be rejected as an illusion. On this picture, the practice of equity is not special or exceptional—all adjudication is equitable to the extent that any is.

On Hart's view, the law is both rule and discretion. His theory would seem to imply that equity is necessary and appropriate in the penumbra, where decisions must be discretionary, but suspect in the core, where decisions to depart from the rule undermine the vary basis for legal decision making.

Of course, the four pictures that I have sketched are simplifications of views that are much more subtle and complex. Nonetheless, all four pictures share a common assumption that is worth noting. On all four theories, legal decision making is either guided by rules (albeit, perhaps complex metarules) or legal decision making is discretionary. The picture that comes closest to attacking the distinction itself is Dworkin's theory. Legitimate equity, according to law as integrity, would be based on the application of a set of principles discovered by attending to coherence within the entire set of legal materials; legitimate equity could not be a matter of attending to the uniqueness of particular cases. In the end, all four views of rule and discretion postulate a distinction between rule and discretion that implies tension (in theory or practice) between equity and the rule of law.

3.3 Deontological and consequentialist views

The third and final approach to the conflict between law and equity proceeds at the level of moral theory. The concerns of principle and policy that support the ideal of the rule of law seem to be in tension with the concerns that motivate the practice of equity. This tension is explored by examining both a deontological and a consequentialist view of the relationship between law and equity.

Viewed from the perspective of deontological moral theory, the ideal of the rule of law can be seen as motivated by the principle of respect for the autonomy and equality of persons. Thus, the idea that the law should treat like cases alike can be seen as applying a principle of political morality—that is, the precept that persons have fundamental rights of equality—to the adjudication of disputes.

Similarly, the requirements of legal publicity and generality operate to protect spheres of individual autonomy. The requirement of publicity ensures that each individual can make decisions with advance knowledge of the legal consequences, and likewise constrains government actors from infringing on individual autonomy when legal rules have not been announced in advance. The requirements that legal rules be framed to apply generally and that the rules apply to government officials provide incentives for lawmakers to protect the autonomy of citizens.

Finally, in societies with popularly elected legislatures, the rule of law operates to preserve the operation of democratic government, by requiring judges to apply democratically promulgated legal rules, unless the constitution itself would be violated. Assuming that participation in government is itself a right, founded on the equality of persons, the rule of law preserves that right by ensuring that the voter's legislative will is respected by judges.[36]

From a deontological perspective, the practice of equity seems to violate a number of moral or political rights of personhood and citizenship. Indeed, each of the features of the rule of law that has been identified can be restated as an individual political (or legal) right that is potentially infringed when a judge departs from public and general rules in order to do justice in a particular case. For example, the requirements of publicity and generality are reflected in the constitutional practice of the United States in the right to due process of law, and the constitutional guarantees against ex post facto laws and bills of attainder. Legal cases produce winners and losers. Even though the facts of a particular case may generate arguments for doing equity in order to assure fairness to the winner, the loser in such a case seems to have a legitimate complaint that his or her political rights have been infringed if a judge departs from public and general rules in order to accomplish the equitable result.

The case that the rule of law and equity are in conflict can also be made from a consequentialist perspective.[37] At first blush, consequentialism seems to welcome equity with open arms; doing equity could be seen as departing from the rules in order to produce good consequences in particular cases. There is, however, a consequentialist case to be made for the rule of law. The rule of law provides predictability to the law, allowing individuals to coordinate their behavior through a system of stable expectations. In addition, the rule of law acts as a prophylactic against the abuse of official discretion. The requirements of publicity and generality reduce the risk that adjudicators will use their discretion to obtain private gains at the expense of public goods. The practice of equity undermines the predictability and stability of the law and loosens the constraints against official abuse. Consequentialists would balance these costs against the benefits of equity. A utilitarian case can be made for allowing the practice of equity when the benefits produced by departure from the legal rule in the particular case outweigh the costs of instability, unpredictability, and risk of abuse. Nonetheless, from a utilitarian or consequentialist perspective, the benefits of equity trade off against the benefits of the rule of law; the two are usually in tension.

To sum up, we have now examined the conflict between law and equity at three levels. First, there is a conflict at a conceptual level. Elaboration of the ideal of the rule of law reveals certain conflicts with the practice of equity. Second, there is a conflict at the level of theories about the role of rule and discretion in legal adjudication. Equity seems to require discretion, and rule by discretion is antithetical to the rule of law. Third, these conflicts at the level of conceptual elaboration and legal theory can be grounded in arguments of moral theory; both deontological and consequentialist arguments can be made for the proposition that the rule of law conflicts with the practice of equity. The goal of this chapter is to overcome the conflicts identified in this section. Accomplishment of that aim must be postponed, however, pending the development of a virtue-centered theory of judging in the following section.

4. Reconciling equity and the rule of law

My claim is that a virtue-centered theory of judging grounds a reconciliation of equity with the rule of law. A caveat needs to be introduced at once. A virtue-centered theory of judging will not work magic. There is no mystic quality of virtuous decision that will dissolve the real tensions between some of the values that underlie the rule of law and some of the reasons that motivate the practice of equity. The fact that equity is done by a virtuous judge cannot change the fact that equity involves judges going beyond the letter of the law and will (sometimes) be less predictable than strict adherence to the letter of the rules might be. The reconciliation I propose will provide an explanation as to why the practice of equity is consistent with the ideal of the rule of law at the most fundamental level, but some tension inevitably remains.

4.1 The judicial virtues and practical wisdom

A fuller account of the judicial virtues is offered elsewhere in this anthology.[38] Following Aristotle, we might divide the judicial virtues into two categories, moral and intellectual. The moral virtues can be conceptualized as dispositions to the mean with respect to moral neutral emotions. Take the clearest example, courage. The corresponding morally neutral emotion is fear. The disposition to fear that is disproportionately large in relationship to the actual threat is the vice of excess—cowardice. The corresponding vice of deficiency might be called rashness—the disposition to fear that falls short of the real danger. The virtue is courage—the disposition to fear that is proportionate to the situation.

From Aristotle's picture of the moral virtues we can sketch the emotional makeup of a well-functioning or excellent judge. Such a judge will be courageous—and hence not subject to easy intimidation or decision making that is distorted by fear of either physical violence or loss of social status. Likewise, an excellent judge will be good tempered, neither easily provoked into anger nor overly tolerant of insulting or outrageous behavior. A good judge will have his or her desires in order and therefore will not have his or her judgment distorted by the intemperate desires for material goods or intoxicating substances. That is, an excellent judge will possess civic courage, a judicial temperament, and be "sober as a judge."

In addition, excellence in judging requires the intellectual virtues. These include *sophia* or theoretical wisdom and *phronesis* or practical wisdom. The ability to understand complex legal rules requires skills that are similar to those deployed in logic or mathematics. Excellent judges comprehend complicated logical relationships, such as those exhibited by the rule against perpetuities or in the Internal Revenue Code. In addition to theoretical wisdom, a good judge must have practical wisdom, which can loosely be captured by the qualities we call "good judgment" or "common sense."

The form of practical wisdom that is manifested by excellent judges might be called *judicial wisdom*: the good judge must possess practical wisdom in the choosing of legal ends and means. Practical wisdom is the virtue that enables one to make good choices in particular circumstances. The person of practical wisdom knows which particular ends are worth pursuing and knows which means are best-suited to achieve those ends. Judicial wisdom is simply the virtue of practical wisdom as applied to the choices which must be made by judges. The practically wise judge has developed excellence in knowing what goals to pursue in the particular case and excellence in choosing the means to accomplish those goals.

This abstract account of judicial wisdom can be made more concrete by considering the contrast between practical wisdom and theoretical wisdom in the judicial context. The judge who possesses theoretical wisdom is the master of legal theory, with the ability to engage in sophisticated legal reasoning and insight into subtle connections in legal doctrine. But a judge who possesses judicial intelligence is still not necessarily a good judge, even if he or she affirms the correct decision procedure for judicial decision making. A judge can be smart and learned but lack common sense—crafting a rule that is elegant in theory but unworkable in practice.

4.2 Practical wisdom and the law

As Aristotle understands the law, "the law *is* intelligence, it has its own rationality or *logos*."[39] But legal disputes cannot be resolved by the written laws themselves; rather, a case ought to be decided by the best judgment of those whose experience enables them not only to apply the written law but to improve upon it.[40] The foundation of this position is Aristotle's view of moral perception. In order to deal with a legal dispute, one must comprehend the case itself. It is only through an appreciation and understanding of the facts of a dispute that one can move to the question of what legal rules may apply. Legal perception, we might say, comes to scene before legal judgment.[41]

For Aristotle, moral perception is "informed by the virtues."[42] Judges differ in their ability to *see* the salient features of a legal case; just as all moral actors differ in their ability to *see* the morally relevant dimensions of occasions for action. As Nancy Sherman puts it, "Accordingly, much of the work of virtue will rest in knowing how to construe the case, how to describe and classify what is before one."[43] The point is this: a virtuous judge is able to perceive the morally and legally relevant factors of a dispute more completely than a nonvirtuous judge. The most relevant virtue is *phronesis* or practical wisdom. *Phronesis* is the ability to respond appropriately to the particular situation; a *phronimos* is able to respond appropriately, because she or he has the experience to discern what is morally relevant about that situation.

Equity is the tailoring of the law to the demands of the particular situation. Doing equity requires moral vision or legal perception, the ability to comprehend the morally and legally relevant features of the particular case. For this reason, equity can (or should) be done only by a *phronimos*, by a person of practical reason. In my taxonomy, equity can (or should) only be done by an adjudicator who possesses the judicial virtues—most particularly, the virtues of judicial wisdom and judicial integrity.

My claim is reinforced by considering what happens when equity is done by a judge who lacks these virtues. Lacking judicial integrity, a judge who departs from the rules is likely to be imposing his or her own preferences and not the principles imminent in the law. Lacking judicial wisdom, a judge who attempts to do equity will not perceive the relevant features of the particular case and so in departing from the rule is more likely to do harm than good.

How does this account of equity provide the basis for reconciling the practice of equity with the ideal of the rule of law? First, when equity is done by a virtuous judge, departure from the rules is not the exercise of arbitrary discretion. An adjudicator with judicial integrity cares about the coherence of the law, and is motivated to ensure that his or her departure from the letter of the rules accords with their spirit. Equity done by a judge with judicial integrity does not substitute the rule of an individual for the rule of law. The purposes and values imminent in the law itself still hold sway, despite the departure from the letter of the law. As Judith Shklar summarized this point, "In Aristotle's account the single most important condition for the Rule of Law is the character one must impute to those who make lawful judgments. Justice is the constant disposition to act fairly and lawfully."[44]

The point that equity is not arbitrary discretion can be explicated by a comparison of a virtue-centered theory with Dworkin's view of law as integrity. Modern legal theory tends to view adjudication as either discretion or following the rules. Dworkin argues that even outside the core of a legal rule, a decision can be based on legal principles. Recall that Dworkin's imaginary judge Hercules approaches a case by constructing the normative theory of law that best fits and justifies the political structure and legal doctrine of their community. From his normative theory of the law of his community, Hercules derives those rules and principles that apply to the particular case, and then he applies those rules and principles to the particular case.[45] Of course, this is a very simplified statement of Dworkin's views, but it will suffice for this occasion. The differences between law as integrity and a virtue-centered theory can best be brought into focus by distinguishing between trial judges and appellate judges, because the different roles highlight different aspects of the process of adjudication.

At the trial level, a virtue-centered theory of the practice of equity has two characteristics with no counterpart in Dworkin's views. First, a virtue-centered view emphasizes the role of practical judgment in particular and the virtues in general in organizing the judge's perception of a case. Dworkin's theory does not address the question as to how judges find facts; he explicitly sets that issue aside.[46] Second, the practice of equity, as interpreted by a virtue theory, is particularistic in nature. The virtuous judge does equity guided by practical wisdom; when he or she departs from the rules, he or she does so because it is the right thing to do in the particular case. For Dworkin, the decision of a trial judge (fact-finding aside) is no different in principle than the decision of an appellate judge. On the trial bench, Hercules would decide all of the cases on his docket on the basis of rules and principles of general application.

At the appellate level, the contrasts between a virtue theoretical practice of equity and Dworkin's views come into sharper focus. This issue can be approached via a familiar criticism of law as integrity—that Hercules is a myth for two related reasons: (1) no real judge could construct the grand theory of the law that Hercules does, and (2) real judges decide cases more instinctively.[47] Dworkin acknowledges that these points are true of real judges but denies that they have any force against his theory. Rather, "Hercules shows us the hidden structure of [real judge's] judgments and so lays these open to study and criticism."[48] The difference between Hercules and a real judge is that Hercules works more quickly, and hence can do a more complete job of theory construction than real judges do. But during the course of their careers, real judges do develop a working theory of law on which they rely, "perhaps unthinkingly" in making their decisions.[49]

Let me re-express Dworkin's points in Aristotelian terms. Legal decision making, at bottom, is in fact a matter of theoretical wisdom and knowledge of the law. What judges really do ("the hidden structure") is to develop a theory of the law that fits and justifies existing legal practice. Dworkin's argument suggests that he wishes to save the appearances—that judges frequently decide intuitively on the basis of "hunches" about correct outcomes rather than on the basis of elaborate theories—by two devices. First, judges do develop a working theory of the law over time. This theory is unconsciously present and determines the content of their intuitive judgments or hunches. Second, because real judges are relatively slow when they engage in legal theory building, they develop "skills of craft husbandry and efficiency" that enable them to reach conclusions without undertaking lines of theoretical reasoning that are unlikely to be fruitful.[50] *Phronesis* or practical wisdom is simply the name we give the unconscious exercise and efficient truncation of theoretical wisdom.

The practice of equity, then, could be explained in the following way. When a judge does equity, he or she may believe that he or she is departing from general rules and principles because of unique features of the particular case. In fact, however, the judge is unconsciously relying on a theory of the law upon which the case before him or her is governed by a general rule or principle. Articulation of the full justification for the decision would be very time-consuming, so the judge uses the category of "equity" as a shortcut. This shortcut does no harm if there are unlikely to be many future cases of a similar sort.

The virtue-centered account of the practice of equity denies that Dworkin's explanation is adequate to all the cases. (Of course, Dworkin could be correct about some cases.) *Phronesis* is not simply unconscious or truncated theoretical wisdom. It is a distinct form of judgment that is both a prerequisite for and distinct from the application of *sophia* to situations of practical choice. More simply, no matter how brilliant and learned in the law, Hercules would not be a very good judge if he lacked the experience of particulars that is required for practical wisdom.

Thus, the first argument for the compatibility of equity and the rule of law can be summarized as follows. A virtue-centered theory of judging can incorporate Dworkin's insight that the law can guide decisions beyond the narrow confines of its letter, but it supplements Dworkin's explanation of the mechanism by which this process occurs. A virtue-centered theory can accept that judges sometimes engage in Herculean theory building in order to construct legal principles, but virtue theory insists that judges with practical reason sometimes depart from the general rules and principles on the basis of their legal and moral perception of the facts of the particular case. This perception is guided by the virtues including the virtue of judicial integrity. Concern for the coherence of the law as a whole constrains the way that a judge with practical wisdom will depart from the rules in order to do justice in a particular case.

The second argument for reconciliation of the rule of law with the practice of equity is that the notion of *moral and legal vision* that grounds the practice of equity is also necessary to understanding the application of legal rules. Rules do not apply themselves. Rule application can only take place after a judge comprehends the facts of the case. Moral and legal vision is required in order to reveal that a case is governed by a rule. This is another way of putting Lon Fuller's famous responses to Hart's picture of core and penumbra.[51] For this reason, the application of legal rules (in any case that is not trivial) and the practice of equity *both* require the virtue of judicial wisdom or *phronesis*.

This insight allows us to see how the practice of equity may actually reinforce, rather than undermine, the values of predictability and regularity that ground the ideal of the rule of law. We all know that it is possible to produce arbitrary and unpredictable results by strictly adhering to the letter of the law. Perhaps the most familiar example of this phenomenon is a nonlegal one—the practice of labor unions disrupting a work environment by working to the book, adhering strictly to the letter but not the spirit of the rules. This takes us back to Aristotle's discussion of the basis for equity: no general rule can be framed with sufficient precision to yield the *expected* outcome in all particular cases. In some cases, the practice of equity will make outcomes conform to expectations and hence make the law more, rather than less, predictable.

The third argument for the reconciliation of law and equity is that the recognition of equity as a distinct practice may serve to increase the regularity and predictability of rule application in the legal system as a whole. Without a publicly acknowledged practice of equity, the pressure to do justice in particular cases may be relieved by loosening the constraints that legal rules place upon judicial decision in general. "Equity will out," we might say.[52] Undergirding this argument is the assumption that the degree to which a system of rules constrains the actual decisions made by adjudicators is a matter of social practice: a system can be tightly rule-bound or loosely rule-guided.[53] In a system where equitable departure from legal rules is an accepted and acknowledged (but limited) exception within a general practice that legal rules determine outcomes, the constraint of binding rules is tolerable. If this safety valve is not provided, then judges will have good reason to engage in interpretive practices that given them considerable freedom of choice in every case and not just the exceptional one. For this reason, the open practice of equity in some cases may serve to increase the adherence of the system as a whole to the requirements of the rule of law.

The three arguments that I have offered for the reconciliation of equity and the rule of law do not eliminate all the tension between them. There will be cases in which doing equity produces surprise or unfairness. Moreover, not all judges are virtuous. Allowing the practice of equity will permit some judges to act arbitrarily and unjustly. Indeed, any given society must decide to what extent its legal institutions should encourage the practice of equity based on the social conditions that prevail in the particular society and not solely on the general theoretical considerations explored in this chapter. The fact that equity and the rule of law *can* be reconciled does not guarantee that they will be.

5. Conclusion

Acceptance of a virtue-centered theory of judging has implications for a number of topics in legal theory and practice. By way of conclusion, consider an additional thought about the criteria for judicial selection. In the United States, there has been a great deal of emphasis on what is called "judicial philosophy" in debates about the selection of judges, especially for the Supreme Court. Of course, there is talk about character, and if it can be proven that a particular candidate for judicial office has engaged in some particularly bad conduct, the nominee is not likely to be confirmed. But the talk about character seems hackneyed and sterile, almost ritual, in nature. By contrast, there is intense interest in questions such as, "Do you believe cases should be decided in accord with the original intentions of the framers?" or "Will you use natural law in your decisions?" Senators, the press, and academic commentators have all focused on these questions, with zeal and enthusiasm.

My suggestion is that this priority should be reversed. This is not to deny that judicial philosophy is important. We do not want to ignore the question whether a particular judge affirms natural law or originalism as a theory of constitutional interpretation. Nor do I mean to suggest that a focus on character will end the divisiveness of battles over confirmation of nominees to the Supreme Court. The content of judicial virtue is open to contest, and no doubt liberals and conservatives would continue to battle if the disputed territory is expanded to include judicial character. Finally, I do not mean to suggest that members of the Senate Judiciary Committee should pore over the *Nicomachean Ethics*; the articulation of a virtue-centered theory for a wide audience must employ the rhetorical resources of our public political culture.

These caveats about the benefits of shifting public focus to judicial virtue should not obscure the fact that constitutional theories play only a limited role in influencing judicial decisions. Both Justice Brennan and Justice Rehnquist made use of the original intentions of the framers in their opinions; both liberals and conservative justices have made appeal to natural law ideas.

We ought, I think, to pay much more attention to the character of candidates for judicial office, and we should broaden our understanding of what constitutes good character. Excellence in judging requires more than avoidance of the worst human vices. An excellent judge must possess judicial intelligence, judicial integrity, judicial wisdom, good temperament, and a sense of justice. Indeed, zealous advocacy of a particular decision procedure—whether it be originalism or natural law—may actually be inconsistent with the virtue of judicial integrity. A truly excellent judge must be willing to set aside his or her theories and political agendas and attend to the facts of the case before him or her. A truly excellent judge needs the wisdom that can only be developed through experience. A truly excellent judge must possess moral vision. We should insist on truly excellent judges.

Notes

1. Aristotle, *Politics* in The Complete Works of Aristotle (Jonathan Barnes ed., Princeton: Princeton University Press, 1984), p. 1287a20. Page references are to Immanuel Bekker's standard edition of the Greek text of 1831.
2. The notion that the rule of law should be understood as a law of rules is expressed in a recent article by Justice Antonin Scalia. Antonin Scalia, *The Rule of Law as a Law of Rules*, 56 University of Chicago Law Review (1989).
3. Aristotle, *Politics*, p. 1287a20.
4. Universal Declaration of Human Rights (1948).
5. For example, see Morton Horwitz, *The Rule of Law: An Unqualified Human Good?*, 86 Yale L. Rev. (1977), pp. 561–566, E. P. Thompson, Whigs and Hunters: The Origin of the Black Act (New York: Pantheon Books, 1975), pp. 263–265, and Allan Hutchinson and Patrick Monahan, *Introduction* in The Rule of Law: Ideal or Ideology (Allan Hutchinson and Patrick Monahan, eds, Toronto: Carswell, 1987).
6. An admirable survey is that of Geoffrey de Q. Walker, The Rule of Law (Melbourne: Melbourne University Press, 1988), pp. 1–48.
7. The distinction between concept and conception I employ is a technical philosophical usage. See Ronald Dworkin, *Hard Cases*, Taking Rights Seriously (Cambridge: Harvard University Press, 1977), p. 103; Gallie, *Essentially Contested Concepts*, 56 Proceedings of the Aristotelian Society 167 (1955–56).
8. On the idea of family resemblance, see Ludwig Wittgenstein, The Blue and Brown Books (New York: Harper, 1958), p. 17; Ludwig Wittgenstein, Philosophical Investigations (3rd edn, G. E. M. Anscombe, trans., New York: MacMillan, 1958), ¶67, p. 32e.
9. A. V. Dicey, Introduction to the Study of the Law of the Constitution (10th edn., London: MacMillan, 1960), pp. 202–203.
10. John Rawls, A Theory of Justice (Cambridge: Harvard, 1971), p. 235.
11. One significant change has been made in Rawls' presentation of the rule of law precepts and their implications. I have substituted "ought" or "should" for "must" throughout. In Rawls' original presentation, the sense that the requirements of the rule of law are necessary for a system to be characterized as legal comes through very strongly. For the purposes of this chapter, and indeed, I think for Rawls' own purposes, the question whether there can be law without the rule of law does not need to be answered.

12. For a discussion of this idea, see Ronald Dworkin, *Political Judges and the Rule of Law* in A Matter of Principle (Cambridge: Harvard University Press), p. 9.
13. J. H. Baker, An Introduction to English Legal History (2nd edn, London: Butterworths, 1979), pp. 83–100. For an interesting discussion, see Roscoe Pound, *The Decadence of Equity*, 4 Colum. L. Rev. 20 (1905).
14. A. Mitchell Polinsky, An Introduction to Law and Economics (2nd edn, Boston: Little Brown and Company, 1989), p. 7.
15. *Hecht v. Bowles*, 321 U.S. 321, 329 (1944).
16. For an enumeration, see United States Department of Justice, Report to the Attorney General, Justice Without Law: A Reconsideration of the "Broad Equitable Powers" of the Federal Courts (Washington, Government Printing Office, 1988), pp. 86–94, 161–166.
17. Aristotle, *Nicomachean Ethics* in The Complete Works of Aristotle (Jonathan Barnes, ed., Princeton: Princeton University Press, 1984), pp. 1137b9–1137b24.
18. *Nicomachean Ethics*, p. 1137b23. Of course, Aristotle's view of the role of intentions of the legislator in judicial decision making is different from some contemporary versions of "originalism" as a theory of constitutional interpretation.
19. Aristotle, Rhetoric, p. 1274a29.
20. Aristotle, *Nicomachean Ethics*, p. 1137b28.
21. United States Department of Justice, Office of Legal Policy, Report to the Attorney General, Justice Without Law: A Reconsideration of the "Broad Equitable Powers" of the Federal Courts, p. 148 (emphasis in original).
22. John Rawls, A Theory of Justice, p. 238.
23. *Id.*
24. For an excellent discussion of the relationship between rules and law, see Frederick Schauer, *Rules and the Rule of Law*, 14 Harvard Journal of Law and Public Policy 645 (1991). On the role of discretion in law, see David Leonard, *Power and Responsibility in Evidence Law*, 63 So. Cal. L. Rev. 937 (1990).
25. Indeed, in modern parlance, the practice of equity is sometimes referred to as "equitable discretion." United States Department of Justice, Office of Legal Policy, Report to the Attorney General, Justice Without Law: A Reconsideration of the "Broad Equitable Powers" of the Federal Courts, p. ii.
26. Of course, this is Roscoe Pound's mechanical jurisprudence. See Roscoe Pound, *Mechanical Jurisprudence*, 8 Colum. L. Rev. 605 (1908). For contemporary neoformalism, see *The Supreme Court In Bondage: Constitutional Stare Decisis, Legal Formalism, and the Future Of Unenumerated Rights*, 9 University of Pennsylvania Journal of Constitutional Law 155 (2006).
27. See Randy Barnett, *Foreword: Unenumerated Constitutional Rights and the Rule of Law*, 14 Harv. J. L. Pub. Pol. 616–617 (1991).
28. Thus, Jerome Frank wrote,

> *The judge, at his best, is an arbitrator,* a "sound man" who strives to do justice to the parties by exercising a wise discretion with reference to the peculiar circumstances of the case. He does not merely "find" or invent some generalized rule which he "applies" to the facts presented to him. He does "equity" in the sense in which Aristotle—when thinking most clearly—described it.

Jerome Frank, Law and the Modern Mind (New York: Anchor Books, Doubleday, 1963), p. 168. See also Randy Barnett, Foreword: Unenumerated Rights and the Rule of Law, 617.

29. H. L. A. Hart, The Concept of Law (Oxford: Oxford University Press, 1961), pp. 121–150. Interestingly, "equity" does not appear as an entry in the index to *The Concept of Law*.
30. Hart, The Concept of Law, pp. 141–142.
31. Ronald Dworkin, Law's Empire (Cambridge: Harvard University Press, 1986); Ronald Dworkin, A Matter of Principle (Cambridge: Harvard University Press, 1985); Ronald Dworkin, Taking Rights Seriously (Cambridge: Harvard University Press, 1978).
32. Ronald Dworkin, *The Model of Rules I* in Taking Rights Seriously, pp. 31–39.
33. Ronald Dworkin, Law's Empire, p. 243.
34. The topic "equity" is not included in the index to any of Dworkin's monographs.
35. Ronald Dworkin, *Hard Cases* in Taking Rights Seriously, p. 116.
36. For a similar argument, see United States Department of Justice, Office of Legal Policy, Report to the Attorney General, Justice Without Law: A Reconsideration of the "Broad Equitable Powers" of the Federal Courts, pp. 158–159.
37. Roscoe Pound's statement of the consequentialist case for the Rule of Law is the classic one. Roscoe Pound, *Justice According to Law I*, 13 Colum. L. Rev. (1913), 709–712.
38. See also Introduction.
39. Nancy Sherman, The Fabric of Character, p. 15 (italicization of *logos* added). The quoted passage refers to *Nicomachean Ethics*, pp. 1134a29–1134b2. For an elaboration of Aristotle's views, see Ernest J. Weinrib, *The Intelligibility of the Rule of Law*, in The Rule of Law: Ideal or Ideology (Allan Hutchinson and Patrick Monahan, eds), p. 59.
40. Aristotle, *Politics*, p. 1287a25.
41. See Lawrence Blum, Moral Perception and Particularity, p. 702.
42. Nancy Sherman, The Fabric of Character, p. 29.
43. *Id.*
44. Judith Shklar, *Political Theory and the Rule of Law*, in The Rule of Law: Ideal or Ideology (Allan Hutchinson and Patrick Monahan, eds), p. 3. Shklar's presentation of Aristotle's view does not emphasize equity or practical wisdom.
45. This statement of Dworkin's theory is adapted from the provisional summary in Law's Empire. See Ronald Dworkin, Law's Empire, pp. 254–255.
46. See *Id*, pp. 11–12. Dworkin does acknowledge the role of law in shaping the perception of judges: "Their craft trains them to see structure in facts and doctrine at once; that is what thinking as a lawyer really is." *Id.*, p. 265.
47. See *Id.*, p. 264.
48. *Id.* at 265.
49. *Id.* at 256.
50. *Id.*, p. 265.
51. See Lon Fuller, *Positivism and Fidelity to Law: A Reply to Professor Hart*, 71 Harv. L. Rev. 630 (1958). A similar point has been made by Michael Moore.

See Michael Moore, *The Semantics of Judging*, 54 S. Cal. L. Rev. (1981), 151, 291–292.

52. The idea that equity will out was inspired by Dean Pound, who expresses it as follows, "The conflict between the two ideas, justice according to law and justice without law will not down. To the extent that equity represents the latter idea, Dean Ames is perfectly right in calling it fundamental and eternal." Roscoe Pound, *The Decadence of Equity*, Colum. L. Rev. 23–24. The conclusion he drew is similar to mine: "Law must be tempered with equity, even as justice with mercy. An if, as some assert, mercy is part of justice, we may say equally that equity is part of law, in the sense that it is necessary to the working of any legal system." *Id.*, 35.
53. The point that it is possible for legal systems to be more or less rule bound has been made clearly by Frederick Schauer. See Frederick Schauer, Rules and the Rule of Law, pp. 653–661.

6

Natural Justice: An Aretaic Account of the Virtue of Lawfulness*

*Lawrence B. Solum***

1. Introduction: natural justice in context

Let me start with the heart of the matter. Justice is a natural virtue. Well-functioning humans are just, as are well-ordered human societies. Roughly, this means that in a well-ordered society, just humans internalize the laws and social norms (the *nomoi*)—they internalize lawfulness as a disposition that guides the way they relate to other humans. In societies that are mostly well ordered, with isolated zones of substantial dysfunction, the *nomoi* are limited to those norms that are not clearly inconsistent with the function of law—to create the conditions for human flourishing. In a radically dysfunctional society, humans are thrown back on their own resources—doing the

---

 An earlier version of this essay was delivered as the 2006 Natural Law Lecture, Natural Law Institute, Notre Dame University School of Law and published as *Natural Justice*, 51 American Journal of Jurisprudence 65 (2006).

**John E. Cribbet Professor of Law, University of Illinois College of Law. I owe thanks for comments provided when this paper was delivered to The Table, the Legal Theory Workshop at Columbia, the Committee on Law and Philosophy at Arizona State University, the law faculty of Saint Louis University, the law faculty of Florida State University, the law faculty of Notre Dame University, the law faculty of Ave Maria School of Law, the law faculty of the University of Illinois, the philosophy faculty of Georgia State University, the law faculty of Northern Kentucky University, the law faculty of the University of Colorado, and to a group including members of the law and philosophy faculties at the University of Cincinnati. I am especially grateful to Sharon Lloyd and Randy Barnett for extended discussions over many years of the ideas that are developed in this article. I am also indebted to Stephen Burton, Antony Duff, Kent Greenawalt, Rosalind Hursthouse, Stephen Macedo, Richard Posner, Phillip Pullman, Ian Shapiro, Roger Shiner, Mark Tushnet, and Linda Zagzebski for comments on prior work that laid the foundations for virtue jurisprudence.

best they can in circumstances that may require great practical wisdom to avoid evil and achieve good. Justice is naturally good for humans—it is part and partial of human flourishing. All of these are natural ethical facts.

Those are the central claims of this essay, but before we examine them, some context is required. The title, "Natural Justice," may be enigmatic and even puzzling to many readers. Such puzzlement could have many sources—a general skepticism about naturalist approaches to morality, a more particular skepticism about a naturalistic approach to justice, or even a radical skepticism about the very idea of human nature itself. In this introduction, I shall not attempt to apply salve to these skeptical itches. Instead, my aim is to provide a sufficient context so that the argument for natural justice that is the main focus of the essay becomes intelligible.

A variety of approaches to morality, justice, and law could be called "naturalist," and the phrase "natural justice" could have a variety of meanings. The sense in which this essay uses the phrase "natural justice" is related to what might be called "moral naturalism." Abstractly, moral naturalism is simply the view that moral facts are natural facts—they are not "supernatural" or "transcendent" or "queer" in Mackie's wonderfully contentious expression.[1] Moral naturalism, if it can be sustained, is attractive for a number of well-known reasons. It enables realism about morality while avoiding the metaphysical embarrassment of queer entities, and it suggests that moral knowledge could be understood on the model of knowledge of the natural world. More colloquially, moral naturalism captures the essence of commonsense morality—that good and evil, right and wrong, are real features of the natural world that human reason can comprehend.

Debates about moral naturalism are well known to contemporary moral philosophers and especially to those immersed in contemporary metaethics, but these debates have not been at the center of contemporary philosophy of law and they are virtually unknown to those who practice normative legal theory from perspectives that are not informed by contemporary academic philosophy—those trained in economics, political science, or law itself. This puts us in an awkward position. Tracing even the broad outlines of the contemporary debates about the metaethics of moral naturalism will take us too far afield, but saying nothing at all will leave many readers with the feeling that "natural justice" is completely implausible. My strategy will be to provide a very brief introduction to some of the general worries about moral naturalism and to sketch the broad outlines of some of the answers to these worries.

My hope is that skeptical readers will come to see that debates about moral naturalism are far from settled and that the case for naturalism in ethics is far stronger than they may have assumed.

Outside the community of moral philosophers, two distinct objections to moral naturalism are likely to be run together and confused with something else, the "fact-value distinction." One of the objections is based on Hume's discussion of the derivation of an "ought" from an "is" and the other based on G. E. Moore's open-question argument. Let us begin with Hume and then discuss Moore.

Here is the famous passage from Hume's *A Treatise on Human Nature*:

> I cannot forbear adding to these reasonings an observation, which may, perhaps, be found of some importance. In every system of morality, which I have hitherto met with, I have always remark'd, that the author proceeds for some time in the ordinary way of reasoning, and establishes the being of a God, or makes observations concerning human affairs; when of a sudden I am surpriz'd to find, that instead of the usual copulations of propositions, is, and is not, I meet with no proposition that is not connected with an ought, or an ought not. This change is imperceptible; but is, however, of the last consequence. For as this ought, or ought not, expresses some new relation or affirmation, 'tis necessary that it shou'd be observ'd and explain'd; and at the same time that a reason should be given, for what seems altogether inconceivable, how this new relation can be a deduction from others, which are entirely different from it. But as authors do not commonly use this precaution, I shall presume to recommend it to the readers; and am persuaded, that this small attention wou'd subvert all the vulgar systems of morality, and let us see, that the distinction of vice and virtue is not founded merely on the relations of objects, nor is perceiv'd by reason.[2]

What Hume meant in this paragraph is much debated, but one popular understanding is that Hume's argument established the "fact-value distinction," the existence of which entails that no normative conclusion can ever be derived from an argument with factual premises. Whatever Hume's argument does, it does not do this. For example, if we read Hume as making a claim about the logical form of normative arguments, his point might be that arguments from fact to value must include some premise that establishes the link—that is, an argument that has entirely nonnormative premises cannot establish a normative conclusion. This is not an argument against moral naturalism, because moral naturalism is a theory that supplies premises that establish a connection between natural facts and moral facts, or, to put it differently, moral naturalism just is the view that there are "natural ethical facts."[3]

The popular imagination frequently confuses Hume on "is and ought" with another famous philosophical argument—G. E. Moore's so-called "naturalistic fallacy," which hinges on his open-question argument.[4] To appreciate the argument, we need a distinction between "open questions" and "closed questions." We can say that it is a closed question whether bachelors are married men, if being an unmarried man is the meaning of being a bachelor. It simply does not make sense to say, "Yes, I know that Ben is a bachelor, but is he married?" The answer must be "no"; this question is closed; asking it suggests that the person who asks is confused about the meaning of the term "bachelor." On the other hand, the question whether bachelors are over 40 is an open one. It does make sense to ask, "Yes, I know that Ben is still a bachelor, but is he over 40 yet?" From the fact that Ben is a bachelor, it does not follow that he is (or is not) over 40.

As applied to moral naturalism, the open-question argument takes the following form. If someone asserts that the meaning of "x is good" is the same as the meaning of "x is N," where N is some natural property, we can sensibly ask the question, but is N good? Thus, if someone asserts that "x is good" if and only if "x is pleasurable," we can reply, "Yes, I understand that x is pleasurable, but is it good?" The question "is it good?" is, according to Moore, an open question, and from the fact that it is open, we can infer that goodness is not the same as pleasure. And therefore, to equate the nonnatural property "good" with the natural property "pleasurable" is to commit the naturalistic fallacy.

The debate over Moore's argument is almost endlessly complex, but it is possible to give an example of how the debate goes that will show that Moore's argument may have started a conversation but it cannot be said to be a conversation stopper. Moore's argument is based on the idea that an assertion that "x is good" if and only if "x is pleasurable" is a claim about meaning. What Moore seems not to have noticed is that "goodness" and "pleasure" might denote the same property, but not mean the same thing. This possibility is famously illustrated with the example of "water" and H_2O. We can agree that all water is H_2O but, at the same time, believe that the meaning of "water" is different than the meaning of "H_2O." We know this is true because chemists had to discover that water was H_2O—prior to the discovery, the relationship of water to the elements, hydrogen and oxygen, was unknown or imperfectly understood. But it is not just the case that being water and being H_2O are merely coincident properties, as being a member of the Illinois philosophy department and not having grown up in Japan are merely coincident. Water is H_2O. It was an open question whether water was H_2O at one time, but this did not preclude the possibility that water just was H_2O.

A much better version of this reply to Moore is famously associated with David Brink,[5] and there is much more to be said with replies and further arguments.[6] (Whole volumes, in fact.) The point of the argument is that Moore's open-question argument hinges on the assumption that for a moral property to be identical to a natural property, the meaning of two concepts must be identical—and that assumption, the argument purports to show, is false. This argument is embedded in a larger philosophical controversy—about the role of conceptual analysis and the analytic-synthetic distinction, but for my purpose, the only claim that you need to accept is that it is an "open question" whether the open-question argument defeats moral naturalism.

Having said this much, I want now to step back from philosophy and turn to culture. The three ideas that I have been discussing—(1) the fact-value distinction, (2) deriving ought from is, and (3) the open-question argument—play a role in contemporary intellectual culture. Most college students encounter some version of the fact-value distinction, especially if they have even a smattering of liberal arts education. The version of the distinction that holds sway in the popular cultural is not, I would submit, either Hume's point about the logical structure of arguments that move from "is" premises to "ought" conclusions or Moore's open-question argument. Rather, in the popular culture, the idea is that factual beliefs are, in principle, demonstrably true or false, whereas moral beliefs are neither true nor false, but simply matters of opinion and culture or the products of relations of power and subordination. That is, the fact-value distinction that holds sway in the popular imagination is tied to philosophically naïve versions of moral relativism, sometimes infused with a smattering of dimly comprehended noncognitivist metaethics.[7]

What I have said so far is not intended to convince you that moral naturalism is the correct view in metaethics—the arguments for that conclusion would take a monograph (or several) and could not even be meaningfully mentioned or described in a few pages. Rather, what I hope to have done is to challenge the preconceptions and prejudices of those who find moral naturalism to be wholly implausible or to be based on an obvious fallacy. Moral naturalism may ultimately be incorrect, but if this is so, it is not because the proponents of moral naturalism commit a naïve philosophical mistake. Quite the contrary, the naïve philosophical mistakes are to assume that a metaethically potent fact-value distinction is self-evident or to assume that Hume and Moore produced knock-down arguments that demonstrate against the view that there are natural ethical facts. Those assumptions are quite simply wrong.

2. The virtue of justice

We have now cleared the ground for the claim that justice is a natural virtue. In this part, I shall offer a very brief sketch of the relationship of the virtue of justice to the other virtues and then explore two conceptions of the virtue of justice. The first conception is justice as fairness; the second is justice as lawfulness. The central point of this section is to argue that humans who possess the virtue of justice are nomimos—they have internalized the *nomoi* or deeply held and widely shared social norms of their communities.

2.1 The virtue of justice in context

Justice is not the only human virtue. Indeed, one of the chief insights of virtue ethics in general and virtue jurisprudence in particular is the realization that not all of the work of morality needs to be done by the virtue of justice. Other virtues, including courage, beneficience, good temper, and most especially practical wisdom, address ethical issues upon which the virtue of justice is silent. One way of stating this insight plays off the title of T. M. Scanlon's book, *What We Owe to Each Other*.[8] The domain of morality does include our duties to one another: the domain of justice is central and crucially important to our understanding human ethical life. But this does not entail that justice is the exclusive or paramount virtue. An account of morality that limits itself to moral duties and permissions is radically incomplete. It cannot account for what we do *not* owe to each other, but nonetheless is morally salient.

One particularly perspicuous context for appreciating this fact about the virtue of justice is the law in general and the judicial virtues in particular. One might think that the law and judging would be the realm in which justice's claim to be the sovereign virtue would be strongest. Indeed, it might be plausibly claimed that if a judge has the virtue of justice, then the other virtues play supporting roles at best. Of course, supporting roles may be essential to the success of the play. So justice without courage, good temper, or sobriety might be unreliable.

A cowardly judge might act contrary to justice out of fear. An angry judge might act out of bias against an offensive defendant. And an intoxicated judge might act contrary to justice in ways that are foolish, careless, or simply blind. But if the other virtues played only supporting roles, then justice could still claim to be the master virtue—the one that does the important work of guiding decision.

In contemporary virtue ethics, there is a virtue that is sometimes understood as playing the leading role. But that role is not assigned to justice, but is instead assigned to practical wisdom or *phronesis*. Indeed, virtue ethicists sometimes call the fully virtuous human, the *phronimos*, reflecting the view that *phronesis* is the highest or most complete virtue. Practical wisdom is the virtue that integrates and directs the rest—that changes the picture of the virtues from a cacophany of competing voices to a well orchestrated choir—with practical wisdom playing the role of director, giving beneficience, courage, good temper and the rest their cues.

In the context of the judicial virtues, I have argued elsewhere in this anthology that *phronesis* plays this same role in a complete account of the judicial virtues. It is *phronesis* or legal vision that enables judges to discern when legal rules apply and what they mean. And it is *phronesis* that enables the virtuous judge to do *equity*, correcting the inherent generality of the law with an appreciation of what the law's purposes require in particular fact situations. In this regard, consider this passage from Barbara Herman's *Moral Literacy*:

> In the course of the very productive encounter between Aristotelian and Kantian ethics, some things seem to have been established. In particular, from the Aristotelian side, it has been argued and is now widely accepted that moral judgment is not a practice of applying fixed rules to particulars in the manner of a legal system. There is, on the one hand, the recognition that what is right to do *here* is often, if not typically, a function of what is specific to the given situation, and on the other, the requirement of salience—much of the work of moral judgment takes place prior to any possible application of rules in the eliciting of relevant moral facts from the particular circumstances.[9]

Virtue jurisprudence embraces Herman's observation with one important correction—the model of mechanical application of fixed rules is inadequate *even in the case of a legal system*. Justice, like beneficience, courage, good temper, and the rest, sings in the choir that practical wisdom directs.

2.2 Two conceptions of the virtue of justice

But what does the virtue of justice require? In this section, I shall examine two different conceptions of the virtue of justice: *justice as lawfulness* and *justice as fairness*. (For short, I will use the phrases "the fairness conception" and "the lawfulness conception" to refer to these ideas.) I shall argue that conceptualizing the virtue of justice as fairness necessitates intractable disagreements about which judges are excellent and that the competing conception, emphasizing the idea that excellent judges are lawful, opens the door to agreement in judgments about who is just. My investigation begins with the fairness conception of the virtue of justice and then moves to the notion of justice as lawfulness.

2.2.1 Justice as fairness

One influential conception of the virtue of justice begins with the premise that the just and the lawful are separate and distinct. Of course, the view is not that all laws are unjust or that no just norms are law. Rather, the idea is that there is no necessary connection between legality and justice.[10] If this were so, then the most plausible conception of the virtue of justice might be articulated as follows:

> *The Virtue of Justice as Fairness: A person, P, has the virtue of justice as fairness, V(j-f), if and only if P is disposed to act in accord with the best conception of fairness, F, in situations, S, where fairness provides salient reasons for action.*

One might think that a judge who possessed *V(j-f)* would act solely on the basis of fairness[11] with reference to the law, but this is not the case. If this were true, it would provide the basis for a devastating objection to the fairness conception—because it would require each judge to substitute his or her private judgments about what fairness requires for the duly enacted constitutions, statutes, and rules. The just judge would entirely disregard the law. Although I shall not provide the argument here, it seems plain that this would be a recipe for chaos.[12]

But a defender of the fairness conception need not admit that a judge who acted on the basis of fairness would disregard the law entirely. *Why not?* Because the existence of legal norms will frequently give rise to considerations of fairness that will transform the moral landscape, creating salient reasons of fairness that motivate a judge who has *V(j-f)* to act in accord with the law. An example may help to clarify and illustrate this point. Suppose there is a dispute between Ben and Alice over Greenacre—a vacant and unimproved parcel of land. The law gives Ben title to Greenacre, which he has purchased, but Alice has begun to use Greenacre by planting a garden. In the absence of the institution of property law, it might be the case that Ben would have no claim on Greenacre—how would he acquire such a claim without some use or improvement of the land?—but that given the existence of property law, Ben would have a claim of fairness, because he has paid for Greenacre and has reasonably relied on the legal institution of property. If this is so, then the law has created a claim of fairness that otherwise would not exist and a judge with *V(j-f)* would decide in favor of Ben—assuming, of course, that there were no other circumstances that created an overriding reason of fairness to decide in favor of Alice.

Nonetheless, the fairness conception faces a formidable objection because of the role that private judgment plays for judges with *V(j-f)*. To articulate this objection, we need to highlight the distinction between two questions about fairness—which I shall call "first-order" and "second-order" questions of fairness. A first-order question of fairness is simply the question, "Which action is fair given the circumstances?" A second-order question of fairness concerns whose judgment about first-order questions will be taken as authoritative. Thus, the question, "Given the fact of disagreement about the correct answer to a first-order question of fairness, whose judgment should be taken as authoritative?," is a second-order question of fairness. One possible answer to a second-order question of fairness is that one ought to rely on one's own *private* judgment about what action is fair. A quite different answer is that one should rely on some source of *public* judgment. For example, one might rely on duly enacted and public laws.

The fairness conception implicitly requires judges to exercise private judgment about first-order questions of fairness. In exercising that judgment, the judge may conclude that expectations generated by reasonable reliance on the law provide reasons of fairness—as in the case of Ben, Alice, and Greenacre—but this is a conclusion of private judgment. One judge might conclude that Ben's reliance on property law was reasonable, and hence that fairness required a decision for Ben. A different judge might conclude that no one could reasonably rely on property law in cases in which they were allowing valuable land to lie fallow when others could make productive use of the land—and therefore decide for Alice. Yet a third judge might conclude that because of pervasive economic inequalities, the whole institution of property is unjust and awards the land to a third party, Carla, who was in greater need than either Ben or Alice. Because each judge makes a private judgment about the all-things-considered fairness of following the law in each case, these judgments can (and we expect will) differ with the moral, religious, and ideological views of the particular judge.

The objection to the fairness conception of the virtue of justice is that disagreements in private judgments about fairness would undermine the very great values that we associate with the rule of law. Because the fairness conception requires each judge to exercise his or her own private judgment about what fairness requires—all things considered—and because such judgments will frequently differ, the outcome of disputes adjudicated by judges with *V(j-f)* will be systematically unpredictable. If this were the case, then the law would be unable to perform the function of coordinating behavior, creating stable expectations, and constraining arbitrary or self-interested actions by officials. How bad this would be is a matter of dispute. A Hobbesian answer to this question is *very bad indeed*—in the absence of coordinating authority, life would be "solitary, poor, nasty, brutish, and short."[13] A Lockean answer is that reliance on private judgment leads to "inconveniences,"[14] but even an optimistic realist would surely concede that the inconvenience of a society that cannot secure the rule of law would be serious.

One way to test the fairness conception of the virtue of justice is to consider its application to the questions, "Who are the good judges?" and "Who should we select as a judge?" If the fairness conception was correct, then the excellent judges are those who have the right beliefs about fairness and who are disposed to act on those beliefs. If we agreed on the content of the right beliefs about fairness, this would not be a problem, but we do not agree. So the fairness conception leads to disagreement about who has the virtue of justice. We can provide a crude translation of this point into the language of political ideologies of the left and right. For the left, only left-wing judges are just; because only left-wing judges have what the left considers true beliefs about what fairness requires. And of course, whereas for the right, the left-wing judges are unjust precisely because they have what the right considers false beliefs about fairness. Even the uncontested virtues—such as incorruptibility or courage—become problematic once the fairness conception has been accepted. For the left, an intelligent, diligent, and courageous right-wing judge may be worse than a judge who lacks a keen intellect, is somewhat lazy, and who will succumb to the pressures of public opinion. And vice versa for the right.

It gets worse for the fairness conception. Anyone who holds the fairness conception is naturally tempted to apply a double standard of judicial excellence. The double standard works like this:

> *For judges with whom I agree, the fairness conception supplies the content of the virtue of justice. Right-thinking judges are excellent when they act on the basis of their convictions about what is fair. But when it comes to judges with whom I disagree, a different standard applies. Wrong-thinking judges are excellent when they stick to the rules. For them, the lawfulness conception provides the standard for the virtue of justice.*

You may say, "That's ludicrous, no one could hold such a blatantly inconsistent set of positions about the meaning of justice." In reply, I suggest that you pay careful attention to the political rhetoric that attends debates about judicial role and judicial selection.

2.2.2 Justice as lawfulness

If the fairness conception of the virtue of justice is unsatisfactory, is there an alternative? In the *Nicomachean Ethics*, Aristotle suggests an alternative understanding of justice as lawfulness, but to understand Aristotle's view, we need to take a look at the Greek word *nomos* which is usually translated as "law." For the ancient Greeks, *nomos* had a broader meaning than does "law" in contemporary English. Richard Kraut, the distinguished Aristotle scholar, explained the difference as follows:

> [W]hen [Aristotle] says that a just person, speaking in the broadest sense is *nomimos*, he is attributing to such a person a certain relationship to the laws, norms, and customs generally accepted by some existing community. Justice has to do not merely with the written enactments of a community's lawmakers, but with the wider set of norms that govern the members of that community. Similarly, the unjust person's character is expressed not only in his violations of the written code of laws, but more broadly in his transgression of the rules accepted by the society in which he lives.
>
> There is another important way in which Aristotle's use of the term *nomos* differs from our word "law": he makes a distinction between *nomoi* and what the Greeks of his time called *psēphisma* — conventionally translated as "decrees." A decree is a legal enactment addressed solely to present circumstances, and sets no precedent

> that applies to similar cases in the future. By contrast a *nomos* is meant to have general scope: it applies not only to cases at hand but to a general category of cases that can be expected to occur in the future.[15]

We can restate this last point by using our distinction between types of judgments (first and second order, private and public). If judges rely on their own private, first-order judgments of fairness as the basis for the resolution of disputes, then it follows inexorably that their judgments will be decrees (*psēphisma*) and not decisions on the basis of a second-order, public judgment—in other words, not on the basis of a *nomos*. In other words, a judge who decides on the basis of his or her own private judgments about which outcome is fair—all things considered—is making decisions that are tyrannical in Aristotle's sense.

"How can this be?" you may ask. "Aren't decisions that are motivated by fairness the very opposite of tyranny?" But framing the question in this way obscures rather than illuminates the issue. Of course, if there were universal agreement (or even a strong consensus) of first-order private judgments about fairness, then decision on the basis of such judgments would be *nomoi* and not *psēphisma*. But our private, first-order judgments about the all-things-considered requirements of fairness do not agree. So in any given case, a decision that the judge believes is required by fairness will be seen by others quite differently. At best, the decision will be viewed as a good faith error of private judgment about fairness. More likely, those who disagree will describe the decision as a product of ideology, personal preference, or bias. At worst, the decision will be perceived as the product of arbitrary will or self-interest. In no event, will a decision based on a controversial first-order private judgment of fairness be viewed as outcome of a *nomos*—a publicly available legal norm.

Rule by decree (*psēphisma*) is tyranny. Decision on the basis of private, first-order judgments about fairness is the rule of individuals and not of law. From Aristotle's point of view, a regime that rules by decree does not provide the stability and certainty that is required for human communities to flourish.[16] Kraut continues,

> We can now see why Aristotle thinks that justice in its broadest sense can be defined as lawfulness, and why he has such high regard for a lawful person. His definition embodies the assumption that every community requires the high degree of order that comes from having

> a stable body of customs and norms, and a coherent legal code that is not altered frivolously and unpredictably. Justice in its broadest sense is the intellectual and emotional skill one needs in order to do one's part in bringing it about that one's community possesses this stable system of rules and laws.[17]

And with that point in place, we can now formulate the lawfulness conception of the virtue of justice:

> *The Virtue of Justice as Lawfulness: A person, P, has the virtue of justice as lawfulness, V(j-l), if and only if P is disposed to act in accord with the nomoi (positive laws and stable customs and norms), N, in situations, S, where the nomoi provide salient reasons for action.*

On the lawfulness conception, the virtue of justice does not require action in conformity with one's private, first-order judgments of fairness. Justice as lawfulness is based on a second-order judgment that judges (or more generally, citizens) should rely on public judgments. The content of the public judgments is the *nomoi*—the positive laws and shared norms of a given community. Someone with the virtue of justice is disposed to act on the basis of the *nomoi*. In other words, the lawfulness conception holds that the excellent judge is a *nomimos*, someone who grasps the importance of lawfulness and is disposed to act on the basis of the laws and norms of his or her community. A judge who is *nomimos* cares about the laws and norms of his or her community. She is disposed to do that which is lawful, because she respects and internalizes the *nomoi* of his or her community.

Finally, we are now in a position to compare the fairness conception and the lawfulness conception. Which of these offers a more satisfactory conception of the virtue of justice? On the surface, it might appear that the fairness conception is more satisfactory—after all, who can deny that we ought to do what fairness requires—all things considered? Although there is much more to be said in a full account of these matters, the argument advanced here provides good reasons to doubt that the fairness conception can offer a satisfying account of the virtue of justice. A view of justice must take into account the distinctions between first- and second-order judgments and between public and private judgments. Once these distinctions are introduced, the need for second-order agreement on a public standard of judgment becomes clear. The lawfulness conception of the virtue of justice answers to this need; the fairness conception does not.

2.2.3 A virtue-centered theory of judging.

For the sake of simplicity and clarity, I shall formulate a virtue-centered theory of judging in the form of four definitions:[18]

> *A judicial virtue* is a naturally possible disposition of mind or will that when present with the other judicial virtues reliably disposes its possessor to make just decisions. The judicial virtues include temperance, courage, good temper, intelligence, wisdom, and justice.
>
> *A virtuous judge* is a judge who possesses the judicial virtues.
>
> *A virtuous decision* is a decision made by a virtuous judge acting from the judicial virtues in the circumstances relevant to the decision.
>
> *A lawful decision* is a decision that would be characteristically made by a virtuous judge in the circumstances relevant to the decision.[19] The phrase "legally correct" is synonymous with the phrase "lawful" in this context.

Thus, the central normative thesis of a virtue-centered theory of judging is that judges ought to be virtuous and make virtuous decisions. Judges who lack the virtues should aim to make lawful or legally correct decisions, although they may not be able to do this reliably, given that they lack the virtues. Judges who lack the judicial virtues ought to develop them. Judges ought to be selected on the basis of their possession of (or potential for the acquisition of) the judicial virtues.

Reliable excellence in judging requires that the judge possess all of the judicial virtues (and the requisite knowledge and skill as well), but a virtue-centered theory places special emphasis on two virtues—practical wisdom and justice. An excellent judge must be both *phronimos* and *nomimos*.

2.3 Transition: from virtue jurisprudence to natural goodness

In this part, I have offered a sketch of the judicial virtues including a more textured account of the virtue of justice in the context of an aretaic theory of judging. That theory is offered as an illustration of the content of a larger view in normative legal theory, virtue jurisprudence. In the next part, we approach the virtue of justice from another angle—the relationship of the virtue of justice to the idea of natural goodness. That relationship raises foundational questions about the status of justice as a virtue. Is justice a natural virtue—a natural characteristic of well-functioning humans? Or is justice an artificial virtue—an artifact of human culture that is "constructed" or "invented" by humans?

3. From natural goodness to natural justice

There is much to be said about the question whether goodness or justice is natural. A full discussion would properly be the subject of a long monograph or series of monographs, far exceeding the limitations on this article. My approach will begin with the idea of "natural goodness," as it has been developed by Philippa Foot[20] and Michael Thompson,[21] and then proceed to the application of those ideas to justice.

3.1 Natural goodness

Is goodness natural? In the introduction, we glanced briefly at Hume's discussion of the derivation of "ought" from "is" and Moore's open-question argument. Having set those arguments to the side, let us go straight for the affirmative case for the thesis that human flourishing is a natural good. This case is not my own—it is borrowed from the account offered by Philippa Foot in her book *Natural Goodness*.

One entry point into Foot's argument is this observation: "Judgements of goodness and badness can have, it seems, a special 'grammar' when the subject belongs to a living thing, whether plant, animal, or human being."[22] A word of clarification here—when Foot uses the word "grammar," she means it in its Wittgensteinian sense[23]: this is "conceptual grammar" or "depth grammar" and not the agreement of nouns with verbs. Michael Thompson's explanation of the distinctive grammar of statements about living creatures is particularly perspicuous:

> "They have four legs," we say of cats or of cat-form; "They bloom in spring," we say of cherries or of cherry-form. "It has four legs," we say of this cat hic et nunc; "It bloomed last spring" we say of the cherry tree in the garden. The properties expressed by these predicates may be said to "characterize" the life forms cat and cherry respectively; we may say, by contrast, that they "hold of" the individual cat or cherry tree in question. The predicates may of course fail to hold of many individual bearers of the life forms they characterize; it may even, in suitable cases, fail to be true of most of them. Where the characterizing predicates do fail to hold—where a cat has three legs

> or a cherry does not bloom—we have natural defect, a failure of elementary "natural goodness." Thus judgments of goodness and defect make implicit reference to the species or life form that the individual bears.[24]

Of course, we humans are not cats or cherries. Among our characteristics as a species are the following:

> Humans are social creatures.
> Humans use language.
> Humans engage in deliberative practical reasoning.

As with cats, so with humans. Not all humans are social, language-using, or engage in practical deliberation, but these activities are characteristic of the species. Well-functioning humans have these characteristics; when an individual lacks these capacities, that individual lacks a form of natural goodness. There is much more to say about Foot and Thompson's position, but this very brief discussion is sufficient to give a lively sense of the line they have taken.

How does this view connect up with virtue ethics and virtue jurisprudence? Michael Thompson puts it this way: "[T]he traditional table of virtues provides an apt characterization of the *specifically human* form of practical rationality... [C]onsiderations of justice, benevolence and prudence are among those a well-reasoning human being will act upon, even where they conflict with other objectives."[25] In other words, the virtues are natural for humans—they are characteristic of well-functioning humans as social, communicative, and rational beings. Human beings need the virtues to function well. Intemperate, stupid, foolish, cowardly, and bad tempered humans do not—characteristically—do well in life. Or to put the point from an Aristotelian perspective, the virtues are required for a flourishing human life, that is, for human happiness.

3.2 Natural justice

And that brings us to justice. Is justice an aspect of natural goodness for humans? My discussion of this question will proceed in three steps. First, I shall lay out the intuitive idea—that justice is a natural virtue for rational social creatures. Second, I shall identify some problems with the intuitive idea. And third, I shall address the question, "In what sense is justice as lawfulness a natural virtue?"

3.2.1 The intuitive idea: justice as a natural virtue for language-using rational social creatures

Because humans are social creatures, they need to get along with one another in order to flourish. At a minimum getting along requires us to avoid injury and interference. Because we are vulnerable creatures, we can kill and injure one another. Because we engage in complex projects, interference can frustrate our aims. Beyond the minimum, both the satisfaction of basic needs and the completion of complex projects require cooperation. Complex cooperation is only possible with stable expectations about social practices such as promising and legal practices such as contracting. Social norms and legal rules ground stable expectations and hence enable complex cooperation. And the virtue of justice—the internalization of social norms and legal rules—is required for all of this to work. Humans who lack the virtue of justice will interfere with the flourishing of others and undermine their own flourishing. I take it that these points are not controversial, because they rely on very "weak" (where "weak" means "uncontroversial") premises. The instrumental value of justice for human flourishing is a well-established social fact, beyond serious argument.

Much more could be said about the function of justice, but if we can (tentatively) be satisfied with this very abstract sketch, we shall then be able to get to the thorny problems that appear near the surface of any attempt to naturalize justice.

3.2.2 Two problems with natural justice

So what are the problems for a naturalistic account of justice? Let us begin with what I shall call "the objection from artificiality."

3.2.2.1 The first problem for natural justice: the objection from artificiality. Is justice really a natural human excellence? One problem is that justice does not fit the pattern that Aristotle lays out for the other natural virtues. Courage is a disposition with respect to the morally neutral emotion of fear, as is good temper with respect to anger. The disposition to too much fear is cowardice; the disposition to too little fear is rashness. Courage is the disposition to fear that is proportionate to the circumstances. We can easily see how virtues like courage can be viewed as "natural": although the moral virtues may require cultivation and education, they are natural capacities of the human animal. But justice does not fit this pattern. There is no morally neutral emotion that relates to justice as does fear to courage. Unlike the other moral virtues, justice does not seem to be a mean with respect to corresponding vices of deficiency and excess (as is courage with respect to rashness and cowardice).

This problem was famously explored by Bernard Williams in his essay, "Justice as a Virtue." Williams suggests that the notion of a just action or outcome "is prior to that of a fair or just person. Such a person is one who is disposed to promote just distributions, look for them, stand by them, and so on."[26] "The disposition of justice," Williams continues, "will lead the just person to resist unjust distributions—and to resist them *however they are motivated*."[27] On Williams's account, then, it might seem that some theory of fairness is prior to the virtue of justice. To be just is to have the right views about fairness and to be disposed to act upon those views.

We can take this objection one step beyond Williams. Here is the way it might go. Having the right views about fairness—it could be argued—is to have the true, correct, or best theory of fairness. But theories of fairness—the argument continues—are not natural attributes of humans as members of the species. Theories of fairness are constructions (or inventions) of human reason. The capacity for reason and deliberation may be natural—so the argument goes—but the products of this capacity are artificial. So justice is artificial—just as other products of human reason (novels, the theory of natural selection, or automobiles) are artificial.

And this objection seems equally potent when applied to justice as fairness and justice as lawfulness. If justice is fairness, then the virtue of justice is the disposition to act in accord with some theory of fairness and that theory is a human artifact. If justice is lawfulness, then the virtue of justice is the disposition to act in accord with the positive laws and social norms of a particular human culture, and those laws and norms are human artifacts. In either case, justice is an artificial virtue.

The answer to this objection rests on a strategy of confession and avoidance. Confession first. Justice does not fit the pattern of the other moral virtues—it is not a mean with respect to a morally neutral emotion. And yes, positive laws and theories of fairness are human artifacts. So there is a sense in which the virtue of justice could be said to be an artificial virtue—its operation depends on the products of human reason and those products can sensibly be characterized as artifacts.

Now for the avoidance. Nonetheless, the virtue of justice is a natural virtue. A well-functioning human is naturally *nomimos*. It is natural for humans to act in accord with the shared social norms and positive laws of their cultures. Of course, not all humans share this disposition to lawfulness. Some humans are outlaws—they prey on the lawful, usually in ways that are ultimately self-injuring. But this is not different than any other natural quality of humans or other species. Not all larks can fly. Not all humans have normal intelligence. Moreover, the natural capacity for lawfulness will not develop in all possible human circumstances. In conditions of extreme deprivation or in radically dysfunctional societies, many or most humans may never develop this natural capacity. But once again, the same is true for the other virtues—such as courage or good temper.

My claim—that justice as the capacity for a disposition to lawfulness is natural—is, of course, an empirical claim about the human species. And like any empirical claim, it can be contested on the basis of relevant evidence. In this case, it might be argued that observable human behavior in well-ordered human societies does not support the idea of a natural capacity for a disposition to lawfulness. Or it might be argued that biology (or evolutionary biology) demonstrates that there is no possible mechanism for such a capacity. In this essay, I shall put these issues to the side and simply assume, for the sake of argument, that there is good evidence that humans have a natural capacity for lawfulness—or, in the alternative, that there is no decisive evidence against the existence of such a capacity.

One further qualification is in order. I am not claiming that "positive law" is natural in the same sense as is the virtue of justice as lawfulness. Constitutions, statutes, rules, regulations, and opinions—all of these are artifacts. Although positive law may be a "natural solution" to the inherent limitations on unwritten or customary social norms, this is not the same kind of naturalness that I claim for the virtue of justice itself. Moreover, the content of particular positive laws will be nonnatural in the sense that a variety of different laws or legal regimes can be compatible with a well-ordered society of flourishing humans.

3.2.2.2 The second problem for natural justice: the uneasy relationship between lawfulness and fairness. There is a second problem with the interpretation of natural justice as a virtue of lawfulness. If lawfulness is a virtue, then what do we say about fairness? This problem seems particularly acute, given the strong association in contemporary moral and political theory between justice and fairness. Indeed, one important political philosopher, John Rawls, called his theory "justice as fairness." And Aristotle recognizes a connection between justice as fairness—offering theories of both distributive and corrective justice (as fairness) in Book V of the *Nicomachean Ethics*. Even if justice is partially or even primarily a virtue of lawfulness, must not it be the case that fairness enters into the picture in some way—supplementing or constraining lawfulness?

Moreover, there is another difficulty with justice as lawfulness. Viewed from the point of the lawmaker, it might be thought that "justice as lawfulness" fails to fulfill an important function of an account of justice. Should not our theory of justice tell us what the law should be? If the lawmaker wishes to know which laws are just, she does not want to know which laws are lawful. She wants to know which laws are fair.

What can we say about the uneasy relationship between lawfulness and fairness? The first point that we should make is that justice does not need to do all the work in an aretaic theory of legislation. The end of law is not justice: it is human flourishing. More particularly, the aim of law should be to create the conditions for the development, sustenance, and exercise of human excellence. The idea that justice is the primary or sole criterion for good laws may have some currency for certain variants of deontological normative legal theory, but virtue jurisprudence need not (and should not) take this idea on board. Of course, justice is one of the virtues. So the law should aim at lawfulness—the very great values of the rule of law. And to the extent that fairness is part of the virtue of justice, legislation should aim at fairness as well.

So what is the role of fairness in the virtue of justice? Fairness is not the primary end of law, but it is a supplement to and constraint on the content of the laws. The idea of fairness as a supplement to lawfulness is taken up in connection with the third problem for natural justice, which immediately follows this discussion. The notion that fairness acts as a constraint on the proper content of both positive law and social norms is taken up in Section 4.

3.3 In what sense is justice as lawfulness natural?

We have examined the idea that natural justice can be understood on the model of natural goodness and that this idea can be given content by the lawfulness conception of the virtue of justice, suitably qualified by the complimentary idea that a fully virtuous judge is both *nomimos* and *phronimos*—and hence that justice as lawfulness can be tempered by the practice of equity. In what sense is this conception of the virtue of justice "natural"? A deep answer to this question would require an explication of the concepts of the natural and naturalness—but that enterprise cannot be undertaken on this occasion. The shallow answer to the question that was outlined above[28] was that the virtue of justice as fairness can be seen as a condition for the flourishing of humans and their communities. It might be argued, however, that the criteria for naturalness are provided by science in general and evolutionary biology in particular. So it might be argued that the naturalness of the virtue of justice as lawfulness can only be established by sociobiology—that is, by a showing that the disposition to internalize social norms is the product of human evolution and is, in some sense, "hard wired." For the purposes of this essay, I shall simply put that argument to the side. I do not mean "natural" in that sense. My claim is that the virtue of justice as lawfulness is natural in an ordinary and pretheoretical sense of the term "natural."

4. Conclusion: from the natural justice to natural law

What is the relationship between natural justice and the natural law tradition? My remarks about these connections will be programmatic and sketchy, but they are informed by a particular conception of the perennial debate about natural law and positivism. Some legal theorists see the "What is law question?" through the lens of contemporary analytic legal philosophy. To those theorists, the debate between natural law and positivism is a debate about the concept of law; analytic philosophy and conceptual analysis provide the appropriate tools for determining the "essence" or "necessary conceptual content" of law. My conception of the debate between natural lawyers and legal positivists is quite different.

The question "What is law?" and the theoretical positions that are labeled as "natural law" and "legal positivism" can be understood in three related but distinct ways. First, we might follow contemporary academic practice and understand this debate as conceptual: how can the concept of law be analyzed and what are the necessary and sufficient conditions for its application? Second, we might understand the debate as empirical: in a particular social context, are the criteria for legal validity based exclusively on the sources or are there moral criteria for the validity of at least some legal rules? Third, we might understand the debate as essentially normative: should the complex social practice that we call law limit itself to source-based criteria for legal validity or should moral criteria play some role? Although these questions are distinct, they are related. For example, strong conceptual legal positivism might entail that the empirical and normative questions are "nonsense," on the one hand, while the intelligibility of normative arguments for moral criteria for legal validity might cast doubt on the plausibility of strong conceptual claims about the strong separation of law and morals or what is called "exclusive legal positivism."

With this understanding of the debate between natural lawyers and legal positivists in mind, let us turn to the lawfulness conception of the virtue of justice. It might be argued that my account of natural justice is radically inconsistent with the natural law tradition. At the center of that tradition, the argument might go, is the idea that *unjust* laws are not *true* laws—*lex injusta non est lex*. From this, it might be argued that the natural law tradition is committed to the fairness conception of the virtue of justice. That is, it might be thought that each human is obligated to act in accord with his or her own first-order private judgments of fairness. If this were so, it would not establish that the idea of a virtue jurisprudence or of a natural virtue of justice is inconsistent with the natural law tradition. Rather, it would establish that the versions of virtue jurisprudence that are compatible with the natural law tradition are ones that incorporate the fairness conception of the virtue of justice.

Nonetheless, I shall claim that a virtue jurisprudence that incorporates the lawfulness conception of the virtue of justice can be reconciled with the natural law tradition. There are two steps to this reconciliation. The first step focuses on the relationship between the social norms and positive law. The second step focuses on the relationship between the status of a norm as a *nomos* and the relationship of the norm to human flourishing.

The virtue of justice as lawfulness is a disposition to act lawfully—to internalize the *nomoi*—the social and legal norms of a given human society. Up to this point, I have not said much about the relationship between social norms and legal norms. There are at least three possible relationships that are relevant to the issue at hand:

First, the content of a legal norm can be congruent with content of a social norm (or set of norms).

Second, a legal norm can be supported by a social norm (or set of norms) that recognizes the legitimate authority of institutions with the power to create, modify, or extinguish legal rules.

Third, a legal norm can be inconsistent with a social norm (or set of norms), either because of conflict between the content of the two norms or because the institutions that are the source of the legal norm lack legitimate authority, given relevant social norms.

Each of these three relationships requires some explanation.

The first relationship is that the content of a legal norm can be congruent with content of a social norm (or set of norms). For example, the legal rule prohibiting and punishing murder is congruent with a social norm. Congruence is not the same as identity. The social norm may be vague or underspecified in comparison with the legal norm. For example, the social norm may sanction or require punishment for murder, but the legal norm may specify a particular punishment, such as imprisonment or execution. Congruence requires that the legal norm express the social norm in a way that enables the internalization of the social norm to provide direct support for the legal norm.

The second relationship is that a legal norm can be supported by a social norm (or set of norms) that recognizes the legitimate authority of institutions with the power to create, modify, or extinguish legal rules. For example, it is possible that there would be no social norms that govern speed limits on the highway or the times that one may use a public park. If this were the case, these legal norms might nonetheless be internalized on the basis of a more general social norm that recognized the legitimate authority of the legislative body that promulgated the norm. Of course, the first and second relationships may coexist—that is, a given legal norm may have content that is congruent with the content of a social norm and also be supported by a social norm that grounds the legitimate authority of the source of the legal norm.

The third relationship obtains when a legal norm is inconsistent with social norms. That inconsistency can take one of two different forms. The first form of inconsistency is based on content. For example, if there were a legal norm that prohibited driving at more than 55 mph, but a social norm against driving less than 60 mph, the content of the legal norm would be inconsistent with the content of the social norm. Likewise, if there were a legal norm authorizing arbitrary murder by the secret police, but a social norm against such murders, the two would be inconsistent. The second form of inconsistency is based on illegitimate authority. For example, if a coup or foreign invasion were to result in the institution of a government with coercive power but without legitimate authority, there could be a social norm that disapproved of the internalization of the content of laws issued by the government.

With these three relationships in mind, let us return to the natural slogan, "an unjust law is not a true law." On the lawfulness interpretation of the virtue of justice, it might appear that this slogan expresses a very odd idea. If we substitute "unlawful" for "unjust," we get "an unlawful law is not a true law." Is the notion of an "unlawful law" an oxymoron? Not necessarily, that expression could refer to a statute that was not enacted through the processes prescribed by law or a statute that was inconsistent with the constitution. But this is not what natural lawyers mean by their slogan. There is, however, another way in which we can interpret the slogan, once we recall that the lawfulness conception of the virtue of justice is based on the *nomoi* rather than positive law. On this interpretation, the phrase "true law" refers to positive laws that stand in one of the two right relationships to social norms—either congruence or socially recognized legitimate authority. Positive laws that have content that is inconsistent with the content of social norms or that are promulgated by institutes that lack legitimate authority are not true laws.

There is another sense in which a virtue jurisprudence that embraces the lawfulness conception of the virtue of justice can incorporate the natural law slogan that an unjust law is not a true law. This sense derives from the notion that it is a condition for a norm to count as a *nomos* that the norm must be such that it could be internalized by any fully virtuous human. That is, the norm must be internalizeable by any fully virtuous agent—in possession of the intellectual and moral virtues. In short, we can say that for a norm to be a *nomos* it must be such that it could be embraced by the *phronimoi*—by those humans in full possession of the human excellences. Social norms or positive laws that clearly hinder rather that enable human flourishing could not be internalized by a fully virtuous agent who has grasped the *telos* or proper end that *nomoi* serve.

When these two restrictions on the content of law are conjoined, it becomes apparent that the lawfulness conception of the virtue of justice gives a distinctive interpretation of the natural law slogan that an unjust law is not a true law. First, a positive law that is inconsistent with social norms is not a *nomos*. Second, social norms and positive laws that could not be internalized by the *phronimoi* are not *nomoi*. The lawfulness conception of the virtue of justice entails that a fully virtuous agent is *nominos*—disposed to act in accord with the *nomoi*. But a fully virtuous agent is not disposed to act in accord with social norms that would undermine human flourishing; nor is a fully virtuous agent disposed to act in accord with positive laws that have content that is inconsistent with social norms or that lack legitimate authority. In this sense, a fully virtuous agent with the virtue of justice as lawfulness will not be disposed to act in accord with unjust positive laws or social norms. From a virtue theoretic perspective, that is the cash value of the slogan, "an unjust law is not a true law." The virtue jurisprudential version of the slogan is, "defective norms are not true *nomoi*."

Our investigation of natural justice has been expressed in three movements. From virtue ethics, we have developed the idea of virtue jurisprudence. From natural goodness, we have derived the notion of natural justice. And from natural justice, we have come around to natural law. Let me conclude with a confident but controversial assertion. This movement, from virtue ethics to a distinctive interpretation of the natural law tradition, is no coincidence, no mere "happy accident." Thinking about natural law is rooted in Aristotle's ethics. There is a "natural" fit between natural law and natural justice—a match made explicit by the virtue of justice as lawfulness. In normative legal theory, it is virtue jurisprudence that can provide the best contemporary expression of the natural law thesis that there is an essential connection between law and justice.

Notes

1. J. L. Mackie, Ethics: Inventing Right and Wrong (Harmondsworth: Penguin, 1977), ch. 1, sec. 9.
2. David Hume, A Treatise on Human Nature (David Norton and Mary Fate Norton eds, Oxford: Clarendon Press, 2000), bk. 3, ch. 1, sec. 1, para 27.
3. See William D. Casebeer, Natural Ethical Facts (Cambridge, MA: MIT Press, 2003).
4. G. E. Moore, Principia Ethica, rev. ed. (Cambridge: Cambridge University Press 1993), pp. 62–69.
5. See David Brink, Moral Realism and the Foundations of Ethics (Cambridge: Cambridge University Press, 1989).
6. Terence Hogan and Mark Timmons, *Troubles for New Wave Moral Semantics: The Open-Question Argument Revisited*, 21 Philosophical Rev. 153 (1992).
7. Something similar to the popular view may once have had philosophical currency. See A. J. Ayer, Language, Truth, and Logic (1946), ch. VI; and Charles L. Stevenson, Ethics and Language (Yale, 1944).
8. T. M. Scanlon, What We Owe to Each Other (Harvard University Press, 1999).
9. Barbara Herman, Moral Literacy 1 (Harvard University Press, 2007).
10. This conception of the virtue of justice bears an affinity to the separation thesis—a central tenet of legal positivism. Cf. H. L. A. Hart, The Concept of Law, 2nd edn (Oxford: Clarendon Press, 1994) (discussing legal positivism and the separation thesis, but not in the context of the virtue of justice).
11. For our purposes, the content of fairness does not need to be specified. The content of fairness could be provided by consequentialist, deontological, or aretaic theories.
12. Of course, there may be some theorists who believe that judges do and should act on the basis of their sense of fairness rather than the law. Moreover, those who adhere to the radical or strong indeterminacy thesis contend that the law never constrains the choices of judges. See Lawrence B. Solum, *On the Indeterminacy Crisis: Critiquing Critical Dogma*, 54 University of Chicago Law Review 462 (1987).
13. Thomas Hobbes, Leviathan (Edwin Curley ed., Indianapolis, IN: Hackett, 1994), p. 76.

14. John Locke, Two Treatises of Government (Peter Laslett ed., Cambridge: Cambridge University Press, 1988), p. 276.
15. Richard Kraut, Aristotle (Oxford: Oxford University Press, 2002), pp. 105–106.
16. Ibid., 106.
17. Ibid., 106.
18. This definition has been offered in slightly different form in prior work. See, e.g. *Virtue Jurisprudence: A Virtue-Centered Theory of Judging,* 34 Metaphilosophy 178 (2003), reprinted in Moral and Epistemic Virtues (Michael Brady and Duncan Prichard eds, Oxford: Blackwell, 2003).
19. The distinction between virtuous and correct decisions is introduced to distinguish a fully virtuous decision (made by a virtuous judge acting from the virtuous) from a merely correct decision (made for the wrong reasons). In order to be legally correct, a decision need only be the one that would have been made by a virtuous judge, it need not be made for the right reason. In order for a decision to be virtuous, it must be both correct and made for the right reasons.
20. Philippa Foot, Natural Goodness (Oxford: Oxford University Press, 2003).
21. Michael Thompson, *The Representation of Life* in *Virtues and Reasons* (Rosalind Hursthouse, Gavin Lawrence, and Warren Quinn eds, Oxford: Clarendon Press, 1995), corrected version available at http://www.pitt.edu/~mthompso/1LIFE.doc; *The Living Individual and its Kind,* 21 Behavioral and Brain Sciences 591–592 (1998); *Apprehending Human Form*in Modern Moral Philosophy (A. O'Hear ed., Cambridge: Cambridge University Press, 2004), pp. 47–74, available at http://www.pitt.edu/~mthompso/ansco652.doc; Michael Thompson, Three Degrees of Natural Goodness, http://www.pitt.edu/~ mthompso/three.doc.
22. Foot, *supra,* note 20, 28.
23. See, e.g. Ludwig Wittgenstein, Philosophical Investigations (G. E. M. Anscombe and R. Rhees eds, trans. G. E. M. Anscombe, Oxford: Blackwell, 1953), pp. 371, 373; see also Anat Biletzki and Anat Matar, *Ludwig Wittgenstein* in Stanford Encyclopedia of Philosophy (Summer 2005 Edition) (Edward N. Zalta ed., URL: http://plato.stanford.edu/archives/sum2005/entries/wittgenstein/ (visited September 26, 2006).
24. Thompson, Three Degrees, *supra,* note 21, 2.
25. Ibid., 5.
26. Bernard Williams, *Justice as a Virtue* in Essays on Aristotle's Ethics (Amélie Oksenberg Rorty ed., Berkeley, CA: University of California Press, 1980), pp. 196–197.
27. Ibid., 197 (emphasis in original).
28. *See infra* Section 3.2.1, The Intuitive Idea: Justice as a Natural Virtue for Language-Using Rational Social Creatures.

7
Virtue, Vice, and Criminal Liability

Antony Duff

1. Explanatory note

This is an edited version of a longer paper, from which I have excised the first three sections. Section 1 noted the recurrent and familiar yearning among criminal law theorists for a grand, unitary theory of criminal liability—a yearning both admirable and dangerous—and the way in which it has recently taken an Aristotelian turn.[1]

Section 2 sketched the context from which this Aristotelian turn emerged, in particular the controversies between "choice" theories of criminal liability[2] and their "character" theory opponents.[3] An Aristotelian virtue-based theory might hope to do justice to the considerations that motivated a rejection of "choice" theories, whilst avoiding the problems of the Humean conception of character on which "character" theorists had typically relied.

Section 3 tackled an important preliminary question: when it is said that criminal liability should be grounded in choice or in character, is this to say that choice, or character, should be the *object* of criminal liability, or a *condition* of criminal liability? That is, are we to be held criminally liable for our criminal choices, or for our defective character traits; or are we to be held criminally liable for something else, on condition that it is suitably related to a choice or to a character trait—for instance for a criminal action on condition that it flowed from choice, or on condition that it reflected a defective character trait?[4] Although theorists often talk as if they intend choice, or character, to be the proper object of liability, I suggest that it would be more plausible to see them as possible conditions of liability for something else, in particular for actions: partly because, as I have argued elsewhere, it is more plausible to see action as the primary object of criminal liability;[5] and partly because that enables the character theorist to sidestep problems about our responsibility for our characters.[6]

In the remainder of the chapter, which is reprinted here, I first (Section 2) sketch some key features of Aristotle's conception of virtue and vice, to show why the criminal law should not be concerned with virtue and vice in their fully Aristotelian senses. Section 3 then discusses the main ways in which theorists have thought that some (roughly) Aristotelian conception of virtue or vice should nonetheless figure in an account of criminal liability and its conditions. The conclusion, in Section 4, is that whilst we can find a useful role for some etiolated ideas of virtue and vice in explaining some aspects of criminal liability, the grander ambitions of Aristotelian theorists are misguided: criminal liability is not, and should not be, generally grounded in the manifestation of anything like Aristotelian vice.

2. Aristotelian virtue and vice

Those who look to Aristotle as inspiration for a virtue-based account of criminal liability are appealing to a particular, and particularly rich, conception of virtue and vice. We should note some of its central features.[7]

First, Aristotle's account gave a central role to the "*pathe*"—emotions, feelings, appetites, and desires—as partly constitutive of human excellence and flourishing. The *pathe* are not merely non-rational forces which by "reason" must quell or resist (on a crudely Kantian model), or serve as a "slave" (on the Humean model):[8] they are aspects of our rational nature, which can be so structured by our rational grasp of the good that they come to "speak . . . with the same voice as" reason;[9] they involve some (albeit often inchoate or ill-formed) evaluative conception of their object. The *pathe* can of course be irrational: they can portray as valuable what even the agent himself recognizes is not valuable; an irrational fear portrays its object as dangerous and fearful (worth fearing) when, as even the agent might recognize, it is not. What makes such *pathe* irrational, however, is not that they are *pathe*, but rather that they are misguided or misdirected *pathe*,[10] which embody an ill-founded or irrational evaluation of their object; and we can hope to remedy them by ordinary methods of rational argument.

This Aristotelian conception of the *pathe* is a clear ancestor of, sometimes the inspiration for, more recent accounts of emotions as having an essential cognitive or evaluative dimension—as rational, rather than non-rational, aspects of our psychology.[11] It has also inspired recent attempts to give the emotions a more significant role in analyses of the grounds of criminal liability,[12] and it could offer support to theorists who seek a partial, in principle rationale for criminal punishment in the rational propriety of such emotions as anger and resentment.[13] Of more relevance here, however, is the difference that this conception makes to Aristotle's own account of virtue and vice.

For, second, "virtue" and "vice" do not constitute an exhaustive classification of ethically significant conditions: they rather mark the end points of a spectrum of four possible kinds of states of character, the other two of which are *enkrateia* (self-control, or "continence" in more traditional translations) and *akrasia* (weakness of will or "incontinence").[14]

In the person of true virtue, reason and passion "speak with the same voice"; his/her actions manifest an integrated unity of reason and passion. For virtue consists not merely in a reliable disposition to act appropriately, or to deliberate and act appropriately, but also in dispositions of feeling and appetite: a virtuous person's emotions and appetites are oriented toward, and structured by his/her understanding of, the good, so that what he/she feels or wants is appropriate to his/her situation; and his/her actions express those appropriate emotions and appetites. He/she therefore does not have to resist temptation, or overcome contrary feeling or inclination, in order to act as he/she sees he/she should, since there is nothing in his/her character that would motivate him or her against what is appropriate. Finally, virtue of character both enables, and is structured and guided by, practical wisdom—the rational excellence by means of which we can recognize the good and what we must do to achieve it; and since the variegated and complex circumstances of human life cannot be captured by any set of rules, practical wisdom requires a well-trained, virtuous "eye of the soul" to discern the good and thus to guide action:[15] which is to say that true virtue also involves appropriate dispositions of thought, of attention, and of observation.

The "self-controlled" person also manages to act appropriately, and does so for the right reason in that he/she does so because he/she sees it to be appropriate. His/her actions, however, are not wholehearted in the way that those of the virtuous person are, since he/she has contrary passions or appetites that he/she must resist in order to do what is right. Faced by someone in need whom it would be appropriate to help, the virtuous person is at once or spontaneously moved to help by the compassion he/she feels—a compassion structured by his/her recognition of the other's need, of the appropriateness of helping, and of what would help.[16] In the same situation the immediate response of the self-controlled person might be irritation, or contempt, or an inclination to turn away: but he/she realizes that that response is inappropriate, and that he/she should offer help—and so he/she overcomes his/her initial disinclination, and helps as he/she should.[17] But he/she will, or should, see the feelings that he/she must resist not merely as unfortunate obstacles to appropriate action, but as defects of character. They are not vices, since he/she does not identify himself/herself with them: but they show him/her to be ethically lacking, since they are an ethically inadequate response—a response which portrays the needy person not (as the compassionate eye sees them) as a fellow being whom he/she can and must help, but as an irritant, an intrusion, an annoyance. This is not to deny that a self-controlled person merits admiration and praise for his/her successful struggle to overcome his/her own feelings and to do what he/she sees to be right; nor is it to say that we, or he/she, should *blame* him/her for those feelings (since it might not be just to hold her responsible for them). But it is to say that he/she is ethically defective in a way that the truly virtuous person is not: for his/her passions are not unequivocally structured by an appropriate conception of the good; they fail—even though he/she does not ultimately fail—to recognize the other's humanity.

A weak-willed person likewise lacks the unity of reason and feeling that characterizes the person of true virtue: although he/she does in some sense recognize and aspire to the good, he/she has emotions and appetites which tempt him/her away from the good. But, unlike the self-controlled person, the weak-willed person gives in to, or is conquered by, that temptation: he/she does what he/she in some sense knows to be wrong. This is not the place for a discussion of the problem of weakness of will—of whether it really is possible to act voluntarily in a way that I truly think is wrong or irrational: all we need note here is that whilst a weak-willed person culpably does wrong, and is motivated by ethically inappropriate emotions or appetites, he/she is different from the truly vicious person. For a vicious person can display, as does the virtuous person, a unity of reason and passion, and a wholehearted commitment to his/her actions—whereas neither self-controlled nor weak-willed agents are thus wholehearted, since both act out of inner conflict. The trouble with the vicious person is that he/she is wholeheartedly oriented toward evil rather than good; his/her reason and his/her passions mutually reinforce each other's misdirection.

Aristotelian virtue and vice are thus richly complex conditions of the soul. To determine whether someone is truly virtuous or merely self-controlled, or whether he/she is truly vicious, or merely weak-willed, we need to examine not just his/her behavioral dispositions to act rightly or wrongly, nor just his/her deliberative dispositions—the kinds of reasons by which his/her actions are guided: we must examine his/her emotional and appetitive dispositions too, the patterns of feeling and desire which help to constitute his/her character. We might then suspect—a suspicion which the following section will show to be fully justified—that the criminal law should not take an interest in virtue or vice in this rich sense: that whatever role the Aristotelian conception can properly play in an account of moral life and action, it can have no proper role in an account of the grounds of criminal liability in anything that purports to be a liberal polity. We surely cannot believe, as Stephen could believe, that "criminal law is in the nature of a persecution of the grosser forms of vice,"[18] at least or especially if "vice" is understood in its Aristotelian sense; or that the criminal law should serve "the greater good of humanity...by promoting virtue,"[19] at least or especially if "virtue" is understood in its Aristotelian sense.

It might be objected at this point that I am demanding too much of a virtue theorist of the criminal law: that we need not mobilize the entire Aristotelian apparatus to find a useful role for notions, even roughly Aristotelian notions, of virtue and vice in explaining and grounding criminal liability. That is obviously true: there are non-Aristotelian conceptions of virtue and vice; and we can properly make use of some aspects of an Aristotelian account without taking on board the whole structure. An important general question does arise here, however, about the role or ambitions of "virtue theory" in relation to criminal liability.

We could make it a truism that anyone who commits what a (just) system of criminal law (justifiably) defines as a crime, without what the law should recognize as a justification or an excuse, displays some vice, or lack of virtue: for a virtuous citizen would never act thus—he/she would be reliably disposed not to act thus; in acting thus the offender displays a lack of civic virtue, or the presence of a civic vice. But this would make the reference to virtue and vice a merely rhetorical flourish: the notions would be doing no substantive work in explaining or in grounding criminal liability. For, first, "virtue" and "vice" are now purely behavioral notions: vice simply consists in culpably wrongful action. Second, that the offender lacks virtue or has a vice is now simply entailed by the prior finding that he/she culpably committed a crime: the reference to virtue or vice neither explains nor grounds his/her culpability.

If "virtue theory" is to make a substantial rather than a merely rhetorical difference to our understanding of criminal liability, it must give "virtue" and "vice" more substantial meanings and a more substantive role than this. In the following section, I turn finally to the question of whether it can do so.

3. What role(s) for virtue or vice?

The question then is this: what substantive roles, if any, can be played by substantial notions of virtue and vice in explaining or in grounding criminal liability? I will work through several possible roles, drawing both on the role of virtue and vice in moral thought, and on the claims made by theorists who want to give virtue and vice a central role in criminal law theory.

3.1 Constituting the character of the agent

The most familiar role for notions of virtue and vice in moral thought is as determinants, not of right action or of proper deliberation, but of moral goodness or badness of character. A good person, we might say, is not just one who reliably does what is right; nor even, if we are unpersuaded by the austerities of Kantianism as it is usually portrayed, one who reliably does the right thing for the right reason, or because he/she sees it to be right. The good person will also have appropriate dispositions of feeling, of attention, of observation: he/she will notice morally relevant features of the world around him/her; he/she will attend to them, and to other people, in the appropriate spirit; his/her appetites and emotions will express his/her conception of the right and the good.[20] Nor are these aspects of goodness valuable only because they make it more likely that their possessor will reliably identify and do the right thing: they are valuable as constituting the person's wholehearted orientation toward the good. Similarly, vice is a matter not just of acting wrongly, or of acting for the wrong kinds of reason, but of failures of feeling (the lack of appropriate feeling, the presence of inappropriate feeling), attention, and observation.

Such a view gives substantial notions of virtue and vice a substantive role in explaining moral goodness and badness; they are not analyzed in behavioral terms; their ascription is not simply an inference from the agent's (even intentional or deliberate) actions. But it is also quite ill-suited to ground an argument that criminal liability should depend on, or should be explained by reference to, vice or lack of virtue: not even the most aspirational perfectionist is likely to want to give the criminal law this kind of interest in its citizens' virtues or vices.

We can show this quite simply (and without having to spell out the liberal ideals which would figure in a more detailed argument) by noting how implausible it would be to say that the criminal law should attend to the distinctions between virtue and self-control, and between weakness of will and vice. Such distinctions are, as we saw, crucial to Aristotle's account of virtue and vice, and any substantial notions of virtue and vice will incorporate some account of the proper role of emotions and appetites: but they are surely not relevant to the criminal law.

The distinction between virtue and self-control could not be generally relevant, since so long as we do not commit what the law defines as crimes, the law has no interest in why we do not commit them—in whether our non-criminal conduct expresses virtue, self-control, a self-interested concern to avoid sanctions, or whatever. Nor, however, is it relevant in those contexts in which the law might attend more closely to agents' reasons for what they do. For even those who argue that the courts should attend to the defendant's reasons for action in determining whether he can avail himself of a justificatory defense do not think that the law should require virtue rather than self-control—for instance, that one who pleads a justifying necessity must show that he/she did not have to resist a cowardly temptation not to do what he/she saw needed to be done.[21] Even if we agree that certain kinds of excuse work by showing that the defendant lived up to "the standards of character which were demanded of [her],"[22] she need not show that she exhibited virtue as distinct from self-control.

Nor is the distinction between vice and weakness of will relevant to criminal liability: it cannot plausibly be argued that one whose commission of a crime exhibited weakness of will rather than true Aristotelian vice should therefore be acquitted, or should be convicted only of a lesser offense. Whether the offense is serious (murder, rape, and so on), or relatively minor (such as many driving offenses, or petty theft), we can imagine it being committed either through weakness of will by one who gives in to a temptation that he knows, in some sense, he/she should resist, or through vice by one who is wholeheartedly involved in the wrong he/she does: but both commit, and should be convicted of, the same offense. It might be argued that the distinction does become relevant at the stage of sentencing: that someone who gave in to temptation in a moment of tragic weakness deserves a lighter punishment than one whose commission of the crime reflected his own corrupt values; and perhaps that this helps to explain the idea that the offender's remorse entitles him/her to some mitigation of sentence (for the weak-willed offender is more likely than the vicious offender to be remorseful), and that prior criminal record can make a harsher punishment appropriate (for the vicious offender is more likely to be a regular offender). But neither remorse nor lack of prior record are reliable indications of weakness of will as distinct from vice: a vicious offender could be remorseful; a weak-willed offender can be weak-willed often enough in a particular way to collect an impressive criminal record.

Perhaps the difference between a vicious and a weak-willed commission of just the same crime could still bear appropriately on sentencing decisions. I think, however, that what is at stake here is better interpreted as a difference in the character of the actions that constitute the crime, than as a difference in the character of the agents who commit them: what justifies the harsher punishment for the "vicious" assailant is the viciousness of the attack itself, not of his underlying character. This leads us to the next possible role for virtue and vice.

3.2 Constituting the character of the action

Sometimes the moral character of an action (if not its character as straightforwardly right or wrong, at least its character as morally appropriate or inappropriate) is determined in part by the attitude it expresses or by the spirit in which it is done.

This is especially true of expressive actions, whose meaning lies to a significant extent in the emotion or attitude they communicate. If I go to visit my sick aunt, the value of my action lies largely in the sympathetic concern that it expresses, or purports to express. Perhaps I feel no such concern: perhaps I undertake this (as I see it) boring, irritating, or unpleasant visit just to keep my place as a beneficiary in her will.[23] My action is then a pretense, a lie; and whilst we can sometimes talk of doing "the right deed for the wrong reason," we might well not want to say this here, even if my aunt is actually cheered up by my successfully deceptive visit: the moral character and worth of my action is at least vitiated by the fact that it flows from greed, rather than constituting a genuine expression of my love and sympathy. So too, what makes a failure to acknowledge a colleague so hurtful and wrong might be the attitude it manifests: of disdain or contempt, of hatred, or even just of indifference.

Sometimes we will describe the attitude or spirit that is displayed in an action in terms of specific virtues or vices. We might see the (dis)value of an action as lying partly or primarily in its courageous, or cowardly, character; in its honesty or its dishonesty; in its kindness or its callousness. Such moral descriptions also break down the distinction between "the right deed" and "the right reason": the action takes its own moral character from the reasons for which, or the spirit in which, it was done.

I do not suggest that this is true across the moral board. In some cases, we might indeed think that an action has no moral worth if it is not done in the right spirit: I should perhaps not visit my aunt at all if I can't visit her out of loving concern. In other cases we might think that the action should still be done, or that it is better that it is done, although its worth is vitiated by its lack of appropriate motivation: at least the homeless person has the money to pay for a room, even if the worth of the gift is seriously qualified by the disdainful spirit or Hobbesian motive of self-aggrandizement from which the giver acted.[24] But in yet other cases, especially perhaps those in which we can talk of what is owed as a matter of justice, the rightness of the deed is more sharply distinguishable from the agent's motive or reason for doing it, and there is then more room to judge the deed as right whilst judging the agent as morally lacking. The debt is paid, the promise is kept, the right grade or the right verdict is given; perhaps even the life is saved: the action is thus right, even if the agent's motives for it are quite disreputable.[25] So too, the moral wrongness of an action is often distinguishable from the motives or reasons for which it was done.

What then of the criminal law? It is equally implausible that the criminal wrongfulness of criminal actions is generally constituted, even partly, by the attitudes or motives they display. The agent's intention might often, if not always, be partly constitutive of the wrong for which he/she is convicted:[26] but the vicious attitudes, motives, or character traits that might be displayed in the action do not generally help to constitute its criminal wrongfulness. This is true of both serious and more trivial offenses: wounding, serious arson attacks, robberies, or burglaries do not take their basic character as criminal wrongs from the attitudes or motives of those who perpetrate them. A vicious motive might aggravate the wrong that the offender commits, if it is displayed in the character of the action that constitutes the crime: but it is not essential to the constitution of the action as a crime. Perhaps sometimes, however, the very identification of an action as a criminal wrong requires reference to something like vice. Gardner argues that in defining theft in terms of dishonesty, the law builds "a standard of character" into the determination of criminality: for part of what makes the thief's action criminally wrongful is its dishonesty, and in judging its (dis)honesty, we apply "exactly the same standard" as that by which we judge a person's (dis)honesty.[27] Similarly, it might be argued that the American doctrine of "depraved-heart murder," which defines one type of murder in terms of the callous or wicked indifference to human life displayed in the defendant's action,[28] defines the wrong (as murder rather than as manslaughter) in terms that make essential reference to the vice displayed by the defendant.

If vice is relevant in such cases, it is relevant as partly constituting the intentional object of liability, not merely as a condition of liability: the defendant's action counts as murder, not as a lesser wrong of manslaughter, because of the wicked indifference that it displayed; or as theft because of the dishonesty it displayed. So can we say that in such cases as these vice is substantively relevant as a ground of criminal liability?

We could say this, but only if we recognize just how etiolated the notion of vice becomes in such contexts. It is thus etiolated not just because it does not attend to the diachronic aspect of vice as a lasting character trait (one vicious action does not constitute its agent as a vicious person),[29] but because it does not distinguish vice from weakness of will. The dishonesty that is displayed in a person's theft, even the "wicked indifference" that his fatal attack displayed, cannot of course (if he/she is a responsible agent at all) constitute nothing more than a momentary lapse which has no connection with any persisting aspects of his/her character: but it could reflect a tendency or a temptation which he usually manages to resist because he/she sees that he/she should; it could, that is, display a momentary weakness of will in an agent who, whilst not virtuous, is generally self-controlled rather than vicious. More generally, vice in any substantive sense of the term involves dispositions not just of action, but of feeling, of motivation, of response, of thought and attention: but the notion of vice in play in these criminal contexts is a far more limited conception. In determining whether the defendant's action was dishonest, we are not interested in whether the appropriation of another's property appeared to him as a temptation which he should (and perhaps even tried) to resist, but to which he gave in; or as an option to be assessed simply in terms of whether or not he could get away with it (we are not, that is to say, interested in his conception of the good). We are not interested in whether he/she was struck down by remorse after the act, or simply enjoyed his/her gains. We are not interested in whether he/she spotted this chance to steal because he/she is sensitive to, even on the alert for, such dishonest opportunities, or because it was such an obvious possibility that even normally honest people might have been tempted.

We are not, that is, interested in whether he/she is a dishonest person: for all the things we are not interested in when determining his/her criminal liability are matters that bear crucially on whether we should ascribe the vice of dishonesty to him/her.[30]

In so far as criminal liability depends and is focused on such matters as the dishonesty of the agent's action, or the attitudes displayed in his action, it is focused on what lies deeper not only than his overt behavior, but also than his choices; it is focused on motives, attitudes, and spirit which are, we might naturally say, aspects of character. But the "character" at issue here is, we should also say, the character or meaning of the action rather than that of the agent: the criminal law should still not make vice, as a substantial feature of the agent's character, either part of the intentional object or a condition of criminal liability. This distinction, between the character of the agent and the character of his/her action, is of course far from sharp: the motives, attitudes, and concerns that help determine the action's character are the motives, attitudes, and concerns of its agent, and would properly figure in any adequate character-based narrative of his/her life. The distinction is thus not between two sharply separate realms of "inner" and "outer," or of "character" and "action"; it is rather between deeper and shallower, or between more and less substantial, interpretations of the person and his/her agency. It is still, however, a distinction that must matter to anyone who wants to set liberal limits on the extent to which the criminal law should be allowed to inquire or intrude into our lives.

3.3 Grounding defenses

Perhaps we can find a larger and more substantive role for notions of vice or virtue, not in the definitions of offenses, but in the articulation of certain defenses: perhaps most notably in explaining the defense of duress and the partial defense of provocation, but more generally in explaining defenses in which the figure of the "reasonable person" plays a criterial role.[31]

Sometimes the reasonable person plays a purely evidential role: that such a person would have foreseen x as an outcome, or would not have believed that p, is evidence from which the jury might properly infer that this defendant foresaw x, or did not believe that p; but it is still open to the defendant to offer evidence or arguments to try to persuade the jury that he might not have foreseen x, or might have believed that p.[32] In these contexts, the reasonable person could be seen simply as the statistically or empirically ordinary person. But in other contexts, the reasonable person plays a criterial role. That a reasonable person would have resisted the kind of threat to which this defendant gave in, or would not have been so provoked as to lose their self-control by that which this defendant claimed provoked him/her into a fatally violent loss of self-control, is not merely (rebuttable) evidence that this defendant could have resisted that threat, or could have controlled himself/herself: it entails the failure of his/her defense.[33] In these contexts, the reasonable person sets a normative standard against which the defendant is judged—he/she is convicted if he/she fails to attain that standard; and as a normative exemplar of this kind, the reasonable person must be understood in normative, rather than merely empirical or statistical terms. We might then plausibly suggest that the reasonable person in such contexts is a person who has and displays those modest civic virtues that the law can properly demand of its citizens—and that those virtues should be understood in roughly Aristotelian terms. I will focus here on the example of duress: but we could offer an analogous account of provocation, though it would need to be complicated to deal with the fact that provocation is only a partial defense.

The reasonable person (the reasonable citizen) fears what is fearful; the threat of what is seriously fearful, because seriously harmful (death or serious injury to oneself or those whom he/she loves, for instance), will make him/her very afraid. He/she also has a proper concern and respect for the interests that the criminal law protects: citizens' interests in life, security, property, and so on; the state's proper interest in such things as the administration of justice. He/she also has a suitable degree of courage—a willingness to face harm or danger for the sake of what is truly valuable. Given those virtues, he/she would often refuse to commit an offense even if threatened with harm by someone who tried to force him/her into committing it: if the harm threatened was not serious, or if the offense was very much more serious than the threatened harm. But he/she would sometimes give in to such a threat. In some such cases this would be because giving in would be justified: at least permissible, if not positively the right thing to do.[34] In other cases, giving in would not be justified: a person of true courage, or a person of such moral strength that his/her proper concern for the interests that the crime would injure would not be undermined even by this threat, would not give in. But the law should not (it cannot reasonably) demand that kind of courage or moral strength of its citizens, on pain of criminal conviction and punishment if they fail to display it: it should set only modest, rather than heroic or saintly, standards for us, and condemn us only if we display a vice which involves the lack even of the modest kind of virtue—of our moral strength, of concern for legally protected interests—that meeting those standards requires.[35]

There are in fact two ways in which duress, on this kind of account, can excuse. First, the threat might be so terrifying that its victim's rational agency is in effect undermined: he/she is so terrified, so destroyed, by the threat of further torture that he/she is no longer capable of the kind of practical reasoning that would ground a rational decision to resist, or to give in; all he/she can think of is how to prevent further agony. Even in this extreme case the reasonable person sets a normative standard. If a reasonable person would not have lost control of himself/herself as this defendant did in response to that kind of threat, we have to judge that in thus losing control of himself/herself the defendant displayed a lack of even the modest level of virtue that the law properly demands of us: an excessive concern for his/her own safety, or an excessive fear of what was not that fearful, or a lack of concern for the interests that his/her action injured. Second, however, this kind of utter loss of control is not plausibly involved in all cases of exculpatory duress: often, the defendant was still capable of, and still exercised, practical reason. He/she is then excused if and because resistance would have required a greater degree of courage or commitment than the law can properly demand of us; if, that is, in giving in he/she did not display a vicious lack of even that minimal level of civic virtue that the law can demand of us, and that is exemplified in the reasonable person.[36]

On this analysis vice (or a lack of even minimal virtue) presumably figures as a condition of criminal liability rather than as part of its intentional object. That is, the defendant is to be convicted and punished not for his cowardice, or lack of strength or commitment, but for the crime that he commits under threat (for perjury, for theft, or whatever), on condition that his commission of that crime manifested the relevant vice or lack of virtue. (In the previous sub-section, by contrast, vice appeared to figure as part of the intentional object of liability.) But does this give a substantial notion of vice a substantive role in grounding criminal liability?

Defenses of this kind do provide the most plausible focus for the virtue theorists' claims: but they still give only a limited role to etiolated notions of vice and virtue.

The role is limited because even if we should explain these defenses in terms of the vice displayed by the defendant, we cannot conclude that vice is a generally necessary condition of criminal liability: the most we can say is that in those—relatively unusual—situations in which one of these defenses is in play, the relevant kind of vice is a condition of liability.

We might be misled about how etiolated the notions of virtue and vice are in this context by the fact that we talk of the "reasonable person": for we might then think that what we must do is compare the defendant, as a person, with the reasonable person, and that we will thus be involved in judging virtue and vice as substantial traits of the agent. But this is just one of the ways in which talk of the "reasonable person" is misleading. What concerns the court in such cases is, essentially, the question of whether this defendant's response and action were within the (fairly generous) boundaries of the "reasonable": was his/her fear reasonable, was his/her response to it reasonable, was it reasonable to give in to that threat? We are, therefore, still concerned with the character of the action rather than with the character of the agent—as is partly shown by the fact that the distinction between vice and weakness of will is as irrelevant here as it is in the other legal contexts we have discussed. Once again, we must look beyond or behind the agent's overt behavior and his/her choices: we must look to the emotions and concerns by which he/she was moved, and judge them to be reasonable or unreasonable. But in doing this we are not trying to reach some judgment on his character, nor do we attend to aspects of his character which would be crucially relevant to the question of whether he/she was virtuous or vicious.[37]

3.4 Virtue, vice, and practical reasoning

We turn finally to the most ambitious of recent Aristotelian accounts of criminal liability as grounded in vice. The purpose of law, argues Huigens, is "to promote the greater good of humanity," and "[t]he criminal law serves that end by promoting virtue." It promotes virtue "by inquiring into the quality of practical judgment displayed by the accused in his actions": what grounds liability is the offender's "faulty reasoning," and what the criminal law "condemns" is "not just harm, but the lack of judgment that results in harm."[38]

Huigens grounds this account of inculpation in Aristotle, but focuses more on Aristotle's discussion of practical reasoning and practical wisdom (*phronesis*) than on his discussions of the virtues of character. Virtue of character, properly speaking, involves practical wisdom; it informs and is informed by the agent's conception of the good, his/her understanding of how that good can be achieved, and his/her perception of what is appropriate in the situations in which he/she finds himself/herself. What inculpates a person, what makes it appropriate to blame and punish him/her as a criminal, is the radical lack of such virtuous practical wisdom that his/her actions manifest: his/her misconception of the good, his/her improper or misguided choice of ends, and his/her faulty practical reasoning. The jury or fact-finder must also exercise *phronesis* in judging the defendant. Cases cannot be decided by the mechanical application of rigid rules, but require sensitive attention to the particularities of the individual case. The fact-finder must in the end decide whether this defendant "made the right choices in her particular situation,"[39] or whether he/she themselves "would have acted in the same way as the accused under the given circumstances,"[40] which involves the exercise of the fact-finder's own practical wisdom.

Now Huigens suggests that "lack of judgment" is a central aspect of the intentional object of criminal liability—it is part of what the offender is condemned for.[41] It might, however, be better to portray lack of judgment as a condition of liability—at least if this account is to be, as Huigens intends, "descriptive of the criminal law as it stands,"[42] and even, I think, if it is to be at all plausible as a prescriptive account. The murderer, the rapist, the thief, might display a lack of practical judgment in committing their crimes: but they are and should properly be convicted and punished for those crimes, for what they did to their victims, not for their lack of practical judgment.

Is "lack of judgment" then a substantial condition of criminal liability? If offenders who are properly convicted have culpably done what they should not do, it does of course follow that there was something amiss with their practical reasoning: someone exercising *phronesis* would not have acted thus, from which it follows that someone who culpably acted thus could not have been exercising *phronesis*. But this is so far to show only that "lack of judgment" can be inferred from criminal liability, not that it constitutes a substantial condition of liability.

Furthermore, Huigens appears to ascribe to offenders a more determinate kind of "lack of judgment" than is warranted; he ascribes vice, though offenders might only exhibit weakness of will. He claims, for instance, that "in judging a person guilty we reject his chosen ends as improper," or "reject the particular conception of the good and the scheme of ends that led the actor into the conflict and to the resulting harm," or "reject and condemn their pursuit of those ends or their use of those means."[43] But offenders might commit crimes through weakness of will rather than true Aristotelian vice, and the weak-willed agent does not have a conception of the good that we should reject, nor has he/she chosen improper ends; his/her trouble is that he/she fails to act in accordance with his/her own conception of the good or his/her own rational ends. Indeed, in an Aristotelian sense of "choice" (as Aristotle's term "*prohairesis*" is often translated) a weak-willed agent does not choose his/her action at all: for choice in this sense is a product of rational deliberation about how to achieve the good as one conceives it; and the trouble with a weak-willed agent is that his/her actions are not structured by any such rational deliberation.[44] So those convicted of the same offense might manifest quite different kinds of defect in their practical reasoning: a vicious offender reasons efficiently from bad ends, from a misconception of the good, to his/her criminal action;[45] a weak-willed offender either fails to complete the appropriate practical syllogism that would lead him/her (in the light of his/her own conception of the good) not to offend, or fails to act in accordance with his/her own practical reasoning.[46] This adds more force to the suggestion that faulty practical reasoning is an inference from criminal liability rather than either a constituent or a condition of it.

Finally, Huigens exaggerates the extent to which fact-finders need *phronesis* if they are to determine guilt, or to which citizens need *phronesis* if they are to avoid committing crimes. A Dworkinian judge might need *phronesis* to carry through his/her Herculean task, and we must of course hope that both fact-finders and citizens will be moderately sensible: but fact-finders will not usually have to determine whether the defendant "made the right choices in her particular situation," or make a "judgment...about the right course of action in the circumstances of the accused";[47] nor will citizens usually need *phronesis* to distinguish criminal from non-criminal actions amongst the options facing them. It is true that, although there are very many cases in which fact-finders and citizens can simply read the criminality of a given action off from such authoritative guidance as is available to them, there are also many cases in which they need to make a judgment about what it is or would be "reasonable" do to: for instance about whether it is or was "reasonable" to take this risk, when the issue is one of recklessness; about whether it is or was "reasonable" to give in to this threat, when duress is the issue; about whether it is or was "reasonable" to use this kind of force in response to this kind of supposed attack, when self-defense is the issue; and so on. But the judgment that a particular action is in this sense "reasonable" is not the judgment that it is "the right course of action in the circumstances"; it is the judgment that the action falls inside, rather than outside, the boundaries of the legally reasonable—and those boundaries are quite generous. We might need *phronesis* if we are to decide what is the right or appropriate course of action in a difficult situation; but we do not need *phronesis*, as a distinctive and quite demanding intellectual and moral excellence, if we are simply to determine whether a particular course of action is "reasonable" in the sense that it is not so clearly wrong or inappropriate that the law should count it as unreasonable.

4. A very modest conclusion

The conclusion of this chapter is both modest and deflationary: etiolated conceptions of virtue and vice can play a limited role in some contexts in an account of the conditions (sometimes also of the intentional objects) of criminal liability. We should not conclude that Aristotelian virtue theory contributes nothing substantial to our understanding of the grounds of criminal liability: but what it can contribute is less both in content (because the relevant conceptions of virtue and vice are much thinner than Aristotle's) and in scope (because it is only in particular and limited contexts that it is useful to talk of virtue or vice) than some Aristotelian theorists would claim.

If that is right, there are two possible ways forward. We could, first, abandon any hope of or aspiration toward a unitary theory of criminal liability, in favor of much more piecemeal, particularist accounts of the different forms, structures, and grounds of liability that we find in existing systems, and that we would expect to find in any acceptable system, of criminal law. Or we could, second, look for some other unitary theory, organized around some other central concept. In more ambitious moods, I still incline toward the second route, and to look to the concept (or a conception) of action to provide the unifying idea—that criminal liability is, at least paradigmatically, imposed not for choices, or character traits, or vices, but for actions.[48] In taking that route we would of course need to take due notice of the various ways in which actions—both in general and as intentional objects of criminal liability—differ in structure, in complexity, in depth of meaning; and at the same time guard against the danger that, in trying to do justice to that diversity, we so empty the concept of action of substantial content that it comes to mean "what defendants are properly held liable for," turning the claim that "actions" are the intentional objects of criminal liability into an empty and uninteresting truism.[49] These are, however, matters for another occasion than this.

Notes

1. For examples of Aristotelian accounts of the grounds of criminal liability (by no means all of which aspire to provide grand, unitary theories), see C. Finkelstein, "Duress: A Philosophical Account of the Defense in Law", 37

Ariz. L. Rev. 251 (1995); K. Huigens, 'Virtue and Inculpation', 108 *Harv. L. Rev.* 1423 (1995), 'Virtue and Criminal Negligence', *1 Buff. Crim. L. Rev.* 431 (1998); D. Kahan and M. Nussbaum, 'Two Conceptions of Emotion in Criminal Law,' *96 Colum. L. Rev.* 269 (1996); J. Gardner, "The Gist of Excuses", *1 Buff. Crim. L. Rev.* 575 (1998); V. Tadros, 'The Characters of Excuse', 21 *Oxford J. Legal Stud.* 495 (2001). See also H. I. Feldman, 'Prudence, Benevolence, and Negligence: Virtue Ethics and Tort Law', 74 Chicago-Kent Law Rev. 1431 (2000); L. Solum, 'Virtue Jurisprudence: A Virtue-Centred Theory of Judging', 34 *Metaphilosophy* 178 (2003).

2. See for example H. L. A. Hart, *Punishment and Responsibility* (1968); A. J. Ashworth, 'Belief, Intent and Criminal Liability' in *Oxford Essays in Jurisprudence* (J. Eekelaar and J. Bell eds, 3rd Series, 1987); M. S. Moore, 'Choice, Character, and Excuse', 7 *Soc. Phil. Pol.* 29 (1990).
3. See for example M. D. Bayles, 'Character, Purpose, and Criminal Responsibility', 1 *Law & Phil.* 5 (1982); G. Vuoso, Background, Responsibility, and Excuse, 96 Yale L. J. 1661 (1987); N. Lacey, *State Punishment*, chapter 3 (1988). For discussion see J. Horder, '*Criminal Culpability: The Possibility of a General Theory*', 12 *Law & Phil.* 193 (1993); R. A. Duff, '*Choice, Character and Criminal Liability*', 12 *Law & Phil.* 345 (1993).
4. For versions of this distinction, see Horder, *supra* note 3, at 204–206; D. Husak, 'Does Criminal Liability Require an Act?' in *Philosophy and the Criminal Law* (R. A. Duff ed., 1998), at 67–73.
5. See R. A. Duff, Criminal Attempts, chapters 3.5, 6.3, 8.4, 11.4, 13.4 (1996); 'Action, the Act Requirement and Criminal Liability' in *Agency and Action* (J. Hyman and H. Steward eds, 2004), p. 69.
6. Aristotle, Nicomachean Ethics III.5; See E. Pincoffs, 'Legal Responsibility and Moral Character,' 19 *Wayne L. Rev.* 905 (1973); P. Arenella, 'Character, Choice and Moral Agency', 7 Soc. Phil. Pol. 59 (1990).
7. Following what has unfortunately remained orthodox practice, I will talk of Aristotle's account of 'virtue' and 'vice,' although these are not happy translations of '*arête*' and '*kakia*'; it would be less misleading to talk of 'excellence' and 'defect' of character.
8. D. Hume, *A Treatise of Human Nature*, II.iii.3.
9. *Nicomachean Ethics*, I.13, 1102b28. Even this understates the extent to which 'reason' and "*pathos*" are interwoven in Aristotle: for it becomes clear in Book VI of the *Nicomachean Ethics* that our grasp of the good is partly constituted by our *pathe*; so Aristotle happily defines 'choice' as 'either desiderative reason or ratiocinative desire' (VI.2, 1139b4–1139b5).
10. See B. Williams, 'Morality and the Emotions' in his Problems of the Self (1973) 207, at 224.
11. See for example R. Solomon, *The Passions* (1993); M. Nussbaum, *Upheavals of Thought* (2001).
12. See for example Kahan and Nussbaum, *supra* note 1; J. Horder, Provocation and Responsibility (1992).
13. See for example Murphy's arguments in J. Murphy and J. Hampton, *Forgiveness and Mercy* chapters 1 and 3 (1988); but see Murphy, 'Moral Epistemology, the Retributive Emotions, and the "Clumsy Moral Philosophy" of Jesus Christ' in *The Passions of Law* (S. Bandes ed., 1999) for some apt criticism.

14. I leave aside here two further kinds of state which do not loom large in Aristotle's account: 'superhuman' or 'heroic and divine' virtue, which transcends ordinary human virtue; and 'brutishness,' which falls below ordinary human vice. See Nicomachean Ethics, VII.1. The main features of Aristotle's account are found in Nicomachean Ethics I.13 (on the different aspects of human psychology); II (on the nature of excellence or virtue of character); III.6–12, IV (on the particular virtues); VI (on practical wisdom and its relation to character); and VII.1–10 (on weakness of will).
15. *Nicomachean Ethics*, VI.12, 1144a29–1144a31.
16. Aristotle's list of virtues of character did not include compassion as I have portrayed here; indeed, it would be alien to his conception of a good human life. I use this example to show how an account of virtue which is Aristotelian in its structure need not be Aristotelian in its ethical content.
17. We will see in Section 3 that this is misleading, since the self-controlled person's lack of proper feeling might sometimes qualify the worth of his/her action, or the sense in which he/she acts 'appropriately.'
18. J. F. Stephen, *Liberty, Equality, Fraternity* (1873), p. 152.
19. Huigens, 'Virtue and Inculpation', *supra* note 1, at 1425.
20. For two versions of this thought, one roughly Platonic and one roughly Aristotelian, see I. Murdoch, *The Sovereignty of Good* (1970); L. Blum, *Friendship, Altruism, and Morality* (1980).
21. For two recent useful contributions on either side of this ongoing debate, see J. Gardner, 'Justifications and Reasons' in *Harm and Culpability* (A. P. Simester and A. T. H. Smith eds, 1996); P. Robinson, *Structure and Function in Criminal Law* (1997), pp. 95–124.
22. Gardner, *supra* note 1, at 598; see also J. Dressler, 'Exegesis of the Law of Duress', 62 *S. Cal. L. Rev. 1331, 1334* (1989). I return to these issues later: see *infra* at notes 34–35.
23. More complex is the case in which I overcome my reluctance from a sense of duty (which would involve recognizing my immediate feelings as morally lacking): depending on how the idea of 'duty' figures in my life, we might or might not still be able to see my action as expressing my love and concern for her. See P. Winch, 'Moral Integrity' in his *Ethics and Action* (1972).
24. See T. Hobbes, The Elements of Law, Part I chapter 9.17.
25. 'The right deed' must of course be done intentionally, under the appropriate description—it must not be a matter of mere chance that what the agent did for his/her own purposes happened to be what he/she ought to do.
26. This is another issue that I cannot pursue here: compare Robinson, *supra* note 21, at 129–137, with G. Fletcher, Rethinking Criminal Law (1978), pp. 475–478, 553–554, 695; see also R. A. Duff, 'Rule Violations and Wrongdoings', in *Criminal Law Theory: Doctrines of the General Part* (S. Shute and A. Simester eds, 2002) 47, at 68–74.
27. Gardner, *supra* note 1, at 575–576: see Theft Act, 1968 ss 1–2; contrast Model Penal Code s 223.2.
28. See S. H. Pillsbury, 'Crimes of Indifference', 49 *Rutgers L. Rev*. 105 (1996), pp. 116–123, 174–182; see also G. Gordon, *The Criminal Law of Scotland* (M. Christie ed., 3rd edn, 2000–2001), pp. 286–300.
29. See Gardner, *supra* note 1, p. 575.

30. So Gardner is wrong to say that 'apart from [the] diachronic aspect, the standard by which we judge a person dishonest is exactly the same standard as that by which we judge an action dishonest,' or that a person 'is dishonest if and only if she tends to act dishonestly.' *Id.* There is much more to being a dishonest person than even a persistent tendency to act dishonestly.
31. See for example Huigens, 'Virtue and Inculpation' (*supra* note 1), pp. 1429–1437 (on justifications generally); Finkelstein, *supra* note 1 (on duress); Kahan and Nussbaum, *supra* note 1, at 305–323 (on provocation and 'heat of passion' homicide), pp. 327–333 (on self-defense), pp. 333–338 (on duress); Gardner, *supra* note 1; Tadros, *supra* note 1.
32. This role is implicit in, for instance, Criminal Justice Act 1967 s 8 (given which, the fact that death was a 'natural and probable consequence' of the defendant's action, that is, one that a reasonable person would have foreseen, is nothing more than rebuttable evidence that the defendant foresaw it); and in Sexual Offences (Amendment) Act 1976 s 1(2) (given which, the absence of 'reasonable grounds' for the belief that the victim consented to sexual intercourse, that is, the fact that a reasonable person would not have believed that, is nothing more than rebuttable evidence that this defendant did not believe that); this provision of the 1976 Act was changed by Sexual Offences Act 2003 s 1(1)—see *infra* note 33.
33. See Model Penal Code ss 2.09 ('a person of reasonable firmness' in duress), 210.3 (homicide 'committed under the influence of extreme mental or emotional disturbance for which there is reasonable explanation or excuse'). For a discussion of the 'role of a sober person of reasonable firmness' in duress, see J. Smith and B. Hogan, Criminal Law (10th edn, 2002), pp. 259–262, 369–375; see also *R. v. Howe* [1987] A.C. 417. For a discussion of the role of the reasonable person in provocation, see Smith and Hogan, *supra*, pp. 367–373; *R. v. Duffy* [1949] 1 All E.R. 932; Homicide Act 1957 s 3. See also Sexual Offences Act 2003 s 1(1): the lack of a reasonable belief in the victim's consent is now constitutive of the fault required for rape, rather than merely evidential.
34. I assume here, with Dressler [J. Dressler, 'New Thoughts about the Concept of Justification in the Criminal Law', 32 UCLA L. Rev. 61, 70–75, 80–87 (1984)] that 'justified' conduct includes permissible conduct—and also that duress is sometimes a justification (a bank clerk who hands over his/her employer's money under plausible threat of death is justified in what he/she does).
35. See Dressler, *supra* note 22, pp. 1367, 1373.
36. Very much more needs to be said about duress than I can say here, and in particular about whether the law can properly sometimes demand heroism of us (as English law seems to do, for instance, in denying duress as a defense to murder): but I hope that I have said enough to show how plausible it is to explain duress in terms of virtue and vice.
37. If we focus on the question of whether this agent's response and action were 'reasonable' or not, we might also manage to undercut the interminable and often radically confused debate about which of the particular agent's characteristics should be ascribed to the 'reasonable person'—a debate which has done so much to obfuscate discussions of both duress and provocation.
38. Huigens, 'Virtue and Inculpation' (*supra* note 1), pp. 1424–1425 (footnotes omitted). This is part of a larger 'republican' theory of criminal law, but

I cannot discuss that larger picture here. Nor can I attend to the way in which Huigens has developed his account in more recent articles: see 'The Dead End of Deterrence, and Beyond', 41 *Wm. & Mary L. Rev.* 943 (2000), 'Rethinking the Penalty Phase', 32 *Ariz. St. L. J.* 1195 (2000), 'Solving the Apprendi Puzzle', 90 *Geo. L. J.* 387 (2002).

39. Huigens, 'Virtue and Inculpation' (*supra* note 1), at 1439.
40. *Id.* at 1463.
41. See *supra* text accompanying note 38.
42. Huigens, 'Virtue and Inculpation' (*supra* note 1), at 1427.
43. *Id.* at 1424, 1439, 1458.
44. See Aristotle, *Nicomachean Ethics*, III.2.
45. See *id.* VI.12 (on 'cleverness' as distinct from practical wisdom).
46. See *id.* VII.3, VII.7 (on 'impetuosity' and 'weakness' as two types of weakness of will).
47. Huigens, 'Virtue and Inculpation' (*supra* note 1), at 1439, 1463.
48. See the works cited *supra* note 5. This would not provide a complete account of criminal liability: it would be an account of its intentional objects, but not of the conditions under which we can be held liable for those objects. See Horder, *supra* note 3.
49. Cf. Husak, *supra* note 4, at 93 n. 19, on interpretations of the supposed 'act requirement.'

8
On Aristotelian Criminal Law: A Reply to Duff

Kyron Huigens

1. Introduction

In a recent article entitled Virtue, Vice and Criminal Liability: Do We Want an Aristotelian Criminal Law?, Antony Duff describes a work of mine as "the most ambitious of recent Aristotelian accounts of criminal liability," in a context in which it is plain that "ambitious" is not a good thing.[1] Neither, for that matter, is "Aristotelian." Aristotelian punishment theory attempts to describe the criminal law in terms of virtue. Virtue, for Aristotle, was not adherence to moral duties against one's inclinations, but a quality of exemplary practical judgment by which the agent does right because the right is what he wants to do—not in the sense that he wishes to comply with a rule, but in the sense that his judgment is so well attuned to the good in ordinary affairs that the right course of action and its objectives are desirable to him. I have argued that the justification of punishment turns on an assessment of whether the defendant exhibited a lack of Aristotelian virtue in the conduct that violated the criminal law, because the inculcation of this kind of virtue is a justifying end of the criminal law.[2] Duff finds this theory not only grand and procrustean but also wrong on the merits.

Duff's warning that grand theorizing runs an unusually great risk of procrusteanism seems questionable. When descriptive fidelity should give way to normative reformism (or vice versa) is a judgment call, and one can and should assess a theory for the adequacy of its implicit judgment calls along these lines. The charge of procrusteanism is a way of saying that one's opponent has let his normative aspirations overbalance his descriptive fidelity (or vice versa). But the hazard of procrusteanism in this sense is universal and is not a function of a theory's aspiration to comprehensiveness. On the contrary, it is a hazard of willful, careless, or inept theorizing on any scale.

Let me give an example of a strongly normative theoretical argument, drawn from a comprehensive theory of punishment, that is not procrustean. I have argued in several places that the Federal Sentencing Guidelines ought to be declared unconstitutional because they feature judicial determinations of positive nonintentional fault considerations—a category described below—in violation of the Sixth Amendment jury trial guarantee.[3] Given that thousands of prisoners have been sentenced under the Guidelines over a period of nearly twenty years, whereas positive nonintentional fault is a novel theoretical category that features in a novel theory of punishment, this contention undoubtedly seems like the worst kind of procrusteanism. It is not. The feature of the Guidelines that I believe renders them unconstitutional is a practice—so-called real offense sentencing—that has been consciously rejected by every other jurisdiction that has adopted a determinate sentencing system. It is the feature that, aside from the sheer excessiveness of Guidelines sentences, has drawn the most criticism from judges and scholars. It is the feature of the Guidelines that logically should doom them under the Supreme Court's developing Sixth Amendment jurisprudence. In short, something is seriously amiss with the Guidelines. And yet all attempts to explain precisely what is wrong seem to run aground. Theorists who have identified the objectionable feature of real offense sentencing have not been able to explain why that feature invalidates the practice under the Sixth Amendment.[4] Given this state of affairs, new tools from an ambitious theoretical project seem to be called for. To use them to explain a conclusion that many conscientious, practical-minded lawyers, judges, and scholars have already reached, but only by intuition, is not procrustean. In spite of its strong normativity—its seemingly drastic recommendation and its coming down hard on one side of a controversy instead of ecumenically reconciling opposing views—my argument makes the theoretical bed fit the practical body, not the other way around.

My arguments also respond to others' procrusteanism. The intentional-states account of fault that Glanville Williams and Jerome Hall insisted upon in the course of the Model Penal Code's drafting remains the leading account of criminal fault. In spite of the Code's many concessions to existing practices—with regard to felony murder and intoxication as a defense to recklessness, for example—the Code is fundamentally committed to an intentional-states account of fault. The same is true of the vast majority of criminal law theorists working today. But a consequence of making this assumption is that a huge number of ordinary criminal law doctrines must be treated as paradoxical, unprincipled, or radically unsettled because they simply do not fit the intentional-states paradigm. One can find writers taking such views of criminal negligence, unreasonable mistake in rape, transferred intent, felony murder, depraved heart or malice murder, strict liability, intoxication as a defense to recklessness, mistake regarding justifying circumstances, conditional intent, accomplice liability premised on negligence, and willful ignorance. Having concluded that one of these doctrines is unsustainable, the theorist urges its abolition, recommends a resigned acceptance of reality, or advances an ad hoc solution. I confess that I find this situation unsatisfactory. It seems to me that these are procrustean responses born of a grand theory and that their accumulation and persistence is a reason not only to discard that theory but to develop a better one that is, of necessity, equally comprehensive.

2. Defects in ordinary punishment theory

A quick review of the leading criminal law casebooks reveals that the theory of punishment breaks down into two camps consisting of utilitarian justifications for punishment and retributive justifications for punishment, respectively.[5] This is all wrong. We ought to make some simple, basic distinctions between a theory of punishment, the justification of punishment, and the ends of punishment. A theory of punishment is a general, systematic explanation of our practices. The justification of punishment is one of the standing issues pertaining to our practices that a theory of punishment might explain—among others, such as the nature of criminal fault, the grounds of excuse, and so on. The end of punishment is the reason or reasons why we punish and might also be called punishment's objective or function. (The end of punishment is actually just another issue to be explained by a theory of punishment, but it is one that has assumed a special, if unwarranted, importance. I separate it out here just so we can see the problem of its unwarranted importance.) The problem with the standard casebook formulation of the theory of punishment is that it refers indiscriminately to both utilitarianism (a theory) and retribution (an end) as justifications of punishment, whereas neither of them is any such thing. Utilitarianism might offer a justification of punishment among its other explanations of punishment's features. And retribution is an end of punishment that can be given a utilitarian explanation—according to which it will have no role in punishment's justification.

This is just one corner of a field that, as Duff suggests, is vast and complicated. There are many conceivable ends of punishment: retribution, incapacitation, general deterrence, specific deterrence, rehabilitation, public catharsis, and the internalization of norms, to name the most prominent. Likewise, there are many issues that a theory of punishment should be able to explain, beyond the question of punishment's justification: the nature of wrongdoing, the nature of fault, the ground of the excuses, the nature of justification defenses, the meaning of proportionality in sentencing, and so on. And, finally, there are at least three major traditions in philosophical ethics on which we might want to draw in order to articulate the ends of punishment and to provide explanations of things such as punishment's justification. These are consequentialism (of which utilitarianism is only one variety), deontological morality, and virtue ethics.

The field of punishment theory might be represented graphically this way:

Ends of punishment	**Theories of punishment**	**Issues requiring explanation**
Retribution	Consequentialist	Justification of punishment
Incapacitation	Deontological	Wrongdoing
Specific deterrence	Aretaic	Fault
General deterrence		Justification defenses
Rehabilitation		Excuse defenses
Public catharsis		Proportionality in sentencing
Internalization of norms		

Looking at punishment theory from this perspective, two important points can be made. First, punishment's justification by a primary end is not what defines theories of punishment. In other words, there is no necessary correlation horizontally between the items in the columns on this chart. Casebook authors confuse theory, end, and justification in the way that they do because they assume that a theory of punishment must take some one end of punishment as the primary justification of punishment, and that which end is chosen for this purpose defines each theory. Hence the so-called retributive theory of punishment, which says that punishment is justified by retribution, the so-called deterrence theory of punishment, in which punishment is justified by deterrence, and so on. But a more careful mapping reminds us that the field is more complex. To expand on the example that I have already noted, we can make connections between retribution as an end, consequentialism as a theory, and justification as an issue in need of explanation: consequentialism will deny that retribution has any justifying force—except perhaps derivatively through the consequence of public catharsis, which then becomes the consequentialist's reformulation of the end of retribution. Connections of this kind are concealed by conventional wisdom, which offers a choice between retribution as our theory and justification of punishment or deterrence as our theory and justification of punishment. To map things more carefully makes the simple but clarifying point that whether or not retribution or deterrence is taken to justify punishment depends on the moral theory that is brought to bear on that function.

Second, this mapping reminds us that there is more work to be done by a theory of punishment than to answer the question about punishment's justification. Consequentialism needs to describe the structure of wrongdoing and explain proportionality in sentencing, as well as to account for punishment's justification. Likewise, everyone knows that Kant justifies punishment by appeal to retribution. But this overlooks the fact that deontological moral theory necessarily has something to say about deterrence and incapacitation in relation to justification—that is, that they do not justify—and that it offers a distinctive take on fault and the excuses as well. This is not to say that theorists are not actually doing this work. For example, Andrew von Hirsch has explained deterrence and incapacitation within a deontological framework as a supplementary prudential reason to comply with the law.[6] And of course the voluntarism of Kantian deontological morality has been invoked in support of the intentional states construction of fault.[7] My point is only that our customary mapping of the theory of punishment tends to obscure the complexity and richness of the field and to make our exploration of it haphazard.

In no respect is this more true than in connection with virtue ethics. Once one makes the appropriate distinctions between theory, end, and justification and once one maps the field as I have done above, then the possibility of an aretaic theory of punishment becomes obvious. Virtue ethics, like any other moral theory, can put a gloss on the ends of punishment and can offer explanations of our practices. This would seem to be an interesting exercise even if nothing of concrete, practical value were to come of it. In fact, the first effort in this direction was made over thirty years ago.[8] But this portion of the field has never developed beyond the stage of a curiosity, and the casebook writers have never made so much as an oblique reference to it.

If the justification of punishment is the principal issue in the theory of punishment, and if the justification at issue is the moral justification of punishment, then it seems to me that it makes sense to divide the field according to the leading theories of moral justification. I find it unnecessarily confusing to run crosswise to this scheme—which is, from the point of view of moral philosophy, the conventional scheme. For example, Duff categorizes H. L. A. Hart as a choice theorist. Now, Hart's work can be described or categorized in a number of ways: he was a legal positivist, a political liberal, and a consequentialist. When Duff calls Hart a "choice" theorist, he has ample textual support, coming mostly from the liberal strain in Hart's thought. Hart famously described law as a "choosing system," meaning that law's basic function is to coordinate society, and that in doing so law could and should give maximum scope and effect to individuals' choices about their lives. But Duff also notes the importance of Kant to "choice" theories of punishment, and it is here that the confusion sets in. Kant is indeed important to "choice" theories because Kantian voluntarism dovetails with a view of culpability and excuses that goes back to Blackstone.[9] The problem is that no one who reads Hart can fail to notice that he is agnostic at best about the role of fault and desert in the criminal law, that he regards the function of punishment to be the promotion of social welfare, and that he is, in short, a dyed-in-the-wool consequentialist. Duff's placing Hart in Kant's school is implausible at best, probably confusing to some readers, and unwittingly obscurantist.

My principal objection to Duff's choice/character/act scheme is that it falls victim to the bad habit of supposing that some one function of punishment justifies punishment and that to identify this justifying function constitutes a theory of punishment. It is misleading from the start to make the inquiry turn on our answer to the question, what do we punish for? Taken as the identifying feature of theories of punishment, that question conflates the issues of end and justification and ignores the other standing issues that a punishment theory ought to address. More disturbingly, it distorts one's view of theories that do not approach the field of punishment in such a narrow way.

3. Reply to Duff

Duff correctly notes that I have argued that "It is not just harm, but the lack of judgment that results in harm that the criminal law condemns."[10] He responds to this by writing,

> Now Huigens suggests that "lack of judgment" is a central aspect of the intentional object of criminal liability—it is part of what the offender is condemned for. It might, however, be better to portray lack of judgment as a condition of liability—at least if this account is to be, as Huigens suggests, "descriptive of the criminal law as it stands," and even, I think, if it is to be at all plausible as a prescriptive account. The murderer, the rapist, the thief, might display a lack of practical judgment in committing their crimes; but they are and should properly be convicted and punished for those crimes, for what they did to their victims, not for their lack of practical judgment.[11]

As I will concede at greater length below, there are a number of errors in the article which Duff is criticizing here. But this is not one of them. I have not argued that we punish because of mistakes in judgment to the exclusion of punishing for the harm or wrongdoing done. And it is surprising that Duff should say that I have so argued when he has just quoted me as saying, "It is not just harm, but the lack of judgment that results in harm that the criminal law condemns." This means that, in some sense, we punish both because of the harm and because of the lack of judgment—as Duff seems to understand when he says I have suggested that the lack of judgment is "a central aspect" of the end of punishment and "part of what the offender is condemned for."

While I may have failed in this early article to spell out clearly what I thought the relationship between harm, wrongdoing, judgment, and fault to be, it was at least clear that I did not mean to use harm and criminal wrongdoing only as evidence of poor judgment or bad character. I argued that because the rules of the criminal law were the accretion of past judgments, the good judgment implicit in them was inferred and employed by the jury in the course of its deliberations. There was no suggestion that the rules of the criminal law were irrelevant, or that the harms and wrongs to which both the rules and good judgment pertain were not the subject matter of the criminal law or part of the justifying purpose of punishment. If Duff has misread me here, it is in part because I was not clear, but also in part because he has superimposed his own scheme over mine. He categorizes me as a "character" theorist and then assumes that this means I believe that good character in the sense of good judgment is what we impose punishment for. But the main thing driving that conclusion, it seems to me, is the fact that this is the question around which Duff's eclectic theory of punishment is organized.

Just as the notion that we punish criminal acts—not choices and not characters—is central to Duff's view of the criminal law, the centerpiece of my reply to Duff is the contention that an aretaic theory of punishment takes the same view. We punish acts that constitute criminal wrongdoing, and we do so because criminal wrongdoing is intimately related to our pre-legal conceptions of wrongdoing. In spite of virtue's obvious relevance to character, to say that virtue is an end of punishment—even to say that it is the principal justifying end of punishment—is not to say that character is what we punish for, to the exclusion of criminal wrongdoing. One must consider questions beyond punishment's principal end, especially the structure of wrongdoing and the nature of criminal fault, if one is to see the relevance of virtue to punishment. Duff takes a step in the right direction when he separates the question of punishment's objectives from the question of the conditions we place on criminal liability. He forgets, however, that these two issues are related. More crucially, he fails to realize that the way in which a theory explains this relationship is an excellent gauge of its adequacy. Consequentialist theories of punishment treat the conditions we impose on punishment as exogenous side constraints that have no necessary bearing on the justification of punishment. The aretaic theory of punishment treats some of the conditions we impose on punishment as endogenous to punishment's justification. The superiority of the aretaic theory goes beyond its greater coherence, however, and extends to areas of special concern to Duff. The aretaic theory fits comfortably into the liberal tradition of limited government and well serves the political ideal of deliberative normative community.

Let me proceed in this part in two steps. First, I will lay out an aretaic conception of criminal responsibility, criminal wrongdoing, criminal fault, the ends of punishment, and punishment's justification. My aim is not only to describe the distinctive features of an aretaic theory of punishment but also to emphasize the familiar appearance of our practices under that account. This will answer not only the charge of procrusteanism but also the charge that the theory is illiberal. Duff makes the latter charge in his recent article, and the second section of this part responds to this and his other objections. Some of my responses will be obvious by that point, but others will not be. Some of my responses will be concessions, and I will try to explain why I do not think these concessions are fatal to the version of the aretaic theory of punishment that precedes them.

3.1 The theory in brief

I have argued above that theories of punishment are not, or should not be, defined by some one end of punishment that is designated as primary. The defining features of a theory of punishment are instead the characteristic concerns, assumptions, arguments, and methods of the philosophical ethics on which the theory draws for its account of punishment's ends, justification, and other standing issues. Consequentialist theories of punishment center around the attainment of an optimal state of social welfare, and a consequentialist theory will make its own characteristic assumptions—about self-interested individuals and consistent preference orderings, for example. Deontological theories of punishment focus on the duties of and pertaining to autonomous individuals. Jean Hampton's account, for example, describes punishment in terms of our duty to restore victims of crime to equal dignity[12]—a concern shared by George Fletcher.[13] The characteristic features of an aretaic theory of punishment include, at a minimum, a concern for human flourishing and an account of practical reasoning that includes deliberations on ends. In the following paragraphs, I will outline a theory of punishment that has these features.

The nature of practical reasoning and the criteria of sound practical reasoning are little understood, and their relevance to law remains largely unexplored. The principal point that has been neglected is this: practical reasoning encompasses more than mere instrumental reasoning toward one's ends: it also includes deliberations on ends. Before I figure out how to support my family, I deliberate about whether or not to have a family. This neglect of rational deliberation on ends is easy to explain. There is a strong tradition in western philosophy that denies that rational deliberation on ends is possible because of the connection between our ends and our emotions. We have the ends we do because we value them, and valuation involves the emotions. As we commonly say, a decision such as the decision to have a family is a value judgment, and value judgments are widely assumed to be beyond the realm of rational debate and deliberation: ultimately, they just feel right to us.[14] However, the connection between ends and emotions does not rule out rational deliberation on ends. Neither emotion nor valuation is reducible to mere feeling, in the sense of an a-rational, noncognitive somatic state.[15] Emotions are intentional (I love her), propositional (I am angry and distraught that she loves another), and fallible (on reflection, I never did truly love her; it was a mere infatuation). Mere feelings are neither intentional (I am cold her?) nor propositional (I am cold that...?) nor fallible (On reflection, I never was cold?). The intentional, propositional, fallible character of emotions gives reason purchase on them and enables us to engage in genuine deliberation on ends.

Similarly, deliberation on ends entails the rational construction of the set of standing motivations that constitutes one's character. The affective component of motivation is a function of the emotions and valuations that lie behind our reasons for action, and motivation is no more reducible to a-rational, noncognitive feeling than emotion or valuation is.[16] Accordingly, character is, or can be, something that one rationally constructs, maintains, and modifies.

Perhaps an example of deliberations on ends and the attribution of responsibility for such deliberations would be helpful at this point. Suppose that Francis is a successful lawyer who works long hours and who often brings work home at night. More and more often lately, Francis finds himself getting angry at his children for interrupting him. Reflecting on these incidents, Francis's first reaction is to appreciate his own father's experience. He now understands the pressure of responsibility as well as the pride and excitement that come with success in one's profession. This, he now sees, can lead a man to be impatient with children, who cannot appreciate any of this. Francis is struck by the irony of his now being in the same position as his father. But then he is struck instead by the memory of the pain he felt as a boy at being shut out and neglected by his busy father. He recalls his own pledge—made not only when he was a boy but also when he married, and again when his children were born—not to be like that. Furthermore, Francis recalls—with some embarrassment now—conversations he had as a law student, in which he invoked his experience with his workaholic father to bolster arguments that traditional gender roles ought to change. Francis therefore promises to spend less time on work and more time with his children.

When the cycle repeats itself after another week or two, Francis recalls how his own father made such promises from time to time and inevitably broke them, just as Francis is doing now. Francis realizes that he is now angry with himself, not only for behaving like his father did but for violating what, on repeated reflection, he still takes to be his deeply held beliefs about the relative value of the roles of lawyer and father—to him and society. As a result of this realization, Francis from that time forward consciously cuts back on his legal work, welcomes interruptions from his children, and prolongs these distractions—giving his children his full attention in order to allow his love for them and the pleasure of their company to dispel his annoyance in the short term and to reorder the distribution of his time and energies away from work and toward his family in the long term.

This is an example of rational deliberation on ends. While not exactly a daily occurrence—by its nature it probably could not be—this kind of deliberation is not only possible, but commonplace in an ordinary life. Furthermore, it does not seem that an ascription of responsibility is any more impossible than the deliberation itself. To deny that one can be responsible for one's character or for the quality of one's deliberation on ends would entail denying that the behavior that Francis exhibits in this scenario can be described as praiseworthy. But it seems implausible to say that Francis's conduct is not even potentially praiseworthy. (Perhaps someone who places a higher value on lawyering than fatherhood would not praise it, but this would not be to deny praise on the ground that the conduct is not an appropriate candidate for responsibility at all.)

This expansive account of practical reasoning contrasts sharply with that which is characteristic of consequentialist ethics. Consequentialism tends to confine its conception of practical reasoning to instrumental reasoning toward stipulated ends—sometimes on the ground that one's ends are impervious to reason, though more often as a studied agnosticism toward the question of rational deliberation on ends. On the other hand, a more expansive account of practical reasoning dovetails neatly with the tenets of Aristotelian virtue ethics—notably with Aristotle's contention that the agent is responsible for her or his character and her or his motivations.[17] If our ends, valuations, and emotions were a-rational, noncognitive somatic states—subliminal givens—then responsibility for character and motivation would indeed be impossible. But if we recognize the rational dimension of the emotions and valuation and the possibility of rational deliberation on ends, then responsibility for one's motivations and character is no more problematic than responsibility for beliefs and actions (which is not to say, of course, that such responsibility is unproblematic). Responsibility for one's character and for the quality of one's practical reasoning—including one's deliberations on ends—is the core of virtue ethics.

In a virtue ethics theory of punishment, responsibility for one's character and for the quality of one's practical reasoning—including one's deliberations on ends—is portrayed as essential to just punishment. People do not commit crimes because they fail to fit means to ends. They commit crimes because their ends are wrong. The failures of reasoning that lead people to commit crimes are not instrumental errors confined to the immediate circumstances of the offense. Crimes are manifestations of callousness, persistent immaturity, narcissism, greed, lack of empathy, impulsiveness, uncontrolled anger, and so on—failures in the rational construction of an agent's motivations, including the standing motivations that make up a character. We hold people responsible for failures of character in ordinary morality, and when failures of this kind result in a violation of a criminal prohibition, we hold people responsible by punishing them. But this is not to say, simplistically, that good character or sound practical reasoning is what we punish for—at least not in any sense that would reduce the criminal act to mere evidence of these qualities. Any theory of punishment has to explain the point of punishment—to explain why the deliberate infliction of pain in punishment is not mere cruelty. Under an aretaic theory, virtue is an end of just punishment and this is to say, in some sense, that we punish people for the sake of virtue. But the relationship between the ends of punishment and the other features of just punishment is no simpler or more obvious in the aretaic theory than in any other.

3.2 Yes, we do want an Aristotelian criminal law

In his Virtue, Vice and Criminal Liability: Do We Want an Aristotelian Criminal Law?, Duff argues that we seldom punish people for vice. We punish them instead for criminal acts, and these acts are not defined by reference to vices.

> It is . . . implausible that the criminal wrongfulness of criminal actions is generally constituted, even partly, by the attitudes or motives they display. The agent's intention might often, if not always, be partly constitutive of the wrong for which he is convicted; but the vicious attitudes, motives, or character traits that might be displayed in the action do not contribute to its criminal wrongfulness.[18]

In the few crimes that are expressly defined in terms of identifiable vices, such as depraved heart murder or theft, we do not punish people for depravity or dishonesty as such. Vice as a component of the crime is etiolated, Duff says, for two reasons: because the diachronic nature of vice—its being a persistent character trait instead of an isolated event—is unaccounted for in the definition of the crime; and because the crime can be committed out of akrasia—weakness of will leading to a failure to do what one knows is right—just as well as it can be committed out of vice.

Duff is right about the place of vice in the criminal law: it is minor at best, as he says. But he is wrong in supposing that Aristotelian theories of punishment need to claim otherwise. Likewise, Duff is right that the notion of vice is etiolated in the criminal law. But he is wrong in supposing that an aretaic theory of punishment necessarily contends that it is not. In his argument, Duff runs afoul of one of the principal barriers to the application of virtue ethics to law, which is the notion that virtue ethics is confined to the explication of the conventional virtues and vices. Were this true, aretaic legal theory would be almost a contradiction in terms. After all, we do not frame legal norms in terms of character traits; we frame legal norms in the form of rules and standards. But while it is true that Aristotle and his successors have much to say about character traits as norms, it is not true that they have nothing to say about rules and standards. Rules are accounted for in virtue ethics in several ways, and it is these features that give virtue ethics its purchase in legal theory.[19] In aretaic legal theory, the role of discrete virtues and vices is correspondingly attenuated. This is why the aretaic theory of punishment that I have presented above emphasizes deliberations on ends and why my earlier accounts of the same theory stressed the end of human flourishing. These concerns are featured in virtue ethics, but they are not absent from law, and the point of an aretaic legal theory is to bring out these concerns in the law as a way of addressing long-standing theoretical and doctrinal difficulties that consequentialist and deontological legal theory has failed to resolve. In this light, it is hardly an argument against the aretaic theory of punishment to note that the vices play no discernible role in the criminal law.

Similarly, Duff's argument that "[i]t is ... implausible that the criminal wrongfulness of criminal actions is generally constituted, even partly, by the attitudes or motives they display"[20] falls just wide of the mark. Criminal wrongdoing sometimes is constituted by attitudes or motives, as Duff acknowledges, but more to the point criminal wrongdoing is constituted by the practical reasoning, including deliberations on ends, that lies behind attitudes and motives. Likewise, this kind of practical reasoning lies behind the actions and intentions that are unquestionably constitutive of criminal wrongdoing. What Duff misses is the substratum of practical reasoning that these features of the criminal law have in common and the extent to which the law governs us as we govern ourselves: by addressing not only how we get what we want but also how we come to want what we want. It is not implausible at all to say that the criminal wrongfulness of criminal actions is constituted at least in part by failures of practical reasoning, including failures in one's deliberations on ends.

Duff's conception of virtue ethics occludes his view of the aretaic theory of punishment but so does his conception of the criminal law, particularly his conception of criminal fault. In the passage quoted above, Duff readily assimilates intentions into criminal wrongdoing but refuses to do the same with practical reasoning in general or with its other products, such as attitudes and motivations. The reason for this difference is that for Duff, as for most criminal law scholars, intentions are not just any product of practical reasoning. For these scholars, intended action is paradigmatic of responsible action and so of actions for which we hold people criminally liable. The more an action departs from this paradigm, the more difficult we are supposed to find it to impose just punishment for that action. Not only intended actions (those done with a purpose, in Model Penal Code terms) but also intentional actions (those done knowingly and recklessly) are proper bases for criminal liability, but beyond this intentional-states boundary line punishment becomes harder to justify.

The aretaic theory of punishment must seem implausible to anyone wedded to these assumptions because intentions have no such paradigmatic status in that theory. On the contrary, it is negligence that is paradigmatic, in that fault generally is taken to be an inference drawn by the jury, in the course of deciding wrongdoing, that the defendant has failed in his practical reasoning, including in his deliberations on ends. Our framing fault in terms of intentional states is a concession to the rule of law that we make in the course of specifying our competing ends concerning wrongdoing. The aretaic theory recognizes the significance of intentions for criminal wrongdoing—that is why they are relevant to our rules about fault to begin with—but it denies that that significance extends beyond what intentions tell us about the quality of the practical reasoning that led to their formation. And on that point, a defendant's attitudes and his character as reflected in his conduct are as relevant as his intentions.

One cannot argue for a gestalt shift, but some such argument seems to be called for at this point. Duff acknowledges the existence of nonintentional criminal fault, such as negligence. He recognizes that nonintentional criminal fault is limited neither to negligence nor to minor offenses: depravity, in the sense of indifference to the value of human life, can premise murder; and an unreasonable mistake does not necessarily, or even plausibly, acquit one of rape on the ground that there is no mens rea regarding nonconsent in such a case. And Duff recognizes that provoking circumstances can reduce an intentional murder to manslaughter, though those circumstances do not negate the murderer's intent to kill. So are these fault doctrines all departures from a paradigm of intentional action? Or is it rather the case that the limitation of criminal liability to cases of intentional action is an aspiration born of rule of law concerns that are exogenous to criminal fault? One obstacle to exchanging the former view for the latter has been the difficulty of seeing what criminal fault does consist of, if not of intentions. But the aretaic theory addresses this need with an alternate definition of fault from which the familiar fault doctrines of the criminal law can be derived—without calling most of them into question.

Because the aretaic account of wrongdoing and fault is premised on a failure of practical reasoning instead of vice as a character trait, the theory also is untouched by Duff's point that crimes are attributable to akrasia as often as they are to vice.[21] Fault is partly constitutive of wrongdoing and fault consists of a failure of practical reasoning. Akrasia is a failure of practical reasoning in the relevant sense: it consists in part of a failure to deliberate well on ends. Duff seems to understand akrasia differently, as consisting of a failure "to complete the appropriate practical syllogism that would lead [an agent] (in light of his own conception of the good) not to offend, or [a failure] to act in accordance with his own practical reasoning."[22] In other words, the akratic agent's ends are in order; it is his reasoning from those ends or something in the execution of the action that goes awry.

However, there is more to the problem of akrasia than this. The actions of the akratic agent seem paradoxical. If the agent does not act in accordance with an end he has, then his contrary actions contradict his commitment to that end. To judge from his action, he must not have that end any longer, if he ever did. And yet the rejected end hangs around, somehow, to condemn or call into question the action that the agent did take. Perhaps the akratic agent is just paying lip service to an end he does not really hold, but more often than not his commitment to the end in question seems quite genuine. The akratic agent seems simultaneously to have, and not to have, the end his action contradicts. One way to resolve this paradox is to recognize that the failure of the akratic agent is not merely a failure to act in accordance with set ends (as Duff's formulation suggests) but a failure to reconcile competing ends in deliberation as well as in action. Such a failure to make one's ends cohere counts as a failure in the agent's deliberations on ends.

If criminal fault is partly constitutive of criminal wrongdoing and if criminal fault consists of a failure of practical reasoning, including one's deliberations on ends, then not only vice—adopting and pursuing bad ends—but also akrasia—the failure to reconcile one's conflicting ends—counts as fault and is partly constitutive of criminal wrongdoing. As Duff says, we punish for akrasia as well as for vice. But in either case, we punish for a failure of practical reasoning.

On a related matter, I must concede Duff's point. In the original statement of my version of an Aristotelian theory of punishment, I argued that a defendant whose actions exhibit phronesis would be acquitted of wrongdoing and that the jury would exercise phronesis in deliberating. Phronesis is a faculty of exemplary practical reasoning that is exhibited by the truly virtuous. It is the full integration of desire and the good that enables the virtuous person to see and pursue the right course of action in any situation. Duff points out that phronesis is not required for innocence; that simple law abidingness will do, even if, as is usually the case, that law abidingness is not a product of exemplary practical judgment. This is clearly correct. Duff is also right when he argues that a jury need not exhibit phronesis in its deliberations. Obviously, most juries fall short of exemplary practical reasoning in their deliberations, but this does not in any way call the legal or moral validity of their verdicts into question.

In response I can only say that I abandoned these arguments some time ago and that Duff's point is not a strike against the theory as I have stated it above or even against another earlier statement of the theory. The interesting thing about phronesis as a quality of practical reasoning is its sensitivity to practical context. I relied on the idea in an attempt to articulate the ways in which the criminal law is concerned with context-sensitive value judgments. But one can describe this concern without appealing to phronesis at all. As I have described in more recent articles relying on and developing the aretaic theory, juries make context-sensitive judgments about wrongdoing when they deliberate about fault if their deliberations are framed in positive law by a concept such as "implied malice" or "extreme indifference to human life." Likewise, our use of thick evaluative terms to describe criminal wrongdoing reflects the context-dependent value judgments that are made in the legislative and constitutional phases of the criminal law.

On another, more basic point, I think that Duff has not offered an argument at all. Duff claims that to say a criminal has failed in his practical reasoning is no more than a truism. Obviously, something has gone wrong in the defendant's reasoning if he has run afoul of the law, but "this is so far to show only that 'lack of judgment' can be inferred from criminal liability, not that it constitutes a substantial condition of liability."[23] This argument does not, of course, engage the arguments about the nature of fault that I have made above. But it also fails, I think, to engage the argument of the earlier article that Duff is criticising. Bracketing my mistaken and misleading reliance on phronesis, I have argued from the outset that sound practical reasoning is an end of punishment because human beings in society are interdependent and rightly demand sound practical reasoning of one another. This much of my argument was at least clear enough to criticise, and it purports to explain why a failure of practical reasoning is more than a coincidental feature of criminal wrongdoing. But Duff rejects it without explanation.

One possible reason for his rejecting my argument from interdependence is that Duff is unpersuaded by its Aristotelian origins. Aristotle described human beings as social animals. The ergon, or distinctive end, of human beings was said to be rationality in action; and our flourishing, the full attainment of that ergon, had to be understood in light of our social nature. The best life, eudaimonia, could not be a solitary life.[24] It is impossible to accept Aristotle's account of human nature and the good as a whole and at face value because it rests on assumptions about logic and the physical world that we no longer share.[25] Perhaps this is why Duff rejects my argument that our interdependence makes sound practical reasoning an end of punishment. However, despite one's doubts about Aristotle's account of human nature (or about contemporary scientific arguments for an identifiable human nature), one would be hard pressed to deny the simple fact of human interdependence. It is not impossible to live a self-sufficient life in a remote corner of the world, but such cases are extraordinarily rare and may evidence illness.[26] Ordinarily, we rely on one another. Paradoxically, this characteristic of ordinary human life has become more pronounced in industrial and post-industrial society, even as technological advances expand the scope and efficacy of individual self-determination. I think Duff must recognize this as a descriptive matter.

The real problem with appealing to interdependence as a basis for a theory of punishment is that it threatens to make the criminal law illiberal. I suspect Duff is concerned about a theory that emphasizes and, in effect, defends the way in which law governs people at the level of ends—that is to say, at the level of their desires and motivations. But the aretaic theory of punishment is not illiberal on this ground. To say that the law governs us at the level of our ends, desires, or motivations is not to say that the law governs us by means of subliminal manipulation.

The jump to this conclusion requires the support of a false premise, which is that our ends, desires, and motivations are established only in noncognitive and a-rational ways, so that subliminal conditioning is the only way that we could be governed at that level. It appears that something like this is Duff's view, for he doubts that we have sufficient rational control over our ends to be held responsible for them. But as I have argued above, the fact that our ends, desires, and motivations have an affective component does not make them mere subliminal givens. Emotion itself is not noncognitive or a-rational; on the contrary it is intentional, propositional, and fallible, and these features give reason purchase on the emotions. For this reason, the affective dimension of our ends, desires, and motivations does not preclude our being responsible for them. We can and do deliberate on ends, and if the law affects those deliberations, in part by holding us responsible for their outcome, then its governance of our desires and motivations is a rational governance.

Properly understood, governance at the level of ends, desires, and motivations actually supports the liberal value of autonomy. The notion that the law governs us only instrumentally is implausible. As Hart pointed out long ago, the law is not a set of commands backed by threats, it is a matter of felt obligation. We do not constantly advert to the threat of punishment; instead, we internalize the law and act within a social fabric constituted by law. This is what Hart meant when he called the law a choosing system. The aretaic theory rejects Hart's consequentialism but dovetails nicely with this aspect of his liberalism. If interdependence is an inevitable feature of human society, then sound practical reasoning by individuals is a necessity—all the more so if we set the expansion of individual self-determination in society as one of our objectives. A society of free individuals is practically impossible unless those free individuals choose the right course of action (speaking broadly) in most situations. The law could not ensure that they do this unless it had the capacity to govern not only practical reasoning toward given ends but also the choice of ends itself. Aretaic legal theory describes this kind of governance.

4. Conclusion

As I noted in the Introduction, Duff has recently argued against Paul Robinson's proposed reformation of the criminal law, under which we would rigorously separate conduct rules from principles of adjudication. According to Duff, crimes are not just prohibited invasions of interests; they are pre-legal wrongs that have been designated as grounds for punishment. This distinction is important for both descriptive and normative reasons. As a descriptive matter, the thickly normative, pre-legal origin of crimes precludes the artificial separation of conduct rules from principles of adjudication, as Robinson would have it. This is particularly true of the intentions that partly constitute crimes. Murder and manslaughter are distinct wrongs, and not merely two infringements of an interest in life that we distinguish only ex post, in adjudication. Were I to commit both a murder and a manslaughter, I would be conscious of doing two very different wrongs because of the enormous difference between intending to kill a person on one hand and, on the other, consciously risking another person's death.

Duff argues that there is also a normative reason to retain the thickly normative phrasing of crimes as wrongs. Because crimes reflect thick, pre-legal norms, our compliance with the law is content-dependent. I do not refrain from killing other people only because I fear that a superior power will punish me if I do. I refrain from killing because I believe it to be wrong—just as my fellow citizens believe it to be wrong. If the criminal law works in the thickly normative and content-dependent way that Duff describes, then I comply with the law as a citizen of a deliberative, democratic community. If I comply with a prohibition on killing only because I fear punishment, then I am merely subject to a superior authority in which I have no voice.

Both Duff's descriptive point and his normative point fit neatly within the aretaic theory of punishment. In the perennial dispute over whether punishment is imposed for the infliction of harm or for wrongdoing, the aretaic theory is firmly in the "wrongdoing" camp. I have described the legislation of the criminal law's prohibitions as the generalization of specific practical judgments, and the adjudication of particular cases as involving a complementary re-specification of the criminal prohibition, from which a context-sensitive inference about the practical reasoning of the defendant is drawn.[27] It should be clear that on this account the criminal law operates on the basis of thick norms: detailed, context-specific prohibitions that have an organic relationship to human history and the human situation and that are cognate with moral norms. Robinson's radically simplified catalogue of harms to be avoided, accompanied by a separate catalogue of limitations on the adjudication of harms allegedly inflicted, cannot be an adequate account of criminal law.

In the end, I suspect that most of the items in Duff's eclectic theory of punishment are responses to two pervasive tendencies in twentieth-century legal theory: the reductiveness of consequentialism and the rule-fetishism of one kind of legal positivism. The aretaic theory of punishment responds to both of those concerns in a systematic fashion. If a systematic, comprehensive theory of punishment threatens to be procrustean, this is so only when it is in the wrong hands. If Duff were to adopt the aretaic theory of punishment as a framework for his theorizing, there would be no such danger. On the contrary, I believe that the strain of humane good sense that is so prominent in his work would be well served. I would be honored to count him as an ally instead of an opponent.

Notes

1. Antony Duff, *Virtue, Vice and Criminal Liability: Do We Want an Aristotelian Criminal Law?*, 6 Buff. Crim. L. Rev. 147, 179 (2003).
2. See Kyron Huigens, *Virtue and Inculpation*, 108 Harv. L. Rev. 1423, 1480 (1995).
3. See Kyron Huigens, *Solving the Apprendi Puzzle*, 90 Geo. L. J. 387, 435–442 (2002); Kyron Huigens, *Harris, Ring, and the Future of Relevant Conduct Sentencing*, 15 Fed. Sent. Rep. 88 (2003).
4. See Michael Tonry and John C. Coffee, *Enforcing Sentencing Guidelines: Plea Bargaining and Review Mechanisms* in The Sentencing Commission and Its Guidelines (Andrew von Hirsch *et al.* eds, 1987), pp. 142, 155; Kevin R. Reitz, *Sentencing Facts: Travesties of Real Offense Sentencing*, 45 Stan. L. Rev. 523, 535 (1993).
5. See, e.g. Joshua Dressler, Cases and Materials on Criminal Law (2nd edn 1999), pp. 33–46 (discussing "utilitarian justifications" and "retributive justifications"); Sanford Kadish and Stephen Schulhofer, Criminal Law and its Processes: Cases and Materials (7th edn, 2001), p. 101 ("Broadly speaking, the justifications for punishment fall into two large groups, retributive and utilitarian"); Paul H. Robinson, Fundamentals of Criminal Law (2nd edn 1995), p. 31 (discussing "retributive justification" and "utilitarian justification").
6. Andrew von Hirsch, Censure and Sanctions 12–14 (1993).
7. Cf. Immanuel Kant, Groundwork of the Metaphysics of Morals 7 (Mary Gregor ed. and trans., Cambridge University Press, 1996) (1785) ("It is impossible to think of anything at all in the world . . . that could be considered good without limitation except a good will . . . A good will is not good because of what it effects or accomplishes . . . it is good in itself").
8. See Edmund L. Pincoffs, *Legal Responsibility and Moral Character*, 19 Wayne L. Rev. 905, 918 (1973) (arguing that punishment represents a demand that one develop and exhibit certain character traits); see also Peter Arenella, *Character, Choice, and Moral Agency: The Relevance of Character to Our Moral Culpability Judgments*, 7 Soc. Phil. Pol'y 59 (1990), reprinted in Crime, Culpability, and Remedy (Ellen Frankel Paul *et al.* eds, 1990), pp. 59, 61 (arguing that the so-called rational choice theory is inadequate to describe the criminal law's concern with character); Claire O. Finkelstein, *Duress: A Philosophical*

Account of the Defense in Law, 37 Ariz. L. Rev. 251, 252–253 (1995) (relying on Aristotle's conception of judgment to give an account of duress in terms of states of character).

9. Blackstone wrote,

> All the several pleas and excuses, which protect the committer of a forbidden act from the punishment which is otherwise annexed thereto, may be reduced to this single consideration, the want or defect of will. An involuntary act, as it has no claim to merit, so neither can it induce any guilt: the concurrence of the will, when it has its choice to do or to avoid the fact in question, being the only thing that renders human actions either praiseworthy or culpable.

4 Blackstone, Commentaries on the Laws of England (1769), pp. 20–21.

10. Kyron Huigens, *Virtue and Inculpation*, 108 Harv. L. Rev. 1423, 1424–1425 (1995), cited in Duff, *supra* note 7, at 179.
11. Duff, *supra* note 14, at 180.
12. Jean Hampton, *Correcting Harms Versus Righting Wrongs: The Goal of Retribution*, 39 U.C.L.A. L. Rev. 1659, 1660–1661 (1992).
13. George Fletcher, With Justice for Some: Protecting Victim's Rights in Criminal Trials (1996), pp. 201–206. The title is misleading. Fletcher's concerns go well beyond standard victim's rights advocacy and extend to the purposes of punishment.
14. See, e.g. Alfred Jules Ayer, Language, Truth and Logic (2nd edn, 1946), pp. 102–120 (arguing for the view that value judgments are merely expressions of noncognitive attitudes).
15. See generally Antonio R. Damasio, Descartes' Error: Emotion, Reason, and the Human Brain (1994), pp. 52–79; Gerald Gaus, Value and Justification: The Foundations of Liberal Theory (1990), pp. 31–34, 106–26, 136; Andrew Ortony et al., The Cognitive Structure of Emotions (1988), pp. 34–47; Justin Oakley, Morality and the Emotions (1992), pp. 7–16; Andrew Ortony, *Value and Emotion* in Memories, Thoughts, and Emotions: Essays in Honor of George Mandler (William Knessen *et al.* eds, 1991), pp. 337, 349–351.
16. Ronald de Sousa, The Rationality of Emotion (1987), pp. 218–220; Michael Smith, The Moral Problem (1994), pp. 104–111.
17. Aristotle, Nicomachean Ethics bk. 3, sec. 3.4, at 66 (Terence Irwin trans., Hackett Pub. Co., 1985).
18. Duff, *supra* note 1, at 171–172.
19. For example,

> But it is hard for someone to be trained correctly for virtue from his youth if he has been brought up under correct laws, since the many, especially the young, do not find it pleasant to live in a temperate and resistant way. Hence laws must prescribe their upbringing and practices; for they will not find these things painful when they get used to them. Presumably, however, it is not enough to get the correct upbringing and attention when they are young; rather, they must continue the same practices and be habituated to them when they become men. Hence we need laws concerned with these things also, and in general with all of life.

Aristotle, *supra* note 17, at bk. 10, sec. 14.21, at 293. Aristotle continued, "For the legislator makes the citizens good by habituating them, and this is the wish of every legislator..." *Id.* at bk. 2, sec. 2.1(3), at 34.

20. Duff, *supra* note 1, at 171.
21. Duff, *supra* note 1, at 181.
22. *Id.*
23. Duff, *supra* note 79, at 18.
24. Aristotle, *supra* note 73, at bk. 9, sec. 11.6, at 257–261.
25. As Bernard Williams put it in one of his last essays,

> If there is such a thing as an essential nature of human beings, there is only one way in which it can rule anything out—by making it impossible. If it has failed to rule it out in that way, it cannot try to catch up by sending normative signals. Such an idea would make sense only if there were more teleology in the universe than is represented by evolutionary adaptation, and one thing we know that Aristotle did not know is that there is not.

Bernard Williams, *Relativism, History, and the Existence of Values* in Joseph Raz, The Practice of Value (R. Jay Wallace ed., 2003), pp. 106, 116; but see George Sher, *Knowing About Virtue* in Nomos XXXIV, Virtue (John W. Chapman and William A. Galston eds, 1992), pp. 91, 99 ("But even if no specific way of life is best for everyone, our background beliefs may still identify various dimensions along which people's lives can be more or less successful").

26. Cf. Jon Krakauer, Into the Wild (1996) (recounting the fatal attempt of a young man to live self-sufficiently in the Alaskan wilderness).
27. See Kyron Huigens, *The Dead End of Deterrence, and Beyond*, 41 Wm. Mary L. Rev. 943, 1028–1029 (2000).

9
Two Ways of Doing the Right Thing

Rosalind Hursthouse

1. Introduction

This chapter is about a standard problem in legal ethics which can be roughly stated as follows. Lawyers' professional role often permits—indeed requires—them to do things that would be wrong if they were acting outside their professional role. The usual general examples of the immoral sorts of things their role might permit or require them to do are: enable a client to defeat a just claim on a technicality if they can (*Zabella v. Pakel*), make opposing truthful witnesses look as though they are lying if they can (*Triangle Shirt Waist*), maintain client confidentiality even when this causes serious harm [including being sent to Death Row (Henry Drake)] to an innocent third party (*Lake Pleasant Bodies*) and, arguably, even when this involves remaining silent about a crime in progress or forthcoming.

These permissions and obligations are usually said to arise from the more general role-obligations of a lawyer in the adversarial (as opposed to the inquisitorial) system. These are, roughly, the obligation to pursue, zealously, your client's interests (not just, for instance, the interests of the clients you morally approve of) and the obligation to respect your client's confidentiality.

Now one might say, well we all know this is true—true that lawyers, *as* lawyers, do such things—but why is it a *philosophical* problem that people who work in legal ethics get tied up in? The answer is that we do not want to say that being a lawyer *necessarily* involves being immoral, the way, say, being a concentration camp commander under the Nazi regime did. We are happy to say that no decent society has any need for concentration camps and hence no need for people to run them, but surely a decent society of some size and complexity does need a legal system and hence does need lawyers. Moreover, surely it needs the adversarial system, so it needs lawyers playing the advocate's role.

Of course, it might be true that a decent society needs advocacy lawyers and it still be true that advocacy lawyers are necessarily immoral. That would be to say that the existence of such lawyers, though an evil, was a necessary evil. That sounds to me like a possible position, but it is not one I have found discussed anywhere, so I will accept here the prevailing assumption. The prevailing assumption in the literature is that, assuming we need advocacy lawyers, it must be possible for a good person to be a good lawyer—that the profession is not necessarily any more inimical to virtue than being a teacher or a business person.

And when we make that assumption explicit, we do indeed have something that looks like a philosophical problem. A lawyer's role sometimes *requires* or *obliges* (we can forget about "permits" at this point) her to do some really immoral things. If she is a good lawyer she will do them when required or obliged. But of course there is no reason why a good person should not be a good lawyer.

Excuse me? How can it be maintained that there is no reason why a good person could not be someone who did those immoral sorts of things? There is surely a compelling reason why this cannot be so, namely that, on the face of it, someone's doing those sorts of things, voluntarily and intentionally, simply entails that they are immoral and lack virtue. So there is our problem; either we give up the claim that the lawyers' role sometimes obliges them to do immoral things or we have to find some way of explaining how it might be that a good, virtuous person—someone who is, for example, just, compassionate and honest—could, if a lawyer, do what, at least prima facie, is unjust, callous or dishonest.

Well, that is what *I* think the problem is, but the prevailing literature in legal ethics does not, as far as I can see, actually tackle that problem, though it pursues debates very close to it.

Some of the debate seems to be about whether acceptance of the adversarial system does indeed entail acceptance of the fact that the lawyer's role within that system obliges him to do quite a startling range of immoral sorts of things. This seems to be a debate with no practical interest in it. Let us suppose, with Freedman, that the adversarial system *does* entail this, that is, that *whenever* the advocate zealously pursues his client's interests, and *whenever* he respects their confidentiality (within the limits of the law) he does what his role obliges him to do, no matter how dreadful, in the particular circumstances it is, or how dreadful the ways in which he does it are.

Well then, the obvious commonsense solution is "so much the worse for the adversarial system *as specified*"; we do not need or want *it*. This does not mean that we want the inquisitorial one instead; we want an adversarial system with some amendments on the general role-obligations—for example amendments that require the breaking of confidentiality to prevent crime or reveal perjury on the part of one's client. (Freedman may insist, as I believe he has, that the obvious amendments are wrong because they are inconsistent with the values intrinsic to the adversarial system, but at that point the debate does seem to have become entirely academic. Objections to this commonsense solution seem to consist of claiming that the whole adversarial system will break down if such amendments are allowed, but thereby ignore the fact that some countries have introduced such amendments and their adversarial systems have survived intact.)

For practical purposes, concentrating on suitable amendments seems an obvious way to go. Why not look for amendments that would significantly reduce the immoral actions (arguably) required by the general role-obligations and then look to see what might still be required and what we could say about them? But I have not found much discussion on such a programme in the legal ethics literature. It seems that the authors either accept the general role-obligations (with all the immorality that the ABA's Model Rules allow) and say that is fine or they aim to reconceive the lawyer's role as somehow not committed to the role-obligations.

So, on the one hand we have, for example, Hazard,[1] who accepts that the role-obligations may require immoral action but insists that, in thus fulfilling their role-obligations, lawyers are doing the right thing. He implies that, as regular doers of the right thing they are not only blameless, but to be admired for voluntarily taking on their unpalatable task. Now that seems to be simply refusing to face the philosophical problem I have outlined. There is still this question—how *can* doing these immoral things count as doing the right thing? How *can* people who do such things count as admirable?

But the legal ethicists who oppose the sort of position Hazard maintains do not seem to do any better. Luban and Kronman[2], for example, agree that *if* you take the lawyer's role in the adversarial system to be specified by those two general obligations, then the lawyer would indeed be obliged to do immoral things. But, they say, what this shows is that we have misconceived the lawyer's role. It is not a matter of deferring to those obligations but of taking on a more ethical, personally responsible, virtuous stance and reaching your decisions about what (as a lawyer) you should do, in some other, more "ethical" way, employing (in Kronman's case) practical wisdom.

Precisely what this "other way" involves is complicated in Luban, and far from clear in Kronman, but in neither of them can I find any clear statement about what the upshot of the (very idealised) lawyer's role would be if instantiated. Is the claim supposed to be that, *if* they reach their decisions about what to do in the recommended way, they will never find themselves deciding to do the immoral things? But this does make it sound as though the original role-obligations just are not going to have any bite at all. Now the problem is not—"How can these people count as doing the right thing or being admirable or good people?" but "How can they count as *lawyers*?"

It seems to me we must bite on the bullet of saying that lawyers, *as* lawyers, *will* sometimes have to do immoral things and look for a way to make that a less awkward fact. We must try to find, as I said above, some way of explaining how it might be that a virtuous person—someone who is, for example, just, compassionate and honest—could, if a lawyer, do what is, at least prima facie, unjust, callous or dishonest.

2. Dilemmas

A good place to start—as some writers in the area do start[3]—is by looking at the fact that it is not only in the case of lawyers that agents' role-obligations may conflict with common morality. Let us, following Hazard, consider whether a good parent can be a good person.

In the days before virtue ethics emerged as a rival to utilitarianism and deontology, expositions of the latter two theories implied (though the issue was not actually raised) that the answer to this had to be "No," because both theories stressed the view that morality must be impartial. But when the issue was raised, and it became clear that they were committed to denying that a good parent can be a good person, naturally they amended their position, and it is now accepted that of course there are many occasions when the right thing for parents to do is *not* to treat their own children in the way they would treat any other child similarly circumstanced, but to give them special, "partial," treatment.

This generates the possibility of conflict or moral dilemmas. Sometimes it is quite obvious that I should benefit my own child rather than another—I help my own rather than another with their homework for example. Sometimes it is equally obvious that I must not benefit my child in circumstances where I would not benefit another in the same way. I must not mark his essay more leniently than I mark others' if I am his teacher for example. But sometimes making the right decision is difficult. Yes, common morality, or the virtue of honesty, generally requires that one not tell barefaced lies, especially to innocent and well-intentioned parties. But one's role-obligations as a parent certainly include protecting one's child from serious harm when one can. So what is the right thing to do when the only way to protect one's child from such a harm is to tell such a lie? It seems that, whichever way you go, you are bound to fail morally in some respect. Either you tell the lie, and then you have done something shamefully dishonest and so cannot be a good or virtuous person, or you do not and thereby fail—through your own intentional omission—to act as a good parent, which is surely a moral failure or a failure in virtue too.

And clearly, other role-obligations also generate dilemmas. Psychiatrists have problems very similar to lawyers' about confidentiality; doctors have rather different ones (do I tell my adolescent patient's parents that she is seeking an abortion). Heads of academic departments have theirs, and also face conflicts between the obligations of that role and those of the common morality of kindness and friendship, and so on.

So good lawyers don't fail to be good people simply in virtue of the fact that their role sometimes compels them to do things which, if virtuous, they would not do if they did not occupy that role. This may happen to all sorts of people who occupy quite different roles. Nor is it simply the fact that they voluntarily took on the role that thus compels them. People voluntarily become psychiatrists, doctors, heads of departments, and, usually, parents. The taking on of *any* such role is giving hostages to fortune, upping the likelihood that bad luck will present one with a moral dilemma, but we do not worry about the question "Can a good occupier of any of those roles be a virtuous person?"

Perhaps we should? Luban, discussing not just the lawyer's role-obligations, but "professional role-morality" in general, claims that "the problem of role-morality stands as a permanent challenge to the coherence of moral thought."[4] He thinks this is so because role-morality, or role-obligation, is "particularistic," whereas (real?) moral obligations are "universal."[5] But this is a mistake. What is fundamentally at issue is not just the conflict between particular, role-specific, moral obligations and the "universal" obligations of common morality, but, quite generally, moral conflicts or dilemmas per se.

These arise in many cases where role-obligations are not at issue. Even if, per impossible, one could avoid taking on any role, one might still be presented with a moral dilemma. Ethical theory literature has long been full of them, since both rule-utilitarians and deontologists constantly come up with cases in which their moral rules give conflicting guidance. Some act-utilitarians were willing to provide brisk resolutions of all such dilemmas, but the rule-utilitarians and deontologists found their resolutions in some cases too unpalatable to accept and continue to disagree amongst themselves about the dilemmas to this day.

So the deep question is not "How can a good occupier of a role be a good person, given that their specific role-obligations may conflict with more universal moral obligations?" but, more generally, "How can anyone be a good person given that their moral obligations may conflict?"

To get clear about this, we must get clearer about dilemmas.

Before virtue ethics appeared on the stage, the standard way to set up discussion of serious (or indeed tragic) dilemmas in normative ethics was as follows. One presented an example in which there were, prima facie, good moral reasons against doing A and against doing B and the agent had to do one of them. (Usually, it was one in which the choice lay between killing, or violating another serious right and causing great suffering, or between killing and letting die, or between killing one person or several.) Then one asked the question "What is the right thing to do in such a case, A or B?" Then one applied one's theory, utilitarian or deontological, resolved the dilemma, and drew the conclusion that A, say, was *the right thing to do*. Full stop.

No one noticed that there was something problematic about such a conclusion but there is, namely that what you do after you have correctly resolved a serious dilemma is bound to be something pretty dreadful—killed someone, for example—and this is not the sort of thing we usually think of when told that someone (good for them) "did the right thing." Choosing to "do the right thing" is after all usually a matter of choosing to do the thing there are good moral reasons for doing, rather than anything there are good moral reasons against. I choose to own up to a mistake rather than lie about it; I choose to stop to help the person who has dropped his shopping rather than pass him by. In such cases, what I do is *the right thing to do*.

But that is not how things are in a serious dilemma—a forced choice between A and B where there are good, even compelling, moral reasons *against* each. If B is even worse than A, then, in deciding to do A, I will have made the right moral decision but my doing A will not thereby be right without qualification. On the contrary, given that there were, ex hypothesi, good, even compelling moral reasons against it which still stand, there must, in some sense, have been something bad or wrong about my doing A.

How can we sort this out? Let us begin by noting how the term "right moral decision" relates to the term "morally right act." Suppose we have a morally right act—a good deed. Such acts merit praise rather than blame; they are the sort of acts that we encourage each other to do, that virtuous agents typically do, that agents can be happy about doing with, as Hume so nicely puts it, that "inward peace of mind" that arises from "a satisfactory review of their own conduct." And the same is true of right moral decisions. Such decisions are the sort of decisions that virtuous agents typically make, that we encourage each other to make. We praise those who make such decisions even when they are ineffective and the act does not come off. When someone makes a right moral decision but, through no fault of their own, fails to do what they intended to do, we say well, that's a shame but still, they made the right moral decision, good for them.

This is because, in many cases, effective right moral decisions result in morally right actions; the two go hand in hand. But there are other cases in which this is not true. Consider an example of Peter Geach's.[6] A feckless man seduces two women, A and B, promising each of them marriage, and makes both of them pregnant. Ashamed of what he has done, he now wants to "do the right thing" and clear his conscience. But, in a way he cannot. Suppose his dilemma is resolvable, the evil of abandoning A being less than the evil of abandoning B (perhaps A is stronger and more independent). Then there is a right, that is, a correct, moral decision to be made about which way to go. So let us suppose that he makes that right decision and carries it through. But a good deed will not result. It is still the case that, in marrying B, he has abandoned A and merits not praise but blame for having landed himself in the circumstances that forced him to do so. He has done the sort of thing that no virtuous man would do, and he is in no position to view his own conduct with satisfaction.

How much of this changes if an agent is faced with a resolvable serious dilemma *through no fault of his own* and resolves it correctly? Anyone, through no fault of their own, may be forced to leave one person to die in order to save five. And not much changes. We will not blame him for having landed himself in the circumstances that created the forced choice, but the fact remains that he has wound up doing something that the immoral rather than the virtuous typically do. He left someone to *die* when he could have saved them, and that is not a good deed. And hence the inadequacy of the way in which the rule-utilitarians and deontologists used to resolve dilemmas and conclude that, say A, was "the right thing to do" without qualification, thereby implying that A was a good deed, morally indistinguishable from an honest or kind act such as owning up or stopping to help.

When they were engaged in resolving serious dilemmas the utilitarian and deontological theorists were not, I think, entirely clear about what they were doing. On the one hand, they were committed, in those days, to providing action-guidance; their theories were supposed to enable their users to reach correct moral decisions. But they also claimed to have identified, in their respective theory's "account of right action," which provided the action-guidance, the "right-making properties" of actions—what it was about them that made them the sorts of actions that the virtuous do and that we all may review with satisfaction. Outside the context of serious dilemmas, the tensions between these two aims were not apparent, since in ordinary cases, an effective right moral decision results in a good deed. But the very reason why we worry about serious dilemmas is that they face us, not with the choice between a good deed and a bad one, but with the unhappy choice between two evils. In such cases there may well be a correct moral decision to be made, the one that latches on to the lesser of the two evils, but no chance that this will result in a good deed.

3. Getting through dilemmas virtuously

As is well known, virtue ethics, rather than focusing on the "right-making properties" of actions, focuses on the virtuous agent. It thereby stands us in good stead when we consider serious dilemmas because it forces on our attention how very different they are from other "Should I do A or B?" questions. Instead of asking us to think "Will A or B have the best consequences?" or "Is it A or B that is in accordance with a correct rule or the highest ranking principle?" and hence think about the actions and their properties, virtue ethics tells us to think about a virtuous agent. Faced with a forced choice between two evils, what would she *do*?

And that is a really *puzzling* question, creating a tension in our thought that the "A or B?" questions do not. When we try to imagine, concretely, a virtuous agent doing one of these dreadful things, each with the weight of such good moral reasons against them, one's mind tends to boggle.

Asking students to imagine it, I have found they are often unable to do so. They start by saying that an *ideally* virtuous agent would never get herself into the circumstances that presented her with a serious dilemma—it is always through some fault of one's own, albeit perhaps, a very minor one, that one is faced with them. But then I give them examples in which this is clearly not so. Or they say, well, she would reject the forced choice and kill herself . With respect to some examples of dilemmas, that is a good answer—after all, as Aristotle rightly remarks "There are some things a man must die rather than do"—but as an answer to all of them, it is dodging the issue. So I produce other examples in which killing oneself would clearly be cowardly or irresponsible so the virtuous agent will not do *that*, and they get stuck again. Eventually, one of them, remembering that I am always telling them that virtue involves feelings as well as actions, will say "Well, I suppose she would have to do A (if that is the way they think the dilemma has to be resolved) but she would feel terrible about it." Right. And now we can start thinking through what she would do in proper detail.

We start thinking about it this way. Anyone, even the immoral, through the normally fallible or venal, to the virtuous agent with practical wisdom, might be faced with a serious resolvable dilemma through no fault of their own. What we are interested in is, what differentiates them? What would we expect the *virtuous* agent would do in such a situation?

We have already noted that when he does A he will feel badly about it. But why?[7] Because, ex hypothesi, A, like B, is the sort of action—unjust, callous, dishonest—that the vicious typically do, not the sort he goes in for. So, when first faced with the dilemma, he is going to be extremely reluctant to do either A or B, and, given that, what would one expect him to do which one would not expect the immoral and the normally fallible to do? Obviously, the first thing *he* is going to do is look for a way to "slip between the horns of the dilemma," in contrast to the immoral, who will not bother to look, and the normally fallible who, lacking practical wisdom, will not think to question whether they really are faced with a dilemma.

Although this too may seem to be dodging the issue, it is, in practice, often indistinguishable from cases that are definitely relevant to it which I will come to in the next paragraph, and it is also an important point to make in the context of teaching legal ethics. It is surely not a good idea to foster in law students the belief that their job is going to face them with a constant stream of forced choices between evils and that, to be good lawyers, they must learn to face the unpalatable choice immediately, identify the lesser of the two evils, grit their teeth and get on with it. The training should consist in directing the students to look *first* for ways of avoiding the presented dilemmas, so they do not have to choose an evil (or such a great one) before moving on to a further step.

Moving on ourselves, let us consider a response to the *Lake Pleasant Bodies Case*. Suppose we think that what a virtuous lawyer would have done in that case was send the authorities an anonymous tip-off about the whereabouts of the bodies.[8] Are we to describe this as slipping between the horns of the dilemma between breaking confidentiality and failing to prevent the grief of the relatives, or simply as resolving the dilemma in favour of breaking confidentiality? It seems to me one could say either. If we opt for the former, then it is an example of the first sort of thing a *virtuous* agent does when presented with an apparent serious dilemma. If we opt for the latter, we find the second instance in which the virtuous agent, faced with a serious dilemma, does not do just the same thing as the immoral or the normally fallible.

Suppose a serious moral dilemma between doing A and doing B is correctly resolvable in favour of A. So the virtuous agent decides that A is "the" way to go. What then? She will not just barge straight ahead but, whenever possible, consider different *sorts of means* of doing A in search of the least bad one and do that (e.g. send the anonymous tip-off). And again, the immoral will not care and so will not bother to search, and the normally fallible will not think to consider anything but the obvious bad means of doing A. So, even when they all decide to "do A," they will not "do the same thing" because the virtuous will look for different means to implement that decision and the others will not. Moreover, sometimes she will find it, and wind up doing A* while the others do A** where A*, though bad, is not as bad as A**.

Now let us confront the cases where doing A is the correct moral decision, and all three really do A, the virtuous agent for the right reasons, the normally fallible or venal perhaps for them, perhaps by luck, and the immoral for whatever. So we are to imagine that our virtuous agent knowingly does something which is the sort of thing that no virtuous agent would typically do—harms his child, hurts a friend, deceives some good and trusting people, breaks a just law, prompts his wife's suicide....[9] If the immoral, the normally fallible or venal and even the ideally virtuous agent all do the same thing, what now can differentiate them?

At this point, we should bring back the student's point and consider its further implications. Given that virtue is concerned with feeling rightly as much as acting rightly, and assuming that our agent is virtuous, we must assume that he will feel about what he has done as he should, with some pain and regret, perhaps great distress. He certainly will not feel pleased about it. So given that is how he feels, what would we expect him *not* to do? Would he congratulate himself on having done the right thing, feeling pleased about what he has done? Obviously not. Will he boast about it? Obviously not. Will he welcome opportunities to discuss his decision and being congratulated on his perspicacity? Obviously not, even if it was very difficult to arrive at the correct decision and did call on all his practical wisdom. It was *painful*, and who wants to dwell on their pain? But the immoral may well do all of these things (in suitable company) and the normally venal be at least tempted to do so.

Will a virtuous agent, conscious of the fact that pure bad luck landed her with the dilemma, and that she did make the correct decision, shrug off the regret as quickly as she can, saying to herself "No use crying over spilt milk?" After all, she is, ex hypothesi, blameless. If she was faced with the dilemma through no fault of her own, and she resolved it correctly, identifying the lesser of the two evils, she can say, truly, "It wasn't my fault – I *had* to do A" and that is a watertight excuse and justification.

Now the normally venal may be content with thus excusing themselves (and the immoral will feel no regrets anyhow), but the virtuous are not content with being blameless and able to justify themselves. *As* virtuous, they are interested not so much in being blameless as in acting well, in the life of virtuous activity. So, landed with a bad job, they do not take the fact that it is not of their making as a reason or excuse for leaving it as it is. They look around for a way or ways to make the best of it.

True, there are undoubtedly situations in which nothing further could be done to ameliorate the upshot of a resolved serious dilemma. And in those cases, having tried, and found nothing, the agent can, without showing himself to be irresponsible or considerably less than committed to acting well, move on past the spilt milk. But there usually is something which makes the doing of A, though still regrettable, a little less bad than it would otherwise have been. And the virtuous agent looks for that, and finds it and does it, whereas the immoral and the normally fallible or venal do not look or (if less venal but still fallible) look but fail to find it.

So we find a number of differences between the way in which the virtuous get through serious dilemmas and how the others do.

What makes it, initially, hard to imagine what the virtuous agent would do when faced with such a dilemma is that it is the general version of the problem of explaining the "awkward fact" I mentioned at the outset. How *could* it be that a virtuous person—someone who is, for example, just, compassionate and honest—does what is unjust, callous or dishonest? When we hear of someone that they killed an innocent person intentionally, or intentionally allowed one of their children to die when they could have done otherwise, our natural reaction is to assume that they *cannot* be virtuous. These are the sorts of things, we think, that only the immoral do, and one thing we can be sure of is that the immoral and the virtuous do not do the same things.

But once we have worked through what a virtuous agent would do when faced with a serious moral dilemma we see what is wrong about that thought. When—but *only* when—faced with a forced choice between evils—the virtuous, even the ideally virtuous may indeed "do the same thing" as someone immoral would do. We see that our initial intuition—that the truly, ideally honest never do what is dishonest, the compassionate never what is callous or unkind, the just never what is unjust—was simplistic. Yes, sometimes they do, *because* they were forced, by the circumstances, to do so.

But it is not enough to say that, resolving a serious dilemma correctly, an agent "did the right thing" with only the qualification "given that they were forced to." There is no virtue in "doing the right thing" in a dilemma unless it is done in a virtuous way. For we also see what is right about the thought that the immoral and the virtuous do not do the same things. When faced with a (apparent) serious dilemma, the immoral and the virtuous do not "do the same thing" in the broad sense of "do." The virtuous get through the dilemma *virtuously*, doing different things before they reach a decision, sometimes reaching a different decision from the immoral, and when they decide on and do the very same specific action as the immoral, they do different things later on. They feel about it all differently too of course, but it is the differences in action that are of practical interest.

So, quite generally, when faced with serious dilemmas, good people can do bad things, and this may be no reflection on their goodness or virtue. When we discover not only that they have done this bad thing but why (it was a forced choice, and they made the right decision) and how (in the virtuous way outlined above) and how they felt about it all, we are sympathetic about the toll it has taken, not shocked and condemnatory.

4. Lawyers' dilemmas

Now let us apply the preceding discussion to lawyers' dilemmas. These are serious moral dilemmas in which there is a forced choice between failing to fulfil one's role-obligation, which (ex hypothesi) is wrong and doing something else that is (ex hypothesi) wrong. And in legal ethics, the question that is standardly addressed is the utilitarians' and deontologists' question—"What is the right thing for the lawyer to do?"—inviting the answer "A (or B) is the right thing to do, full stop."

But if we recast that question in virtue ethics' terms we get "What would the virtuous lawyer do faced with such a dilemma?" and many answers emerge that parallel those in the preceding discussion.

Sometimes the answer is going to be "Reject the forced choice by giving up on being a lawyer and resigning from her job." Like the students' even more drastic response ("reject the forced choice and kill herself") this will sometimes, given some examples, be a good answer and it is a possibility that should not be overlooked. However, as before, thinking of it as the answer to all of them is dodging the issue, and we may assume that such examples will be rare. There are doubtless others in which what a particular virtuous lawyer would do, in the circumstances, is arrange for their client to be transferred to another lawyer, and that should not be overlooked either. But in many cases the answer will be that, since she is a virtuous *lawyer*, she fulfils her role-obligations, resolving the dilemma in favour of them and does what common morality would forbid.

But, as a *virtuous* lawyer, he will get through the dilemma, thus resolved, in the way I have detailed above. He will already have looked to see if he can find a way of slipping between its horns. If he cannot, he will look for the least unjust or dishonest or harmful or grief-causing means of fulfilling his role-obligation, not just barge ahead. In particular, he will not ignore the ABA's Model Rules' grudging permissions to fulfil his role-obligation in a less than hyper-zealous way[10] but take advantage of every single one of them. That would make a substantial difference to what is done in many cases.

A virtuous lawyer will not, while or having fulfilled her role-obligation in such a situation, feel pleased about doing so, nor proud of having done what she has done, nor boast about it, nor write articles or appear on television extolling her perspicacity and legal expertise. She will not congratulate herself smugly on having done the right thing, thinking of what she has done as a good deed. She will, in the course of fulfilling it, and afterwards, be on the look out for ways in which to mitigate the evils of the situation, rather than rest content with having the perfect excuse ("I had to") and she will find any that are going and do them. And every lawyer who fails to do any of these things fails to do what the virtuous lawyer would do and thereby fails to do what they should.

It will now be obvious that what I think is wrong with Hazard's position is the unqualified claim that the lawyers "do the right thing" when (whenever? he leaves it unclear) they fulfil their role-obligations, and thereby his unwarranted inference that, as regular doers of such right things, they are virtuous people and merit our esteem.

When in accordance with their role-obligations, they are forced to do something contrary to common morality or virtue, something that is not right "without qualification," through no fault of their own, lawyers count as "doing the right thing" *only* if they recognise their choice as one side of a serious dilemma and subsequently act (and react) in the way a virtuous agent would. When, and only when, they regularly "do the right thing" in this broad sense of "do" are they candidates for being virtuous people who merit our esteem.

Correspondingly, they are up for moral censure if they fail to find the least immoral means of fulfilling their role-obligations (if there are alternatives), if they congratulate themselves on having done the right thing or make a point of claiming they were blameless, giving the "adversary system excuse"[11] instead of looking around afterwards for ways to ameliorate the situation. All of which seems a far cry from what Hazard has in mind.

So far, so good. Pointing out that virtuous lawyers must "do the right thing" *in the way* a virtuous person would takes us away from Hazard and more towards Luban's and Kronman's call for more "ethical lawyering." A virtuous lawyer has to do a lot more than simply fulfil his role-obligations, and a lot more than fulfil them with an appropriate feeling of regret.

However, we might still wonder whether we have got far enough. In theory, we have found an explanation of the "awkward fact" with which we began, namely that a virtuous person will, if a lawyer, sometimes do immoral things. The explanation is that virtuous people sometimes *do* do immoral things; they do them when presented with a forced choice between two immoral things through no fault of their own (and then do one of them in a special way which involves doing other things). But there are significant differences between the lawyer's situation and the general case of a virtuous person being faced with a forced choice.

In the general case, it is sheer unpredictable bad luck that brings the forced choice. Ordinarily virtuous people leading ordinary lives have no reason to expect that, lying in wait for them, is some horribly serious dilemma. Minor ones (having to break a promise, let someone down or trick them into doing something, tell a serious lie, cause someone distress, keep a confidence with one and bring serious results for someone else) no doubt crop up quite often. But the "bad job" can often be not only ameliorated but sometimes entirely dissipated (especially with people one knows, as is often the case) by a subsequent sincere apology ("I *am* sorry; I had to do it because... and I couldn't confess before because..."). So, even in the virtuous, the regret does not have to be deep and does not last long. With a very serious or tragic one, the regret and pain may be long-lasting, even lifelong, but, in ordinary life, these are rare.

This is not true of lawyers. Their being faced with serious dilemmas is not unpredictable bad luck, but all too predictable. Although each particular dilemma may be one they are in through no fault of their own, it is by their own choice that they are in a profession in which they know such dilemmas will face them. Though many involve only relatively minor acts of dishonesty, deception, manipulation, injustice or unkindness, there is no chance of the lawyers' ameliorating the bad job by subsequently apologising to the strangers they have thus injured. And very serious ones are quite on the cards, not a random blow of cruel fortune which prompts our sympathy when it strikes the virtuous in ordinary life and causes them such distress.

No wonder people claim that lawyers must lack moral integrity! If they were as distressed by acting on their very serious forced choices as the virtuous are in ordinary life, surely they would have broken down and resigned from their profession years ago. How can they have any pretensions to virtue and survive unless they have somehow split themselves in two, leaving their virtuous persona and its emotional reactions at home when they go into the office, and their immoral one (including its consciousness of what it has done) in the office when they go home. And that is not enough for virtue.

So the necessary condition for being a virtuous lawyer, outlined above—that she regularly "does the right thing" in the virtuous way—is not sufficient. If we are going to hang on to the idea that there can be virtuous lawyers, despite their being forced to do the immoral things they do, something more needs to be said.

Let us again go back to Hazard's reminder that lawyers are not the only role-occupiers who can predict, with confidence, that they are going to be faced with very serious dilemmas. Although I doubt this is true of parents, it certainly seems to be true of some doctors, psychiatrists and soldiers. Do we suppose of *all* such role-occupiers that they have either split themselves in two, or are on the verge of breaking down under the stress and distress of having to do the things they do, or are immoral and in it just for the money or because it is a more exciting job than any others available to them? I assume we may think that of many—and sometimes see evidence to support it—but not think it of all. I assume we find, if we know some of them, or can imagine, if we do not, that the virtuous ones see themselves as, overall, dedicated to promoting a truly good end—other people's good, or the relief of their suffering. They are thereby enabled to see their forced choices as inseparable from their job-long service to this worthwhile end, not merely as strokes of misfortune, and hence they are less distressed than virtuous people getting through dilemmas in ordinary life. Moreover, they can take heart from their dedication to such an end, and preserve Hume's "inward peace of mind" and pride in their job.

May we find, or imagine, the same regarding lawyers? Some of them, we may suppose, see themselves as, overall, dedicated to promoting justice. They are thereby enabled to see their forced choices as inseparable, in the inevitable imperfections of any legal system, from their service to that end, and can preserve peace of mind and pride in their job. Well, perhaps—but only if we can find, or imagine, that the dedication is genuine.

An avowal of the dedication, even if manifestly sincere, will not be enough, since self-deception powered by the financial rewards of the profession and the desire for self-esteem is quite enough to guarantee the sincerity. Just as we will doubt the dedication of a psychiatrist with the avowed end of helping others who specialises in wealthy patients suffering from self-indulgence, so, in my view, we may surely doubt the dedication to justice of anyone who has chosen to specialise in corporate law. Even if it were possible for a lawyer to regularly "do the right thing" in the virtuous way in a US corporate law firm rather than getting sacked the first time he tried it (which I gather from the literature is very unlikely), can they reasonably believe that many of their cases would have just outcomes? There can be no just or fair outcome of two Mafia bosses' battle over the territory in which their gangs operate and, analogously, no just outcome of two corporations' legal battle over profits in the adversarial system when both sides are greedy and unscrupulous. Or so I believe, but I realise this may be a very tendentious view.

Is it as tendentious to claim that we could expect a lawyer dedicated to promoting justice to do pro bono work for "persons of limited means?" It appears that not many do pro bono work at all unless required by their state, and that some who say they do, do it not by working for the poor but "by doing free legal work for in-laws and attorneys' country clubs."[12] They thereby compare unfavourably with those who do do more, particularly those who choose to join law firms that specialise in pro bono work and charge lower fees to the needy, even though this means the lawyers wind up with less money. It is this sort of willingness to "go the extra mile" that one would expect of the virtuous lawyer, the one who is truly dedicated to promoting justice.

Indeed, we might think that promoting justice was itself a role-obligation of lawyers and that any lawyer who did not manifest the dedication but only fulfilled their other two general role-obligations was not even a good lawyer. After all, the Preamble to the ABA's Model Rules states [in (1)] that a lawyer, *as* a member of the legal profession, is a public citizen having *special* responsibility for the quality of justice (my italics). To an outsider, this seems to assert that lawyers have a double obligation to promote justice—the one all citizens share, and the one they have in virtue of their role, highlighted here. Still, it might be said, they can discharge the second entirely by discharging the two standard ones effectively; the "special responsibility" does not require anything further of them as lawyers, and hence is not, as such, a role-obligation. You can be a good lawyer without going the extra mile for justice.

All right, let us accept that. We may still point out that the lawyers' role gives them special opportunities to promote justice. A *virtuous* lawyer will, of course, not pass up such opportunities, and these are not exhausted by the possibility of extra pro bono work.

The specific actions which constitute fulfilling the two general role-obligations are in part determined by the content of specific laws. So if a law changes, so do some of the specific actions required. And laws can be changed, sometimes for the better. Lawyers' expertise, experience and authority as lawyers, give them the opportunity to do good and to promote justice in ways that are not open to many others, because they are better positioned than most of the rest of us to be instrumental in changes within the legal system.

A point too obvious to be worth making in the general discussion of getting through serious moral dilemmas virtuously should be made now, namely that only the immoral are indifferent to the prospect of people being faced with a forced choice between two evils and hence doing one of them. The virtuous, and even the minimally decent, just do not want bad things to be done. It is not only that they do not want to do them themselves, they do not want them to *happen*. Given human frailty of course they do happen, and given serious dilemmas they happen, but anything consistent with morality we can do to ensure they happen less often is worth doing. We still do not know what to do about human frailty, and many serious dilemmas arise in ways over which we have no control, but some of the lawyers' dilemmas arise *only* because of imperfections in the legal system, and something can be done about them.

Tim Dare[13] argues that lawyers are the most appropriate people to take on, occasionally at least, the distinct role of "reformer"—one who critically evaluates the constitutive rules of a practice. Defending "the standard conception" of the lawyer's role, he wants to emphasise the necessity of their sticking to their role-obligations. But, as he nicely points out, who would be better positioned than Pakel's lawyer, *after* he had seen the case through, to initiate a change in the relevant statute which would prevent the particular dilemma he resolved in favour of fulfilling his role-obligation from arising again?

Rephrased in virtue ethics' terms we may say that this is exactly the sort of thing one would expect a virtuous lawyer to do. As a lawyer, he pursues his client's interests, venal as they are; as a *virtuous* lawyer, he goes the extra mile for justice and, say, writes to his local law reform commissioner, conforming to the Preamble's (6)—"a lawyer should seek improvement of the law" and "should employ ... knowledge [of the law] in reform of the law."

One would expect too that virtuous lawyers in the US would be campaigning to get the ABA Model Rules more strictly enforced or tightened up. To the naive reader, they seem to forbid many of the practices deplored by legal ethicists (for example, responding "to an interrogatory by delivering to the discoverer tons of miscellaneous documents to run up their legal bills"[14]) but apparently they do not, or not unambiguously enough. Young lawyers with aspirations to being virtuous do not need exhortations to "exercise [...] sensitive professional and moral judgment guided by the basic principles underlying the Rules" [as (9) in the Preamble has it] to find their proper interpretation. They need clearer Rules to which they can appeal, invoking an "ABA Model Rules Excuse," when under pressure from immoral clients.

I have read much in the legal ethics' literature about low morale amongst lawyers and law students. The aim of this chapter has been to show that there are quite a lot of things to be done that would entitle lawyers to think of themselves as virtuous people. Their two, further, general obligations as *virtuous* lawyers are firstly, to do the right thing in a virtuous way, with all the extra doings that entails, and secondly, to go the extra mile for justice. It will not be easy, but virtue never is.

Acknowledgements

Readers interested in a virtue ethics approach to role-generated dilemmas should also read Christine Swanton's rather different version, 'Virtue Ethics, Role Ethics, and Business Ethics' in *Working Virtue* (Rebecca L. Walker and Philip J. Ivanhoe eds, Oxford: Clarendon Press, 2007), pp. 208–224.

I am grateful to my colleague Tim Dare for generously allowing me to read chapters of his book manuscript *The Counsel of Rogues*, forthcoming (Ashgate, 2008) to which I am greatly indebted in this chapter and for commenting on an earlier version.

Notes

1. Geoffrey C. Hazard, Jr., "Doing the Right Thing" in *Legal profession: Responsibility and Regulation* (Geoffrey C. Hazard, Jr. and Deborah L. Rhode eds,), pp. 161–168.
2. Anthony Kronman, *The Lost Lawyer: Failing Ideals of the Legal Profession* (Cambridge, MA.: Belnap Press, 1993); David Luban, *Lawyers and Justice* (Princeton: Princeton University Press, 1988).
3. Hazard, to good effect, *vide supra*, and Richard Wasserstrom "Roles and Morality" in *The Good Lawyer: Lawyers' Roles and Lawyers' Ethics* (David Luban ed., Totowa, NJ: Rowman and Allenheld, 1983), pp. 25–37.
4. David Luban, "Professional Ethics" in *A Companion to Applied Ethics* (R. G. Frey and Christopher Heath eds, Oxford: Blackwell, 2003), p. 595.
5. *Ibid.*, 588.
6. Peter Geach, *The Virtues* (Cambridge: Cambridge University Press, 1977).
7. The idea that serious moral dilemmas could only be resolved "with moral remainder" in the form of regret was introduced into the literature by Bernard Williams and has entered the legal ethics literature to some extent. But, as far as I know, no one does more with it than note that "the agent ought to feel regret." Cast that in virtue ethics' terms and we get "the virtuous agent (unlike the immoral) would feel regret" and can start thinking about why and *what follows* from this fact.
8. David Wasserman, "Should a Good Lawyer do the Right Thing? David Luban on the Morality of Adversary Representation", 49 *Maryland L. Rev.* 392–423, 399 (1990).
9. I heard of a tragic case in which a woman was married to a deeply unhappy and neurotic man who abused their children. When she threatened to leave him, taking them with her, he would cry and say he would commit suicide if she did and promise to reform. And lapse again. Having tried everything else without success, she did leave him. And he did commit suicide.
10. Tim Dare, "Mere-Zeal, Hyper-Zeal and the Ethical Obligations of Lawyers", 7 *Legal Ethics* 24–38 (2004).

11. David Luban, "The Adversary System Excuse" in *The Good Lawyer: Lawyers' Roles and Lawyers' Ethics* (David Luban ed., Totowa, NJ: Rowman and Allenheld, 1983), pp. 83–122.
12. See *Legal Ethics* (Deborah L. Rhode and David Luban eds, New York: The Foundation Press, 1995), p. 794 and preceding.
13. Tim Dare, unpublished manuscript of *The Counsel of Rogues*. He tells me that William Simon makes the same point.
14. David Luban, *Lawyers and Justice*, p. 51.

Index